CONFRONTING EQUITY
ISSUES ON CAMPUS

CONFRONTING EQUITY ISSUES ON CAMPUS

Implementing the Equity Scorecard in Theory and Practice

EDITED BY *Estela Mara Bensimon and Lindsey Malcom*

Foreword by David Longanecker

Sty/us

STERLING, VIRGINIA

Sty/us

Published by Stylus Publishing, LLC
22883 Quicksilver Drive
Sterling, Virginia 20166-2102

Library of Congress Cataloging-in-Publication Data
Confronting equity issues on campus : implementing the
equity scorecard in theory and practice / edited by Estela
Mara Bensimon and Lindsey Malcom.
    p.   cm.
Includes bibliographical references and index.
ISBN 978-1-57922-707-4 (cloth : alk. paper)
ISBN 978-1-57922-708-1 (pbk : alk. paper)
ISBN 978-1-57922-709-8 (library networkable e-edition)
ISBN 978-1-57922-710-4 (consumer e-edition)
 1. Minorities—Education (Higher)—Research—United
States.   2. Academic achievement—Research—United
States.   3. Discrimination in higher education-United
States.   4. Educational equalization—United States.
I. Bensimon, Estela Mara.   II. Malcom, Lindsey, 1980–
LC3727.C63   2012
378.1'982900973—dc23   2011032188

13-digit ISBN: 978-1-57922-707-4 (cloth)
13-digit ISBN: 978-1-57922-708-1 (paper)
13-digit ISBN: 978-1-57922-709-8 (library networkable
e-edition)
13-digit ISBN: 978-1-57922-710-4 (consumer e-edition)

Bulk Purchases

Quantity discounts are available for use in workshops
and for staff development.
Call 1-800-232-0223

First Edition, 2012

10   9   8   7   6   5   4   3   2   1

CONTENTS

FOREWORD

The equity gaps that currently exist in American higher education between White students and students of color are both indefensible and unacceptable. They're indefensible because they run directly counter to American ideals of equality—not only equality of opportunity but equality in life experiences. They're unacceptable because they erode the vitality of our society and undercut the financial viability of our nation.

Despite this, many intelligent people believe that equity gaps in American education are intentional or unavoidable—or both. Some have argued that these gaps result from the intentional efforts of privileged sectors of society, "the haves," to protect their position of superiority over the "have-nots." Others, including some noted scholars within academe, believe that only a small share of our population can benefit from the intellectual rigors of higher education; thus, it's no surprise that our system is de facto exclusive, and equity gaps are simply proof that "some folks" aren't up to the challenge. Neither of these arguments passes muster when we look at the evidence, or consult our reason.

First, we find little evidence of intentional inequality and few examples of deliberate efforts to prevent equality of opportunity within our system. Although American higher education has certainly contributed substantially to the divide between the haves and have-nots, and thus to racial and ethnic inequality, most educators, be they faculty, administrators, or policy folks, believe passionately in bridging equity gaps—a goal that should be achievable but has proved to be remarkably challenging. Our problem is that the elitist foundations of American higher education undercut those passionate desires. Our elitist tradition, which created the original divisions between advantaged and disadvantaged classes in society by presuming higher education was the province of a few privileged individuals, remains unintentionally entrenched within a system that continues to relish serving "the best and the brightest." And too often those of us who plan, administer, and deliver higher education simply don't comprehend our own complicity in maintaining a status quo that fosters exclusion rather than inclusion.

Second, the presumption of some that higher education's exclusivity is both natural and appropriate is thoroughly debunked by the profound and profuse evidence indicating that many more individuals within our society could benefit from a college education—and succeed in attaining it—than have in the past. Indeed, many more *must* attain it, if we are to remain competitive in a world in which a host of other developed countries now surpass us in the share of their young adults receiving a college-level education.

Despite this, a disproportionate share of students of color simply don't prosper at our colleges and universities, although every indication is that they have the ability to do well and a strong interest in succeeding. Why do they fail to thrive under our current system of higher education? That's the question this book asks. And in answering that question, it provides evidence from action research not just on causes but on solutions. Delineating how we can reduce equity gaps, it also shows how we might use American higher education as a tool to radically transform our culture into one that truly values equality, in word and in deed.

Confronting Equity Issues on Campus, written by the researchers of the University of Southern California's Center for Urban Education and their partners at Equity Scorecard campuses, moves the discussion from one of student deficits to one of institutional opportunities. It focuses on what institutions can do, rather than on what students can't. It examines the nature of institutions of higher education as organizations, which (like all organizations) are designed to perpetuate themselves by performing much as they have in the past and are thus unlikely to change without intentional interventions. And it provides two elements essential to that intervention: specific evidence of how our institutions are failing to serve their mission; and, equally important, a solid argument for how change will advance their mission.

Confronting Equity Issues on Campus describes how institutions, through their practices and structure, have unintentionally marginalized students of color. But it doesn't stop there. Instead, it goes on to provide an evidence-based process by which these patterns can be reversed. It demonstrates how leadership within the administration and faculty ranks can transform institutions from ones that create the problem to ones that successfully redress it. The process employs an "equity scorecard" that examines five suppositions or assumptions that are essential to closing institutional equity gaps—elements that are neither radical nor remarkable but that must be in place if this problem is to be solved.

The first presupposition, *doing good,* presumes that an institution's leaders and faculties want to make this change. And in general, when faculty and campus leaders understand the true nature of the equity gaps on their campus and closely examine the ways in which their institution (rather than their students) contributes to these gaps, they tend to act. Awareness heightens these actors' interest in doing good.

The second presupposition relates to the *participatory process* needed to tackle equity gaps and holds that being personally engaged is essential to owning this issue. Without personal engagement, well-meaning folks see the equity gap as someone else's issue, and someone else's fault—an important matter, to be sure, but not their responsibility. The Equity Scorecard, however, engages these individuals in the discovery of their unique personal and corporate roles in addressing the equity gaps and helps them accept responsibility for engaging their colleagues in redressing the equity gaps.

The third assumption concerns *remediating practices* and supposes that our past remedies have failed primarily because we've presumed that the deficits are in our students rather than in our institutions. When we accept responsibility for remediating ourselves and our colleges and universities rather than our students, we see the actions steps entirely differently.

The fourth assumption focuses on *inquiry as a change strategy*. It holds that the agenda is, in great part, a scholarly pursuit—one that must be supported by research, evidence, and a strong theoretical foundation. Thus, it posits that change-focused inquiry is a wholly appropriate academic exercise.

Finally, the presupposition of *racial inequity as a problem of practice* argues that this issue can be practically attacked from within the academy. It holds that we cannot afford to become mired in the broad array of sociopolitical issues that have contributed to racial inequality in the United States but instead must address those practices that we can change and act to improve our own performance.

Confronting Equity Issues on Campus will serve a variety of stakeholders. It stands as a guide for campus administrators and faculty who see the need for change but haven't yet found a way to make it happen. It provides aid to those who have already made the commitment to move forward but require help in convincing their professional colleagues of the need to do so and their institution's ability to do so. It offers hope and valuable research to race theorists and others interested in the scholarship of equality and inequality.

In addition, though the current research focuses on institutions, the Equity Scorecard's five suppositions provide higher education policymakers at the state and national level with a valuable way of thinking about equity gaps and how to close them. Policy, just like practice, relies on good people seeking to do good things, with those who are truly engaged by a topic becoming the agents of change. The change strategy of a policymaker may differ from that of a campus leader—policymakers incentivize change rather than intervene directly to make change happen. But change at both the policy level and within institutions requires evidence, and this book provides it.

Confronting Equity Issues on Campus is a great case study of the potential power, value, efficacy, and joy that can come from action-based research. Enjoy.

David Longanecker
David Longanecker is the president of the
Western Interstate Commission for Higher Education (WICHE)
in Boulder, Colorado.

INTRODUCTION

Estela Mara Bensimon and Lindsey Malcom

The need for this book arose from a recognition that the civil rights victories of the past fifty years, although successful in opening access to higher education, have not translated into equity in educational outcomes for African Americans; Latinas and Latinos; American Indians; Hawaiians; or certain Asian American groups such as Hmong, Vietnamese, Cambodians, and others. Patterns of racial inequity are evident in educational outcomes in public and private institutions, selective and open-access, and two- and four-year colleges. Equity has even eluded these students in minority-serving institutions. Data at the national, state, and campus levels show that Black, Hispanic, and American Indian students have the lowest rate of bachelor's degree attainment.

For those of us who witnessed the birth of the civil rights movement and viewed education as the prime engine for social and economic mobility, the persistence of inequality in educational outcomes is appalling and frustrating. How could it be, one might ask, that fifty years after the passage of the Civil Rights Act, our institutions of higher education have not found ways of reducing the higher education gaps for racial and ethnic groups? How could it be that campuses tout the value of diversity and organize any number of programs to promote interracial "contact," yet inequities in educational outcomes have worsened? How could it be that despite hundreds of journal articles, books, reports, and conferences on the retention of college students and the best practices of diversity, inclusion, engagement, integration, and involvement, the success indicators for the same racial groups, unfailingly, year after year, fall into the unequal zone of performance? How could this be so even in those institutions that qualify as minority serving?

We at the Center for Urban Education (CUE) perceived that access and diversity initiatives by themselves were not sufficient to achieve racial equity in outcomes. We also came to the conclusion that regardless of scholars' efforts to translate their research for practitioners and make it useful, it was unlikely that studies that were designed and written for an audience of peer scholars would be a catalyst for institutional transformation. We decided that an explicit focus on institutional capacity, responsibility, and accountability was essential to "move the needle" toward equity. To address this, we devised a research methodology that required us to create specialized tools to prompt institutional change, and at the same time to document, by means of traditional empirical methods, their effect on practitioners.

Thus, rather than focusing on what students do (or fail to do) to control the quality and outcomes of their own education, we decided to focus on what institutions can do—through their practices and structures as well as their leaders and faculty—to produce equity in outcomes for racially marginalized populations. Rather than doing research to describe problems and prescribe solutions, we were interested in creating the structures and tools that would help leaders and faculty view themselves and their everyday practices through the lens of racial equity. That is, rather than us—the researchers—conducting case studies, interviews, or surveys to document inequity in conference papers, journal articles, or books, we drew on our research expertise and cultural knowledge of academic organizations to create a structure for practitioners to become researchers of their own institutional culture. Drawing on the theory of action research, we hypothesized that direct involvement in a collaborative inquiry into racial equity in one's own institutions would raise awareness of racial disparities among practitioners and a greater chance that they would confront their own practices. By engaging in a structured process of deep and extended inquiry to learn how things are done on their own turf, practitioners might be more inclined to ask: In what ways am I contributing to equity and inequity?

This book is for college leaders, instructors, and support staff who feel the pressure—moral or otherwise—to close the racial equity gap that their institutions produce year after year. As already mentioned, there are many books and articles about student diversity, as well as strategies to increase access and retention. So what can this book offer that is not more of the same? The most important difference between this book and others lies in its accounting of a model of organizational change that is significantly different from traditional views of how change happens. The following five presuppositions highlight the major concepts that undergird the organizational change strategy presented in this book—the Equity Scorecard.

Doing the Good

First, the model of change described in this book presupposes that professionals in an academic community are committed to doing good for others. Therefore, all higher education professionals have the potential to become agents of equity, both within their own areas of responsibility and in the institution at large. However, doing so requires more than the implementation of standard, off-the-shelf solutions. We provide a vision and an approach to assist professionals to develop the knowledge and wisdom to do the good—to become best practitioners—rather than simply prescribe best practices. Expert knowledge in one's profession is essential for doing the good, but it is not sufficient to create racial equity. This book introduces institutional leaders and practitioners to the knowledge base, tools, and case studies to become agents of equity on behalf of racial and ethnic groups with a long history of opportunity denied.

Participatory Process

The second presupposition is that the members of an academic community must be involved as full partners in the development of a strategy to eliminate inequity in access and success. The authentic involvement of faculty members and professional staff is essential in any kind of intervention that aims to change educational outcomes in retention, graduation, completion of remedial education, and participation. Simply put, student outcomes in institutions of higher education are constructed through the quality, frequency, and types of interactions between students and professionals—including instructors, teaching assistants, advisors, counselors, and others—as well as through the contextual conditions in which these interactions occur.

Remediating Practices

The third presupposition is that equity in educational outcomes has eluded us because interventions have focused on correcting the academic deficiencies of students and neglected institutional factors. Inequity in educational outcomes has persisted almost undisturbed because programs to increase diversity, access, and success continue to be the modal solution. But equity may be more achievable if we can focus on remediating institutional cultures, practices, and structures. The tools provided in this book constitute an intervention to remediate practices—in admissions and recruitment, in classrooms, in tutoring centers, in science labs, in counseling services—that are failing students of color, and to create new practices wherever needed. The Equity Scorecard equips practitioners with the tools and inquiry methods to interrogate data and contemplate taken-for-granted practices as if they were brand new and had to be figured out to learn how they work and for whom.

Engagement in a collaborative inquiry into a problem brings practitioners together to share their hunches about data patterns, ask questions that lead to more data, and propose causes for the problems and solutions. It is through the inquiry process that practitioners become aware of patterns of racial inequity that they did not know or that they never looked at so carefully; they learn to ask questions that they had not thought of; and they learn to unbundle practices into their most basic elements to understand how they work, who benefits most, who benefits least, why something is done in a particular way, how it could be done differently, and so on. The learning that happens through inquiry helps practitioners to view their own practices and consider their effect on students of color from the standpoint of equity. Inquiry and learning are the catalyst for individual and institutional change.

Inquiry as a Change Strategy

The fourth presupposition is that change strategies have to be responsive to the unique characteristics of academic cultures. The intervention strategy presented in this book starts from the Deweyan idea that when problems in learning are encountered, it is best to treat them as indeterminate. In other words, assume that the reasons for the learning problem are not known; therefore, solutions should not be prescribed without first inquiring into the problem. An indeterminate situation is one in which the practices being used by a professional—a teacher, therapist, social worker—do not have the expected effect. Following Dewey's logic, this book frames racial inequity in higher education outcomes as a problem of practice that calls for a structured inquiry by educators, administrators, staff, and leaders into their own or the institution's practices.

The Equity Scorecard is equally appealing to administrators and faculty members. The Equity Scorecard has the features of a comprehensive evidence-based approach, and it resonates with current management rhetoric about accountability, performance, and measurable outcomes. The inquiry processes used in the Equity Scorecard are sensitive to the concerns of academics for participatory as well as rigorous and systematic problem solving. Even though faculty members do not receive a stipend or other forms of remuneration for doing the work required by the Equity Scorecard process, it has been remarkably successful in engaging them. The collaborative approach of data interpretation and decisions about indicators and recommendations for change show that the Equity Scorecard operates from an understanding of faculty culture and acceptance of faculty primacy over academic decision making. Gaining the faculty's trust and support is essential because the influence of the Equity Scorecard depends on their willingness to examine their own practices and be open to the possibility that they may contribute to the patterns of racial inequities that are made visible by the Equity Scorecard.

Racial Inequity as a Problem of Practice

The fifth presupposition is that there is a greater likelihood of improving students' outcomes if the focus of the change strategy is on those things within the immediate control of leaders and practitioners. The Equity Scorecard actively discourages participants from becoming mired in a sociopolitical analysis of racial inequity that blames it on history, poorly funded schools, segregation, poverty, language, single mothers, values, or the students themselves. We recognize that racial inequity is a complex problem and that casting it as a problem of practice risks the appearance of naïve reductionism. However, framing inequity as a problem of practice makes it possible for practitioners to envision themselves as the instrument of change. In order for faculty members to change the outcomes for students of color, they must first learn how to change themselves.

In sum, this intervention called the *Equity Scorecard* is based on the concept that when professionals who are committed to doing good become engaged in a carefully structured participatory process of inquiry into their own practices, they are more apt to accept equity as a worthy and viable goal that deserves attention. This book provides the tools that will help leaders and practitioners develop the knowledge and wisdom to do the good for students from racial and ethnic groups who even today continue to be disadvantaged by an education of poor quality, limited resources, and lack of opportunity.

This book is also for scholars and students of higher education who have an interest in the study of organizational change. Although the Equity

Scorecard is a data tool, the processes through which institutional participants create the Scorecard are grounded in theories of organizational learning, practice theory, participatory action research, and critical perspectives
on race. For those with a scholarly interest in organizational change, this
book provides an introduction to (a) the theories of learning and change that
undergird the "practitioner-as-researcher" model; (b) inquiry as a strategy of
bringing about change at individual, organizational, and societal levels; (c)
the methodology of the "practitioner-as-researcher" model (e.g., outsider
researchers working as facilitators engaged with insider teams of practitioners
in a process of collecting data and creating knowledge about local problems
as seen from a local perspective); (d) the mediational means of facilitating
practitioner learning and change; (e) negotiating institutional politics that
resist equity as an indicator of accountability and quality; and (f) methods
of documenting and evaluating learning and change among practitioners.

The Genesis of the Equity Scorecard

The Equity Scorecard model as presented in this book is the result of many
years of collaborative work to understand how inquiry processes induce
learning and change among higher education practitioners and institutions.
Throughout its development and implementation, the Scorecard model has
been refined and revised while maintaining its core concepts and theoretical
principles.

First Generation: The Diversity Scorecard

The first-generation Scorecard was named the *Diversity Scorecard,* and it
was implemented from January 2001 to the end of 2005. Two grants from
the James Irvine Foundation supported the development of the Diversity
Scorecard and its pilot testing in partnership with fourteen[1] institutions:
six private institutions, five community colleges, and three California State
Universities. In order to better understand how the Scorecard process
worked on the ground, the fourteen institutions were each assigned a
research assistant whose sole responsibility was to be a "human recorder"
(i.e., observe and document the social process of meaning construction
among the members of the teams). We were particularly interested in how
and what was learned by teams and members engaged in collaborative examination of data disaggregated by race and ethnicity.

    In the first year of the Diversity Scorecard project, we held 141 site visits
at the partner campuses, which were documented in 1,100 pages of field

notes. Even though the Equity Scorecard's theory, approaches, and tools have undergone many revisions, the foundational concepts—practitioner-as-researcher, deficit and equity cognitive frames, tools such as the vital signs and equity index, and structures such as the evidence teams—were created during the first two years of the Diversity Scorecard. Several individuals, many who are chapter authors, played prominent roles in the Scorecard's developmental phase. Donald Polkinghorne, the holder of the Attallah Chair in Humanistic Psychology at the Rossier School of Education at the University of Southern California until his retirement, joined CUE's research team at the same time that he was researching and writing *Practice and the Human Sciences: The Case for a Judgment-Based Practice of Care* (2004). This book has been profoundly influential in the Scorecard's theory of change and methods because it was here that Don elaborated the idea that the practitioner is the factor that produces change (p. 3). Don's imprint is obvious in the prominent role practitioners play in the Scorecard's theory of change. His wisdom and creativity helped us turn the Scorecard from a technical tool into a process of practitioner learning and change that has made the Scorecard approach distinctive and inimitable.

The Scorecard would not have been possible without the very generous support of the James Irvine Foundation, which gave us the luxury of freedom to be creative, take risks, and learn from our mistakes. We are particularly indebted to Bob Shireman, our first program officer at Irvine, who challenged us to translate abstract ideas into practices that college presidents and others would find of value. Hilda Hernandez-Gravelle, also at the Irvine Foundation, gave us valuable advice and guidance during the preparation of our second proposal to Irvine.

Other individuals at CUE who contributed to the development and implementation of the Scorecard in the first fourteen colleges were Marta Soto, Georgia Lorenz, Michelle Bleza, Melissa Contreras-McGavin, and Lan Hao, all of whom were affiliated with CUE as doctoral students and postdocs. Marcy Drummond, now a vice president at Los Angeles Trade Technical College, was also a key member of the staff during this period. There were also influential team members at the fourteen participating colleges whose language, values, and practices helped us crystallize two key Scorecard concepts, practitioner as researcher and equity-mindedness: Alfredo Gonzalez and Desdemona Cardoza at CSU–Los Angeles; Abbie Robinson-Armstrong and David Killoran at Loyola Marymount University; Rafael Chabran, Tracy Poon Tambascia, and Fritz Smith at Whittier College; Janice Love and Dan Seymour at Los Angeles City College; Mike Tamada, Karen

Yoshino, and Laura Palucki-Blake at Occidental College; Susan Mills and Joan Wells at Riverside Community College; Keith Osajima at University of Redlands; Erlinda Martinez at Cerritos College; and Cherine Trombley at Los Angeles Valley College. We also received great support from the then-presidents Tyree Weider at Los Angeles Valley College, Mary Spangler as Los Angeles City College, Sal Rotella at Riverside Community College, Father Robert B. Lawton at Loyola Marymount University, and Theodore R. Mitchell at Occidental College.

Second Generation: The Equity Scorecard

In 2005 the Diversity Scorecard was renamed *Equity Scorecard,* primarily because it was a more accurate name given the focus of the Scorecard on racial equity. This phase was funded by Lumina Foundation for Education and by a matching grant from the Office of the Chancellor for California Community Colleges. At Lumina we are especially grateful to Sam Cargile, vice president of grant making, and Professor Heather Wathington, who served as our program officer before joining the faculty at the Curry School of Education at the University of Virginia; at the Chancellor's Office for California Community Colleges, we were fortunate to have former chancellor Mark Drummond as one of the early champions of CUE and the Equity Scorecard. These two grants supported further development and pilot testing of the Scorecard in partnership with nine California community colleges.[2]

In this project, called *Equity for All: Institutional Responsibility for Student Success,* we concentrated more intensely on delineating how practitioners learn and change through their involvement in contextualized inquiry to define and resolve problems of practice. We audiotaped the majority of the meetings held by campus evidence teams (the term that refers to the team charged with creating the Equity Scorecard). This project produced a database of more than 1,500 pages of coded field notes of naturally occurring talk (Perakyla, 2005) in ninety-one campus evidence team meetings among fifty individuals between May 2005 and the summer of 2006. This database allowed us to more rigorously describe key concepts that we had begun to name in the Diversity Scorecard but had not fully explained, such as the qualities of an equity-minded practitioner. It helped us understand the role of institutional researchers, why some became ardent advocates of the process while others were skeptical or outright resisters.

An added value of having this database was that it helped us study the methods used by CUE's researchers to facilitate the Equity Scorecard. As facilitators, we were also exercising what Don Polkinghorne describes as "judgment-based" practice. Our role was to assist the evidence teams through the various steps of the Equity Scorecard process, which entailed asking questions, making suggestions, and creating alternative interpretations, particularly when team members expressed ideas that were at odds with racial equity. An important aim of the facilitation process was to assist practitioners to become equity-minded and discourage interpretations that pointed to student deficiencies as the reason for unequal outcomes. The quality of our facilitation depended on our knowledge of the theory, purposes, and tools of the Equity Scorecard and our group facilitation skills.

Because there were varying levels of understanding of critical theories of racial stratification among CUE's researchers, it was important to build our knowledge and experience to more definitively differentiate between forms of talk that were representative of equity and deficit thinking about student outcomes. It was also important for furthering the development of the Scorecard to establish the kinds of facilitation strategies that helped individuals reframe deficit interpretations from an equity perspective. The database from Equity for All provided us with a wealth of knowledge to support our own learning of what worked, what didn't, what needed further development, and what was missing altogether from the model. This learning is reflected in the chapters in the third section of the book authored by CUE's faculty members and senior facilitators.

Our work with the colleges through *Equity for All* was recognized with a Chancellor's Special Recognition Award for Best Practices in Student Equity. This award is reserved for a person, project, college, or district with notable contributions that advance equity in California's community colleges. In addition, Mt. San Antonio College, an *Equity for All* participating institution, was honored with a Chancellor's award for its efforts to advance equity via its *Achieving Student Empowerment Through Equity and Diversity* initiative.

This phase of the Scorecard involved new researchers, among them professors Alicia C. Dowd, Robert Rueda, and Frank Harris III, who became CUE's associate director and is now a faculty member at San Diego State University. Three PhD students were also involved: Leticia Tomas Bustillos and Edlyn Vallejo Peña, both of whom documented the effect of the Scorecard on practitioner learning and change in their doctoral dissertations. Lindsey Malcom (coeditor of this volume) was also a PhD student and research assistant at CUE during this phase of the Scorecard's development. There were also individuals at the participating colleges who contributed to the continued improvement of Equity Scorecard tools and processes. We are particularly grateful to Leticia Suarez, Fred Trapp, Linda Umbdenstock, and Hannah Oh (Long Beach City College); Dan Walden and Ed Hector (Los Angeles Southwest College); Kelly Pernell (College of Alameda); Marion Winters and Andrew LaManque (Foothill-De Anza); Anika Toussaint-Jackson and Audrey Trotter (Merritt College); Philip Maynard, Angel Lujan, and Barbara McNeice-Stallard (Mt. San Antonio College); Henry Gee, Carolyn Russell, Gail Chabran, and Robert Holcomb (Rio Hondo College); and Janice Takahashi and Kathleen Hart (San Joaquin-Delta College).

Other individuals who have been involved with the work of the CUE and have contributed in a variety of ways include Lloyd Armstrong and Mike Diamond, the former provost and executive vice provost at USC who provided the grant to create CUE. The many foundations and officers with whom we have worked over the last eleven years include Greg Anderson, Janice Petrovich, and Jeannie Oakes at the Ford Foundation; Pamela Burdman at the Hewlett Foundation; and Barbara Gombach at the Carnegie Corporation. We are also grateful to Georgia Lorenz and Robin Bishop for reviewing drafts of chapters, providing editorial advice, and assisting with the overall organization of the book.

Overview of the Book

The book has three sections. Part One consists of three chapters that in combination provide an overview of the Equity Scorecard's theory of change and core concepts, description of tools, and an empirical description of high-learning evidence teams. Chapter 1 provides an extended discussion of the theoretical strands that jointly make up the Scorecard's theory of change. This chapter is important because individuals who are not familiar with the theory of change often mistake the Scorecard for a "technical template" that is filled with numbers. In actuality, change comes about through the guided process of creating the Scorecard as members of evidence teams jointly struggle to create meaning of the racial inequities revealed by "routine" data.

In chapter 2, Georgia Lorenz's study reports on an analysis of organizational learning among the fourteen campus teams that participated in the first generation of the Scorecard. In this chapter she describes the differences between teams that were high, middle, or low learning. This chapter provides a behind-the-scenes look at what constitutes evidence of "evidence-based" problem defining. The Equity Scorecard has a deceptively simple look, but its implementation depends greatly on careful planning and attention to details. Chapter 3 describes the nuts and bolts of the Equity Scorecard and is intended to give readers a closer look at what the tools and processes look like on the ground.

Part Two has four chapters, three of them written by evidence team members from Scorecard institutions. In chapter 4, our partners at Loyola Marymount College describe the changes experienced by the team members who created and implemented the Scorecard, as well as the important role played by their president in the institutionalization of the Scorecard throughout the university. The Scorecard process at Loyola Marymount has been the subject of other publications (Bauman, Bustillos, & Bensimon, 2005) because it illustrates the organizational, political, and leadership factors that contribute to successful implementation and change. It is also an example of sustained change in that the Equity Scorecard has been updated annually by all academic units over the last five years.

In chapter 5, faculty members and administrators from Occidental College, along with Professor Edlyn Vallejo Peña, who was a research assistant at CUE while completing her PhD, describe an inquiry project they undertook in order to explore more deeply a problem revealed in their Scorecard data. Occidental's Scorecard showed that African American students had the lowest first-year retention rates and four-year graduation rates. In the Deweyan tradition (Dewey, 1938), the team treated this finding as "indeterminate," calling for further inquiry. With the assistance of CUE's researchers and the continuous guidance of Dr. Edlyn Vallejo Peña, the authors of this chapter designed an "interview" project that lasted for two years. As a consequence of the interview project, the authors of this chapter developed new knowledge about the classroom and institutional conditions that work against the success of African American as well as Latino and Latina students. This new knowledge resulted in important pedagogical changes to be more responsive to minority students. This chapter provides an excellent illustration of the concept of "practitioner as researcher," which is at the heart of the theory of change underlying the Equity Scorecard process.

In chapter 6, Dr. Leticia Bustillos and Professor Rueda, with faculty members at Los Angeles City College, describe a fifteen-month action research project they embarked on after completing the Scorecard Project. The LACC math faculty sought to understand why African American and Latino students enrolled in remedial mathematics courses were performing at lower levels than their White and Asian peers. Similar to the Occidental team, rather than assuming they knew the answer, they examined the problem using a variety of inquiry methods. The results of their efforts led them to have a greater awareness of their students, including their students' perceptions of mathematics and the resources they needed to succeed at LACC. This chapter details the efforts of this group, offers their recommendations to help improve the educational outcomes of their students, and articulates their individual reflections in regard to their involvement with the "Math Project."

Chapter 7 discusses the results of interviews conducted with eight participants of the first generation of the Scorecard. These participants were selected for their having expressed either particularly positive or negative reactions to their Scorecard experiences. In exploring this "insiders' perspective," authors were able to illuminate the factors that either hindered or facilitated practitioners' engagement with the process. The chapter goes on to highlight the importance of practitioner dialogue around data disaggregated by race as a key component of developing awareness of inequities and ultimately becoming an agent of change.

Part Three has five chapters, three of which consist of research studies conducted in California community colleges participating in Equity for All. The last chapter was written by Georgia Lorenz, a dean at Santa Monica Community College, and discusses the uses of this book for practitioners. Using data from the Equity for All project at nine community colleges in California, chapter 8 highlights how the Scorecard uses a "situated organizational learning model" to build communities of practice that allow practitioners to view inequalities as a problem of institutional accountability that calls for collective action. The chapter begins with a detailed overview of national community college data to provide a context for why such work in community colleges is key to addressing inequitable patterns in higher education. The chapter goes on to provide a thorough description of how the theoretical underpinnings of the Equity Scorecard are informed by both sociocultural work in general and activity theory specifically. This analysis includes an emphasis on the importance of seeing each community college setting as a unique sociocultural context, and creating activity settings within these colleges that are designed around the recognition that learning is social and is mediated by the language tools in the environment.

Chapter 9 utilizes case studies to tell the stories of nine institutional researchers involved in the Equity for All project. In particular, it focuses on their development from being simple managers of data to taking on the roles of teachers who assist others in making meaning of data. It further highlights the journey of institutional researchers from neutral presenters of data to equity advocates. In doing so, the chapter illuminates both the difficulties and potential of using data as a learning tool, and it demonstrates how the design of the Scorecard team setting facilitates the development of these functions for institutional researchers.

Chapter 10 highlights the importance of the organizational change concept of double-loop learning, in which a practitioner comes to focus on the root causes of a problem and to ask, "What changes must I make in myself in order to address this problem?" The chapter also returns to the sociocultural concepts presented in chapter 8 by focusing on the mediational means— the tools, language, and other artifacts of an environment—that facilitate such learning. In exploring this, the authors turn the traditional idea of remediation on its head by suggesting the importance of "re-mediation," in which we change the nature and types of mediation in the professional environment in order to create new understandings. The authors illustrate the means by which this was accomplished in their presentation of conversation excerpts from two Equity for All campuses.

Chapter 11 chronicles the change process for three individuals who took part in the Equity Scorecard process. The first individual chronicled is a practitioner who, as a result of ongoing collaborative questioning with teammates, develops a greater tendency to look at data in equity-minded ways. The second story highlights a team leader who learns to more effectively assist team members in their learning and sensemaking as they examine data and ask questions. Finally, the authors present the story of an institutional researcher who develops her capacity to support the learning of others as they analyze and make sense of data. In addition to telling her story, the authors present examples of the graphical representations that she gave to teams at early and later stages in the process to illustrate how she changed her approach to focus on others' understanding, rather than simply the data itself. The chapter concludes with a number of practice and policy changes that were implemented at the nine community colleges that took part in this round of Equity Scorecard inquiry. In essence, through its varied examples, this chapter synthesizes many of the types of learning and change explained in earlier chapters into one cohesive picture.

The book concludes with a reflection from the field by Georgia Lorenz, a dean at Santa Monica College. She shares her professional observation that, although everyone working in higher education has good intentions toward students, not all practitioners are *aware* of inequities and their potential place in these inequities. She speaks to the Equity Scorecard as key to bringing that consciousness to practitioners. Dr. Lorenz also shares a number of key "aha" moments that she witnessed on various Scorecard teams during her former time as a research assistant at CUE. She connects her own learning at CUE to her present-day experiences as a dean and leaves us with a reflection on how the early days of the Equity Scorecard set the stage for its present manifestation.

Notes

1. The fourteen partner institutions are Loyola Marymount University, Mt. St. Mary's College, Occidental College, University of LaVerne, University of Redlands, Whittier College, Cerritos College, Los Angeles Valley College, Los Angeles City College, Riverside Community College, Santa Monica College, California State University–Dominguez Hills, California State University–Fullerton, and California State University–Los Angeles.

2. College of Alameda, De Anza College, Hartnell College, LA Southwest College, Long Beach City College, Merritt College, Mount San Antonio College, Rio Hondo College, and San Joaquin Delta College.

References

Bauman, G. L., Bustillos, L. T., & Bensimon, E. M. (2005). Achieving equitable educational outcomes with all students: The institution's roles and responsibilities. In *Making exclusive inclusive: Preparing students and campuses for an era of greater expectations* (pp. 1–57). Association of American Colleges and Universities.

Dewey, J. (1938). *Logic: The theory of inquiry.* New York, NY: Henry Holt.

Perakyla, A. (2005). Analyzing talk and text. In N. Denzin & Y. S. Lincoln (Eds.), *The Sage handbook of qualitative research* (3rd ed., pp. 869–886). Thousand Oaks, CA: Sage.

Polkinghorne, D. E. (2004). *Practice and the human sciences: The case for a judgment-based practice of care.* Albany: State University of New York Press.

PART ONE

THEORY, ORGANIZATIONAL LEARNING, AND TOOLS AND PRACTICES OF THE EQUITY SCORECARD

I

THE EQUITY SCORECARD
Theory of Change

Estela Mara Bensimon

I n the Equity Scorecard process, student success in college is framed as an institutional responsibility that requires *race-conscious* expertise. The centrality of race-conscious practitioner expertise distinguishes the Equity Scorecard process from the more familiar models of student success. Prevailing models of student success are based on sociopsychological behavioral theories of student development, integration, and engagement. Typically academic success is described and assessed as behaviors, attitudes, and aspirations that represent how college students, ideally, ought to be. The normative model of academic success focuses on the student's self-motivation and the amount of effort he or she willingly invests into the academic activities that signify he or she is taking on the identity of "college student." The normative model of academic success is exemplified by Vincent Tinto's (1987) theory of academic and social integration, Alexander Astin's theory of involvement, and George Kuh's (2003) model of student engagement. Although there is no lack of evidence that these models capture what it takes to be academically successful in our colleges and universities, there is also plenty of evidence showing that very large numbers of students do not have access to the social networks that can help them develop the knowledge, practices, attitudes, and aspirations associated with the ideal college student.

Practitioners and scholars typically respond to evidence of low rates of college completion by asking questions that focus attention on the student: *Are these students academically integrated? Do these students exhibit desired behavioral patterns? Do these students exert effort? How does the effort of these students compare with the effort of such-and-such group? How do the aspirations of high-performing students compare with those of low-performers? Are they engaged? Are they involved? Are they motivated? Are they prepared?*

A premise of the Equity Scorecard process is that questions like these reflect a normative model of academic success. That is, academic success is associated with the experiences, behaviors, and values of the full-time, traditional college-age student. When we come across students who are not engaged or involved, who don't take advantage of support resources, or who rarely ask questions or seek help, we judge them as deficient and in need of compensatory interventions. These students often acquire the "at-risk" label.

The purpose of this chapter is to introduce a theory of student success that focuses on the knowledge and behaviors of practitioners and institutions, rather than on the knowledge and behaviors of students. Instead of speaking about the racial achievement gap, we focus on the knowledge and cultural gap that undercuts practitioners' capacity to be responsive to the students they *get*, rather than the ones they might *wish* for.

The chapter introduces the concept of funds of knowledge for race-conscious expertise, followed by a discussion of the four theoretical strands: sociocultural theories of learning, organizational learning, practice theory, and critical theories of race that represent the principles of change underlying the Equity Scorecard process. The chapter concludes with the attributes of equity-minded individuals.

Funds of Knowledge for Race-Conscious Expertise

In this section we discuss the meaning of funds of knowledge, how they develop, why the prevailing funds of knowledge that practitioners draw on are inadequate to undo racial patterns of inequity, and how practitioners can develop funds of knowledge that increase their expertise to make equity possible.

The terms *funds of knowledge* (González, Moll, & Amanti, 2005; Moll, Amanti, Neff, & Gonzalez, 1992), *background knowledge* (Polkinghorne, 2004), *tacit knowledge, implicit theories, cognitive frames* (Bensimon, 2005), and *cultural frameworks,* among many others, have been used by social scientists to describe historically developed and accumulated strategies (e.g., skills, abilities, ideas, practices) or bodies of knowledge that practitioners draw on, mostly unconsciously, in their everyday actions. They draw on these funds of knowledge as they decide what to pay attention to, what decisions to make, or how to respond to particular situations (Polkinghorne, 2004). A premise of the Equity Scorecard process is that practitioners can make a marked difference in the educational outcomes of minoritized[1] (Gillborn, 2005) students if *they recognize that their practices are not working* and *participate in designed situated learning opportunities to develop the funds of knowledge necessary for equity-minded practice* (Bensimon, Rueda, Dowd, & Harris, 2007).

How do we know that practitioners' funds of knowledge are inadequate for the task of improving the academic outcomes of minoritized populations? Through our work with the many campuses implementing the Center for Urban Education's (CUE's) Equity Model, we have documented the conversations of practitioners as they attempt to make sense of racial patterns of inequity revealed by their own institutional data. The Equity Scorecard process, through its various data tools and data practices, enables practitioners to notice racial disparities in successful completion of remedial[2] courses in English and mathematics; persistence in science, technology, engineering, and mathematics (STEM) majors; transfer to four-year colleges; graduation with honors; and many other fine-grained measures that signify the completion of critical milestones as well as participation in academic opportunities (e.g., studying abroad, doing research with a faculty member, having an internship in a Fortune 500 company, transferring to a highly selective college) that enhance students' likelihood of accessing valued experiences, resources, and social networks.

Our analyses of practitioners' talk consistently show that the prevailing funds of knowledge informing their interpretations of student outcomes reflect widely accepted beliefs about student success. These beliefs are mostly derived from psychological theories of motivation, self-efficacy, and self-regulation, as well as sociological theories of cultural integration. In essence, practitioners have learned to associate academic success with individual characteristics and attributes that signify the motivated, self-regulating, and academically and socially engaged archetype college student. For sure, it is hard to dispute practitioners' desire for college students who are responsible; persist from semester to semester; and graduate, if not in four years, within six. But the reality is that a great many students, particularly those who are first-generation, low-income, immigrant, or from marginalized racial and ethnic groups have been disadvantaged by highly segregated high schools that lacked the resources to prepare them, academically and culturally, for college. Upon entering college these students are further disadvantaged by a college culture that expects them to know the rules and behaviors of academic success: seeking help when in academic trouble, visiting faculty members during office hours, knowing how to study, and having goals and being committed to them.

These students are not an exception. In many colleges, particularly community colleges and four-year colleges with open admissions policies, they are modal students. Viewed through the normative lens of academic success, these students fall so short of the image we have of academic-ready college students that they have become known as *at-risk*. Herein lies a major obstacle to the agenda of equity in educational outcomes for minoritized students: The funds of knowledge that lead practitioners to expect self-directed students, and to label those who fall short of the ideal *at-risk,* reinforce a logic of student success that is detrimental to an equity change agenda.

The logic underlying the notion of at-risk students goes something like this: "If students are not doing well it must be because they are not exerting the effort/seeking help/motivated; or because they are working too many hours/unprepared for college/disengaged." Framing the problem in this manner is defeatist in that patterns of racial inequity seem inevitable and self-fulfilling. This leaves little hope for practitioner agency. It is also unproductive because a focus on the deficits of students discourages practitioners' deeper reflection about their failure to understand the structural production of inequality or the need for institutional responsibility—in practices and ethos—for producing racial equity in educational outcomes.

To bring about institutional transformation for equity and student success, practitioners, including institutional leaders, have to develop funds of knowledge for equity-minded expertise. We pause here to provide an example that contextualizes the meaning of deficit and equity-minded funds of knowledge through an actual conversation among members of a campus team that participated in one of CUE's early field tests[3] of the "Equity Scorecard" (at the time called "Diversity Scorecard"). This excerpt was adapted from "Learning Equity-Mindedness: Equality in Educational Outcomes" (Bensimon, 2006) to illustrate funds of knowledge that represent a deficit perspective of student success. Throughout the rest of the chapter we will refer to it to show how the Equity Scorecard process attempts to remediate this perspective.

Campuses that adopt the Equity Scorecard process create teams of practitioners based on specific criteria: knowledge; leadership attributes; and forms of involvement in decision making, academic governance, and administrative structures. Institutional researchers are required to be members of the teams because the Equity Scorecard process's initial phases involve the review of numerical data as a means of raising awareness of inequality at various stages of educational progress and success.

The team portrayed in the following excerpt had been meeting for several months to create indicators for its campus's Equity Scorecard. One of the perspectives of the Scorecard is "excellence" and teams typically examine indicators that, as mentioned previously, illustrate experiences and relationships that give students access to scarce resources that create advantage for a small number of beneficiaries (e.g., honors programs).

Among community college teams a common measure of equity within the "excellence" perspective of the Scorecard is the proportion of students, by race and ethnicity, who transfer to selective colleges. We encourage community college teams to examine transfer patterns to highly selective institutions, particularly the flagship campuses of their public university system because there is a tendency to ignore racial and ethnic access to high-resourced and elite institutions. For example, if the community college portrayed in the excerpt was located in Texas, then the team would look at transfer to UT–Austin or Texas A&M at College Station; if it was located in Wisconsin, then transfer patterns to UW Madison would be the focus of the analysis. In California, transfer into UC–Los Angeles and UC–Berkeley would constitute important metrics of equity.

The Funds of Knowledge Evident in Team Members' Data Interpretations

The following excerpt from a conversation among three members of a community college Equity Scorecard *evidence team*[4] was prompted by data on transfer patterns to the state's highly selective flagship university, which is located about ten miles from the college. To make it easier for the team members to notice the patterns of inequity, the institutional researcher created two pie charts (see Figure 1.1). The pie chart on the left shows that among the almost 18,000 students enrolled in the college, Latinas and Latinos are the largest group, constituting just over 40 percent of the total head count, followed by Whites (35 percent), Asian Americans (13 percent), African Americans (7 percent), and American Indians (4 percent). The pie chart on the right shows that on the particular year being examined, 141 students transferred successfully to the highly selective public university. As can be seen immediately, Latinos' and Latinas' share of the students who transferred to the flagship university is 23 percent, which is considerably lower than their 40 percent share of the total enrollment. In the case of Latinas and Latinos, to have equity in transfer to the flagship university they would need to increase their share from 23 percent to 40 percent. The pie chart also shows that while White students represent 35 percent of the total student population, their share of the transfer population is 48 percent.

Let's see how three of the team members attempt to create meaning of the equity gaps between enrollment and transfer to the highly selective university campus. As you read the excerpt it is important to concentrate on the language used and reflect on the ways in which unequal outcomes are attributed to students' characteristics, making them the authors of their own inequities.

> **Dean:** More Black and Latino students may transfer to the local four-year college than to the state's leading university because the state college is closer to home.
> **Counselor:** This may be an issue for Latino students because of the pressure from family to remain close to home.

FIGURE 1.1[5]
Members of a community college evidence team comparing the shares of total enrollment and transfers to a selective university by race and ethnicity.

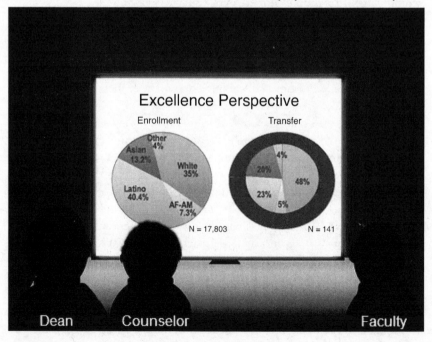

Faculty: It may also be related to financial issues. Many students do not know about financial aid options. They also tend to manage money poorly.

Counselor: Many students don't take advantage of the tutoring and counseling services we offer because they are embarrassed to use them or don't see their relevance to educational success.

Faculty: Or they may not value education intrinsically but see it as a ticket to a well-paying job. Many of our Latino and African American students need remediation due to inadequate academic preparation, but they are not willing to put in the work necessary to be able to transfer. Some of them may need two or three years of remediation even to begin taking courses that are transferable, and this discourages many students.

Based on how these individuals respond to the data, what are they saying and what can be inferred about the funds of knowledge implicit in their interpretations about unequal patterns of outcomes? This is how we read it:

1. The individuals construct a narrative about the pie charts in such a way that inequity, instead of being interpreted as a *racialized* outcome is *rationalized* as a cultural predisposition of Latino and Black students to "stay close to home."

2. The assumption is made that the students may be low income and need financial aid to be able to transfer to the more selective college, but they are not smart enough to take advantage of financial aid opportunities, nor do they have the competence to manage their finances responsibly.

3. The assumption is made that students lack the academic qualifications; therefore, they have to enroll in remedial education courses, taking them longer to get to the college-level courses that will eventually make them eligible for transfer. It is assumed that the students do not help themselves because they don't take advantage of the college's academic support services. Why not? Because, it is assumed, that they are embarrassed to admit they need help or they don't have the motivation; or because they lack the stick-to-itness needed to get through the long sequence of remedial education courses.

4. In addition, it is assumed, these students may not have the cultural or social class predisposition to appreciate education for its own sake. The assumption is that they are more motivated by occupational opportunities than by a general and liberal arts education.

The explanations given by the participants foreground student deficits and take the focus away from the pattern of intrainstitutional racial inequity that is revealed by the transfer patterns in the pie chart. The conversation among the dean, counselor, and instructor bring to mind the "color-mute" (Pollock, 2004) euphemisms that are used in education—"at-risk," "disadvantaged," "underprepared"—to attribute disparities to race and culture without appearing to do so.

The dialogue creates the distinct impression that what *we* interpret as an instance of inequity in transfer patterns these practitioners view as the domino effect of cumulative disadvantages inherent in the students' cultural and social characteristics, which are manifested in lack of self-efficacy, lack of effort, lack of ambition, and avoidance of help-seeking due to hyper self-consciousness. The influence of normative concepts of student success (e.g., commitment, effort, motivation, and integration) are discernable in the team members' attribution of small transfer numbers among Latinas and Latinos to inadequate values, not having the right attitude, and not engaging in desirable behavioral patterns.

Although it is possible that the practitioners in the illustration may not be familiar with the scholarly literature on college student development and success, it is highly likely that they have been exposed to key concepts such as engagement, involvement, effort, and integration in conference workshops, professional development activities, newsletters, and websites, as well as in courses offered in higher education graduate programs in student affairs and administration.

In the context of our theory of change, it is important to note the following: The practitioners depicted previously reacted to the data display spontaneously and in the moment. Their talk was "unrehearsed" (Perakyla, 2005). Their interpretations of the data represented in the two pie charts are informed by their funds of knowledge, which have been acquired over time and which they draw on unconsciously. These funds of knowledge (also called "the background" by Polkinghorne) function mostly below consciousness (Polkinghorne, 2004).

Like the practitioners depicted in this brief conversation, the funds of knowledge that most higher education practitioners have developed do not encourage reflection on ways in which their practices, judgments, and beliefs may contribute to or exacerbate the production of racially unequal outcomes. Entertaining the possibility that inequality may be as much a problem of practitioner knowledge, pedagogical approaches, or "culturally held" ideas about minoritized students (Nasir & Hand, 2006) is not a typical practice within institutions of higher education or among academic leaders and policymakers. This is not because practitioners, leaders, and policymakers are irresponsible or uncaring, but because most of us lack the funds of knowledge to assist us in noticing patterns of racial inequity and, once noticed, to be able to analyze them as a failure of structures, policies, or practices that can be changed.

The challenge, therefore, is how to create the funds of knowledge that are needed to bring about equity-minded institutional transformation. In order for the practitioners in the community college evidence team to reframe their interpretations within the perspective of failed institutional practices rather than failed students, they would need to have the funds of knowledge that help them recognize that the problem depicted in the pie charts is an indeterminate situation (Dewey, 1938; Polkinghorne, 2004). This means that the reasons for the inequities in transfer are unknown and demand a disciplined inquiry into the possible causes. The inquiry needs to start from questions that turn attention to the realm of the practitioner and the institution, rather than to the realm of the students, as was done by the members of the community college evidence team. When inquiry is framed from the standpoint of the practitioner and his or her practices, the questions that can lead to substantive learning and change include (a) How is transfer "done" here? and (b) In what ways might we be "doing" transfer that results in unequal outcomes for African Americans and Latinos and Latinas? Simply put, practitioners need to *learn* how to ask, "In what ways are our practices failing such-and-such students" and *unlearn* to ask, "What is wrong with these students?"

In sum, we lack the funds of knowledge that would enable most of us to notice racial inequities within our classrooms, departments, schools, and institutions. Moreover, when they are brought to our attention we lack the funds of knowledge to ask, "In what ways are my practices, or the practices of this institution, related to racial inequities in outcomes?" "In what ways are institutional practices enabling or reinforcing racial inequities in outcomes?"

Reframing the problem from one having to do with what is wrong with students to one having to do with the inadequacy of practices is a major cultural and intellectual challenge. To question our own efficacy or knowledge goes against our identity as professional experts. Additionally, the suggestion that the solution to the problem of inequity may lie in taking a hard look inward into institutional practices—as well as our own within the classroom, the counseling office, the dean's office, or the president's cabinet—goes against the inclination to externalize the problem and jump to solutions that typically involve the adoption of proven "best practices."

It is also worth pointing out that the Equity Scorecard process attempts a major shift in the ways leaders, policymakers, practitioners, and scholars think about how colleges work (Birnbaum, 1988), how they learn, and how they can change. While this book is not about theories of organizational change, readers will note that the Equity Scorecard process's conceptualization of change, as an outcome of practitioner engagement in situated learning, represents a considerable departure from conventional perspectives. These conventional perspectives center on change as an outcome of rational actions induced by strategic planning, data-based decision making, external accountability systems, instrumental incentives, restructuring, or adoption of best practices.

In the next section we present the key principles of the Equity Scorecard process and we will return to the example of the community college evidence team to illustrate them in action.

The Equity Scorecard Process: Principles of Institutional Change

The aim of the Equity Scorecard process is to assist practitioners in developing new funds of knowledge that empower them with the expertise, know-how, and self-efficacy to produce equity in outcomes within their classrooms, departments, and institutions.

The theory of action used within the Equity Scorecard process draws on principles of learning and change derived from sociocultural activity setting theory, organizational learning theory, practice theory, and critical theories of race. First, it draws on the *sociocultural idea* that (a) learning is social, (b) learning is facilitated by assisted performance that is responsive, (c) learning is mediated by cultural tools and artifacts, and (d) learning takes place in communities of practice and is indexed by changes in participation within these communities (Rogoff, Baker-Sennett, Lacasa, & Goldsmith, 1995; Roth & Lee, 2007; Rueda, 2006; Tharp & Gallimore, 1988; Wenger, 1998; Wenger, McDermott, & Snyder, 2002). Although these concepts of learning have been mostly applied to the study of learning among children, they are relevant to the study of learning among adults, particularly when combined with theories of organizational learning.

Second, *organizational learning* theorists (Argyris, 1977, 1982, 1991; Argyris & Schön, 1996) differentiate between two types of learning: single loop and double loop. Single-loop learners are prone to externalize problems by attributing them to forces and circumstances that are beyond their control. Single-loop learners tend to view evidence of inequities in educational outcomes as evidence of student deficiencies and they resort to compensatory strategies as the solution (Bensimon, 2005). Examples of single-loop learning solutions are a ubiquitous characteristic of college campuses, from the most elite to the least selective. Special support service programs such as TRIO, Puente, the Mathematics, Engineering, Science, and Achievement (MESA) program, and many more reflect single-loop learning solutions in that their focus is to equip students with the academic and cultural knowledge to survive in institutional cultures that may be hostile to their presence and not self-reflective about race and racialized practices. The trouble with solutions based on single-loop learning is that they leave internal values, norms, and beliefs unchallenged. Double-loop learning focuses attention on the root causes of a problem and the changes that need to be made in the attitudes, values, beliefs, and practices of individuals and organizations to bring about enduring results (Bauman, 2005).

Lest we be misunderstood, we are absolutely convinced that without the many special support and academic programs referenced previously, racial and ethnic inequity in higher education would be a lot worse. These programs provide racial and ethnic minority students with access to a network of professionals who often share the students' racial and social class backgrounds and have the experiential knowledge to be responsive to students' needs and, when required, are able to advocate on their behalf. These professionals often see themselves in the students and are able to adjust their practices to the situation of students labeled "at risk." They have the experiential know-how to understand the difficulties of navigating an alienating environment, thus giving them an insight into students' actions that individuals who don't see themselves in the students lack.

In labeling such programs the product of single-loop learning, my intent is not to be derogatory or overlook the extraordinary role these programs have played on campuses everywhere. Quite the contrary, having spent the first ten years of my professional life in various roles associated with "compensatory" programs, I am very cognizant of their critical role in mediating the success of first-generation students from racial and ethnic communities with a history of exclusion. What I am critical of is the hierarchical stratification of institutions of higher education that marginalizes programs for minority students and separates them from the institutional "mainstream," causing students to miss out on the opportunity for double-loop learning.

Given the mission of these programs and the racial diversity of their leadership and staffing, I speculate that they have accumulated valuable knowledge and experience about the ways in which minoritized populations experience the campus. However, their often marginal status prevents them from spreading their know-how throughout the institution. This may be the reason why, despite the myriad of compensatory programs, gaps in educational outcomes persist and even get larger.

Third, the Equity Scorecard process takes a different approach to framing the problem than do theories of student success. Rather than starting out with students' characteristics and poor academic preparation as the culprit for inequity in educational outcomes, we frame *inequity as an indeterminate problem of practice.* We use the term *practice* broadly in reference to the actions of individuals such as an instructor, a counselor, or a dean, as well as to the practices and policies inscribed in an institution's structural arrangements and cultural characteristics. Practice theorists, drawing on the work of Dewey (1938) and Vygotsky (1978, 1934/1987), maintain that practitioners learn and change when they encounter an indeterminate situation that makes them realize their actions are not producing the results they hoped to obtain. According to Polkinghorne (2004), an indeterminate situation is one in which practitioners find that "their practices fail them." We apply these ideas in the Equity Scorecard process by framing inequity in educational outcomes as an indication that practices—at the individual or institutional level—are failing to produce the expected results for students from particular racial and ethnic groups. That is, rather than conceiving of inequity as a sign of student failure, we view it as a sign of institutional malfunction that calls for an investigation to learn what is not working and what changes need to be made. The changes may be in structures, pedagogical approaches, delivery of services, professional development, or policies; they may also need to be changes in individuals' knowledge and beliefs about race that prevent them from making judgments about what to do to facilitate the success of students of color.

In *Practice and the Human Sciences: The Case for a Judgment-Based Practice of Care,* Donald Polkinghorne (2004) focuses on the "practitioner as the factor that produces change" by engaging in "judgment-based" decision making. The notion of the practitioner as the agent of change is essential to understanding the theory of action that distinguishes the Equity Scorecard process from other approaches and interventions. An important premise of the Equity Scorecard process is that the failure of practice (i.e., inequity) is caused by practitioners' lack of requisite knowledge to create successful outcomes for racial and ethnic minority students. For example, practitioners may not be aware of the extra "cultural effort" (Dowd & Korn, 2005; Tanaka, 2002) that is imposed by predominantly White institutional cultures on students who have experienced discrimination, exclusionary practices, and the general sense of being outsiders (Bensimon, 2007; Peña, Bensimon, & Colyar, 2006).

As already discussed, higher education practitioners have been socialized to expect autonomous and self-regulating students who take responsibility for their own learning and they often assume that students know how to be students. Consequently, they may unconsciously attribute the lower rates of success that are experienced by African American, Latina, and Latino students, and other minoritized groups, to individual characteristics and backgrounds rather than to educational practices, institutional policies, and culture. Attributing unequal educational outcomes to students' lack of academic preparation, motivation, help-seeking behaviors, or engagement is problematic because, in addition to blaming the student, race-based disparities are made to appear as a natural occurrence that is not within the control of higher education practitioners.

Fourth, *race-consciousness* is central to the Equity Scorecard process. Being race-conscious requires that individuals learn to see the ways in which race is embedded in everyday practices. Critical race scholars (Harper, Patton, & Wooden, 2009; Ladson-Billings, 2006; Matsuda, Lawrence, Delgado, & Crenshaw, 1993; Solórzano, Villalpando, & Oseguera, 2005; Yosso, Parker, Solórzano, & Lynn, 2004) contend that inequality is produced and maintained by the routine practices of institutions and the cumulative effect of racial micro-aggressions. Thus, from a critical race perspective, the claim that inequity in educational outcomes is race-neutral would be challenged. In order to close the opportunity gaps that disadvantage the educational experiences of racial and ethnic groups, it is necessary to reinterpret inequity in educational outcomes from the perspective of those who experience them, taking into account the social, cultural, and historical context of exclusion, discrimination, and educational apartheid.

These four theoretical strands: sociocultural theories of learning, organizational learning, practice theory, and critical theories of race inspired the principles of institutional learning and change that make up the Equity Scorecard process. In the next section we describe these principles further.

Principles of Change Underlying the Equity Scorecard Process

Principle One: Practitioners learn and change through their engagement in a joint productive activity. (Sociocultural theories of learning)

To develop equity-minded funds of knowledge, the Equity Scorecard process relies on the strategy of creating "activity settings" (Roth & Lee, 2007) that call on practitioners to perform actions requiring new competencies. These activity settings are structured in ways that both draw on and challenge established competencies, placing learners in the "zone of proximal development," where the new competencies for equity-minded leadership are within reach (Tharp, 1993; Tharp & Gallimore, 1988) and obtainable through a process of "situated" inquiry (Bauman, 2005; Lave & Wenger, 1991; Peña et al., 2006). An activity setting consists of individuals who collaborate on a joint productive activity. In the Equity Scorecard process the activity involves the examination of routine data on student outcomes disaggregated by race and ethnicity and the construction of indicators and goals to populate the four perspectives of the Equity Scorecard. The activity setting is designed to raise practitioners' awareness of inequities and to help practitioners learn to examine their own settings to determine how inequities are created and sustained and consider how practices, structures, and policies might be changed.

As already shown in the scenario introduced earlier, the funds of knowledge practitioners rely on are reflected in their dialogues to create meaning out of the data. For example, in the earlier scenario the dominant funds of knowledge that the practitioners call upon to make sense of the data patterns exemplify what some scholars have described as "bootstrap ideology" (Horvat & O'Connor, 2006), deficit paradigms (Valencia, 1997), or culture of poverty (Valencia, 1997). In the Equity Scorecard process, we use the term *deficit-minded* in reference to the funds of knowledge that prevent individuals from seeing racial inequity or cause them to interpret disparities as a deterministic deficiency that afflicts Latinos, Latinas, and African Americans in particular. The change project of the Equity Scorecard process is to assist practitioners to become aware of deficit-mindedness in themselves and others, as well as in structures and policies that may disadvantage minoritized populations.

Principle Two: Inequity in educational outcomes is characterized as an indeterminate situation produced by a failure of practice. (Practice theory)

The development of practitioners into agents of equity for students of color requires that they react to data showing inequity in educational outcomes as evidence that something is not working. The reasons for the dysfunction could be many things; however, in the Equity Scorecard process the possible sources of the dysfunction are restricted to characteristics of institutional structures, policies, practices, and culture that can be changed through the individual and collective actions of leaders, including trustees and practitioners.

To facilitate an understanding of inequity as a symptom of institutional dysfunction, data revealing patterns of inequity, such as those shown in the pie charts in Figure 1.1, are characterized as an "indeterminate situation" (Dewey, 1938)—that is, a situation in which the *institutional basis of malfunction* is unknown. To view disparities in student outcomes as an indeterminate situation triggered by an institutional malfunction requires practitioners to learn how to frame problems so that they, not the students, are the target of change. The interpretation of inequities in educational outcomes as a failure of practice goes against academic culture; moreover, the positing of situated learning (i.e., inquiry) as a strategy of change can prove to be challenging because institutions of higher education are not organized to learn about themselves (Dill, 1999; Garvin, 1993).

In order to overcome the cultural and organizational conditions that stand in the way of practitioners learning to view inequity as an indeterminate situation that calls for inquiry to discover why and in what ways practices are failing to produce expected outcomes, the CUE has created specialized tools, processes, structures, and expert assistance from individuals who are knowledgeable in the four theoretical strands that are foundational to the Equity Scorecard process.

It would be natural to ask, "Why is it necessary to define inequity as an indeterminate situation arising from institutional failure?" We realize that inequities in educational outcomes are multidimensional, complex, and unique. We also recognize that they have been produced over time by the great inequalities in income, wealth, health, and housing that have long divided the United States into separate and unequal worlds (Hacker, 2003). Delimiting the problem of inequity to a failure of institutional practice is a pragmatic decision to define it in a manner that is conducive to institutional action and change.

To make the concepts of indeterminate situation and institutional dysfunction or failure of practice more concrete, let us turn our attention once again to the scenario of the community college evidence team introduced in the previous section. In our model, one approach to defining equity in transfer rates is based on population proportionality. Applying this definition of equity to Latinas and Latinos would mean that the number who should have transferred to the flagship university is 58 (41 percent of 141). Instead, there were only 32 Latinas and Latinos who transferred, 26 fewer than there should have been. Needless to say, we have no idea why there were 26 fewer Latino and Latina transfers to the flagship university. It is an indeterminate situation that causes practitioners to inquire: What might we be doing or not doing that is causing us to be less effective in transferring Latina and Latino students to the flagship university? To answer this question and be proactive to remedy the situation, the Equity Scorecard process engages practitioners in a set of planned inquiry activities to unpack the problem and collect numerical and qualitative data. In education there is currently a big emphasis on data, data-based decision making, and a movement to create humongous data systems. Through our work we have learned that student unit record data are indeed important in helping to pinpoint problems. But we have also learned that unless practitioners or policymakers have the capacity to frame basic and practical questions, neither the quantity nor quality of data can compensate for the lack of good questions. Our experience suggests that the more familiar institutional actors are with particular conditions, structures, or situations, the more difficult it is for them to know what to ask in order to pull apart the "black box" of, say, transfer, remediation, completion of key milestones, persistence in STEM fields, and so on.

In the case of the missing Latinos and Latinas transferring to the elite flagship university, some of the questions that need to be asked to get at what may be causing the discovered inequity include the following:

- What are the requirements to transfer to an elite flagship university?
- How many students, disaggregated by race and ethnicity, meet those requirements?
- Of the students who were eligible to transfer to an elite flagship university, how many actually applied, were admitted, and subsequently enrolled?
- What are the current practices in place to assist students to transfer to elite flagship universities?[6]
- What can be learned about the quality of our transfer practices by talking to Latinos and Latinas who transferred to an elite flagship university?
- What can be learned from institutions that are successful in transferring Latinos and Latinas to an elite flagship university?

The Equity Scorecard process assists evidence teams in arriving at the bulleted questions and to design inquiry activities to answer them. The knowledge that is created by practitioners inquiring into the bulleted questions has several advantages that make the effort and time invested into inquiry worthwhile. Locally generated knowledge is more meaningful to those who have to solve the problem than knowledge produced by an expert consultant; the inquiry focus on the failure of practices, structures, or policies produces knowledge about things that can be acted on (i.e., if they are not working they can be changed or eliminated; if a process or procedure or structure does not exist it can be created; and the results of changing, eliminating, or creating something can be assessed to determine whether or not they are working).

Admittedly, the bulleted questions that have been proposed to get inside the black box of transfer to the elite flagship university appear to be commonsense, perhaps overly simple. But their simplicity is the very thing that prevents institutional actors from asking them. It is difficult to put things that are taken for granted and are assumed to be known and understood, like the process of transfer, under a microscope. As a consequence, asking commonsense, basic questions takes a lot of well-planned and assisted instruction. The Equity Scorecard process provides the data practices and data tools that assist practitioners to implement the methods of situated inquiry and generate locally meaningful knowledge (Lave & Wenger, 1991) to bring about change.

Principle Three: Practitioner-led inquiry is a means of developing awareness of racial inequity and self-change. (Practice theory and organizational learning theory)

As shown in the pie-chart illustration, the Equity Scorecard process employs data practices to make them visible to practitioners, who in turn draw on their experiential knowledge to make sense of them. In the pie-chart illustration, the practitioners' experiential funds of knowledge result in deficit-minded hunches (i.e., inequity is externalized and attributed to student characteristics). The hunches provided by the practitioners are an example of single-loop learning.

To assist evidence team members in reframing their hunches so that they lead to double-loop learning, an experienced facilitator who is familiar with the Equity Scorecard process's theory of change assists participants by redirecting their hunches and focusing them on cultural practices, structures, and policies. Returning to the pie-chart example, let us take a look at how the faculty member's statement can be reframed, from a deficit pertaining to students to a deficit pertaining to the institution.

Deficit-minded framing (Single-loop learning)	Equity-minded framing (Double-loop learning)
Faculty Member: *It may also be related to financial issues. Many students do not know about financial aid options. They also tend to manage money poorly.*	**Faculty Member:** *It may also be related to financial issues. We may not be doing a good job of letting students know about the different options for financial aid. We assume that because the information is available at the financial aid office or on the website, everyone is aware of it. When was the last time any of us looked into how students find out about financial aid?*

The first statement is labeled *single-loop learning* because the faculty member externalizes the problem and blames it on students' lack of knowledge about resources as well as inability to manage their money responsibly. Single-loop learning typically treats the symptoms of a problem without addressing its root causes. Student knowledge about financial aid can be reframed as a double-loop learning problem by asking whether the institution is being responsive to the needs of their students and providing financial aid services actively and in a caring way.

In the rewritten double-loop version, the statement points to some of the potential practices that could be inquired into. The inquiry questions underlying the statement are: (a) In what ways do we currently provide information on financial aid to students? (b) What might be hidden obstacles to getting information about financial aid? (c) What is our expertise in financial aid opportunities for transfer students? A community college that took up this question discovered that the office charged with providing information about scholarships operated only during certain times of the year that coincided with the deadlines for transfer applications. Consequently, the handful of students in the honors program (where minority students were severely underrepresented) were the most likely to get the information because they had a dedicated transfer counselor.

In the Equity Model, the first frame reflects what we have labeled as "deficit-minded" hunches or hypotheses, in which students are blamed for the inequities they experience. The second frame is labeled "equity-minded" because it places the institution as the responsible agent for the unintended creation of inequity and for the actions to correct it.[7]

Admittedly, solutions that focus on student deficiencies may work in the short term, but they will not change the cultural practices, structures, power relations, values, and other contextual factors that produce racial inequities in educational outcomes. In contrast, when "practices" and "practitioners" are the subject of the hunches there is increased likelihood that inquiry will lead to incremental corrective steps and that engagement in the process of inquiry will result in practitioner learning and self-change that has a direct and immediate effect on the students with whom these practitioners come into contact. For example, at an Equity Scorecard process community college, a professor who participated in an inquiry project designed to examine the culture of transfer (Bensimon, Dowd, Alford, & Trapp, 2007) became more conscious of the role he could play in developing students' transfer aspirations and providing them with direct assistance. He took several actions that let students know he cared about their transfer aspirations and was available to provide information about the process and options. A few months after the project was completed he wrote an exuberant e-mail:

> I want to fill you in on some good news. Three of my former students have been accepted to Berkeley for the Fall as philosophy majors. (Is that wild or what?) In addition, a student that I recommended for the Jack Kent Cooke scholarship not only got the scholarship, but he got accepted to UCLA, Berkeley, and Stanford! He's accepted the full ride at Stanford where he will probably major in sociology with a minor in African American studies. And these are just the students who I've run into over the past two weeks!

This example supports the notion that individuals can become agents of change as a result of inquiring into an institutional problem of inequity. On the other hand, the excerpt also points to our unfinished work. To become an equity-minded practitioner means to be race-conscious and aware of who benefits from one's actions and who is not benefitting. The e-mail does not specify whether the three students accepted as transfers to Berkeley were members of the racial and ethnic groups that experience the greatest inequities in transfer to highly selective institutions—African Americans and Latinas and Latinos. Similarly, the only hint about the racial background of the student winning the Jack Kent Cooke scholarship (designated specifically for low-income students) is his intended major.

Principle Four: Equity-minded practitioners are race-conscious. (Critical theories of race)

Creating awareness of inequity is the first step toward change. It is possible for practitioners and leaders to become aware of racial inequities in educational outcomes, willingly engage in inquiry into the problem, enthusiastically endorse the process, yet hold on to an interpretive framework that perpetuates the status quo. Straight talk about race and inequity proves to be a difficult undertaking and practitioners tend to be more comfortable talking about low-income students, or diversity or success for all students, even when educational reform initiatives purport to serve students of color. Essentially, it is extremely difficult to move from creating awareness of inequities to the point where practitioners are able to ask, systematically,

> Why are our practices failing to assist African American students? In what ways might my practices contribute to the formation of inequity in educational outcomes for Latinas and Latinos? In what ways do I use my resources, including power, authority, knowledge, and social networks, on behalf of minoritized student populations?

The political and racial environment of higher education, as well as the culture of the profession, poses barriers to the analysis of inequity as a failure in practice. However, unless practitioners develop the qualities of equity-mindedness, it will be very difficult to accomplish the national goals for college completion. President Obama has declared that the United States will become the world's best-educated country by 2020. To reach this goal will require that the United States produce 8.2 million additional degrees (National Center for Higher Education Management Systems, 2010). Needless to say, in states like California, Texas, Arizona, and New Mexico, as well as in cities like New York, Newark, Detroit, Union City, Paterson, Miami, Chicago, Milwaukee, Phoenix, Denver, and others with a growing concentration of non-Anglo populations, achieving these ambitious college degree completion goals will require a dramatic increase in racial and ethnic equity in college access and completion. To address this challenge we need to develop the qualities of equity-mindedness among policymakers, leaders, and practitioners.

The Attributes of Equity-Minded Individuals

Equity-minded individuals are more aware of the sociohistorical context of exclusionary practices and racism in higher education and the impact of power asymmetries on opportunities and outcomes for African Americans and Latinas and Latinos.

The qualities of equity-minded individuals include:

- Being color-conscious (as opposed to color-blind) in an affirmative sense. To be color-conscious means noticing and questioning patterns of educational outcomes that reveal unexplainable differences for minoritized students and viewing inequalities in the context of a history of exclusion, discrimination, and educational apartheid. Example: Recognizing that help-seeking practices such as going to a tutor, making an appointment with an instructor, or joining a study group require greater or lesser cultural effort based on one's race, social class, and experiential knowledge (Dowd & Korn, 2005; Tanaka, 2002).
- Being aware that beliefs, expectations, and practices assumed to be neutral can have outcomes that are racially disadvantageous. Racial disadvantage is created when unequal outcomes are attributed to students' cultural predispositions or when practices are based on stereotypical assumptions about the capacity, aspirations, or motives of minoritized populations. Example: Not encouraging Latinas in community colleges to consider transfer opportunities to selective colleges because it is taken for granted that they prefer to stay close to home or their families will not allow them to go away.
- Being willing to assume responsibility for the elimination of inequality. Rather than view inequalities as predictable and natural, allow for the possibility that they might be created or exacerbated by taken-for-granted practices and policies, inadequate knowledge, a lack of cultural know-how, or the absence of institutional support. Example: Noticing racial patterns in activities within or outside the classroom that accumulate advantage for students, such as an honors program, leadership positions, tutors, residential advisors, or study abroad.
- Being aware that while racism is not always overt, racialized patterns nevertheless permeate policies and practices in higher education institutions and maintain racial hierarchies despite increasing diversity.

What makes the Equity Scorecard process approach to institutional learning and change effective? Essentially, if practitioners do not recognize that inequities exist and that such inequities are abnormal and unacceptable, then there will be no inquiry into the problem. As mentioned earlier, learning how to view racial patterns of disparity in educational outcomes as an indeterminate situation represents a difficult mind shift for educators who think they know the causes for student success and are not accustomed to admit uncertainty or doubt. For example, the individuals in our pie-chart illustration assume they know the reasons for the inequity in transfer rates to the flagship university.

In order to view the problem as indeterminate, these individuals will need to become aware of their tacit knowledge (Argyris & Schön, 1996; Greenwood & Levin, 2000; Polkinghorne, 2004) about student success. They will need to take notice whether in their search for explanations and solutions, they focus their attention on students' deficiencies or the characteristics of practitioners such as their beliefs, knowledge, and self-efficacy. Becoming aware of one's tacit knowledge requires the assistance of individuals who can model how to differentiate between deficit and equity perspectives. The critical reframing that is essential to the Equity Scorecard process requires a facilitator who is an expert in the theory underlying the technical and procedural aspects of implementing the model. Otherwise, it becomes a data exercise that leaves institutional and individual values untouched.

Unique characteristics of higher education institutions—such as the faculty's control over the curriculum and teaching, and the loosely coupled (Weick, 1976) relationship among academic disciplines and departments and student services (Birnbaum, 1988)—make rational and linear change approaches practically impossible. Nevertheless, the culture of administration and policy making privileges action over questioning because questioning conveys not knowing what to do and not understanding what the problem is; questioning is antithetical to the action-oriented and problem-solving characteristics of administrative culture. On the difficulties of cultivating doubt (Weick, 1979), Dewey (1900) observed, "The natural tendency of man is not to press home the doubt, but to cut inquiry as short as possible. . . . Any prolongation of it is useless speculation, wasting time and diverting the mind from important issues" (p. 466). For this reason, it takes a great deal of discipline and expert facilitation for action-oriented practitioners and leaders to learn to ask *Why? Why? Why?* (Boudett, City, & Murnane, 2005) in response to evidence of inequities, and it is equally important that they learn to limit their *Because, Because, Because* to institutional-level variables within their control, rather than to student attributes.

Challenges Encountered in the Implementation of the Equity Scorecard Process

Why have I spent so much time on the Equity Scorecard theory? One of the barriers to learning the Equity Scorecard process is that practitioners often are impatient for solutions and may see time invested in the foundational aspects of the intervention as wasted time, or they may assume that they know the theory. One of the dangers of not understanding the theoretical underpinnings of the Scorecard is that practitioners may unknowingly turn it into a "lethal mutation" (McLaughlin & Mitra, 2001, p. 307) that undermines or violates the principles of change. One of the vulnerabilities of the Equity Scorecard is that implementers will see it simply as a framework to organize data more coherently. Implementers who view the Scorecard as a "data tool" lose sight of its equity-oriented sensemaking purposes and mistakenly assume that having the capacity for sophisticated data analysis is all that is needed to implement the Scorecard. The data are necessary to engage in equity sensemaking. However, unless the practitioners involved understand that the purpose of examining disaggregated data is to create a context to talk about race and equity, the data itself will not make a difference. Successful implementation of a theory-based change approach depends on implementers' having a deep understanding of the theory and principles and being able to apply them in the context of their everyday practices.

In the tradition of Dewey (1938), the motive of the Equity Scorecard approach is to create an "indeterminate situation" that will spark the realization for practitioners that their actions are not producing successful results for minority students. The inquiry activities that compose the Equity Scorecard are structured to bring into the open practitioners' interpretations of inequalities, increasing their awareness of perspectives that make inequality appear natural, and encouraging them to take responsibility for the educational outcomes of minority students. The purpose of inquiry is to create a situation that prompts practitioners to raise questions such as: "How ought we to teach in order to be responsive to minority students?" "How do we think about our responsibility for minority student outcomes?" "How do we think about equity?" "How do we know who benefits from the initiatives, innovations, and programs that we are so proud of?" "How do the assumptions we make about our students disadvantage them?" "How do best practices take race and equity into account?" "How can we eliminate inequalities in educational outcomes?"

Now that we have explained the theory of change underlying the Equity Scorecard approach, in the next chapters we describe the various means, including tools, activities, language, and processes that we have developed to implement it.

Notes

1. "Minoritized" groups represent "involuntary minorities" (Ogbu, 1990) because their presence in the United States came about as a consequence of enslavement (African Americans), conquest (American Indians, Mexican Americans), and colonization (Puerto Ricans and Native Hawaiians) (Bartlett & Brayboy, 2005). Hence, the term *minoritized populations* is used intentionally to represent more accurately the historical and legal circumstances that resulted in the creation of "minority" populations. The prevalence of educational inequality among minoritized populations is the legacy of exclusionary practices (e.g., forbidding the teaching of reading to slaves), legal segregation, mandatory instruction in English, and inferior schools and resources (Ladson-Billings, 2006).

2. We use the term *remedial* in reference to courses offered in two- and four-year colleges that are categorized as precollegiate level and typically do not count toward requirements for degrees or transfer to baccalaureate-granting institutions. Remedial education courses are also identified as "basic skills" or "developmental education." We recognize that "remedial" is a term that attributes academic deficits to students and its use can perpetuate the deficit-minded thinking the Equity Scorecard process was designed to challenge and eliminate. We use *remedial* because it is the most likely term to be understood by readers.

3. CUE's Equity Scorecard process evolved from a pilot project funded by the James Irvine Foundation that included fourteen two- and four-year public and independent California colleges.

4. In the Equity Scorecard process campus teams are called *evidence teams* because their role is to hold up a mirror to their respective institutions and reflect the status of students on educational outcomes. From an organizational learning perspective, the members of an evidence team have the responsibility of learning on behalf of their institutions and spreading their learning to the campus through various administrative and governance structures.

5. This illustration is excerpted from a longer article (Bensimon, 2006).

6. The Missing 87 (Bensimon, Dowd, et al. 2007), http://cue.usc.edu/tools/Bensimon_Missing%2087%20Institutional%20Report.pdf, describes the inquiry activities of a team of faculty and staff at Long Beach City College in California that set out to find out why transfer-ready students did not transfer.

7. Single- and double-loop learning are not the same as deficit- and equity-mindedness. However, there is some overlap in that both single-loop and deficit-minded statements seek external causes for problems and seek solutions to "fix" people or things without probing into the circumstances, including values and beliefs that may be the cause. Double-loop learning and equity-mindedness are similar in that both are focused on exploring values, assumptions, and organizational

culture that may be contributing to a particular problem. The difference between the two is that equity-mindedness involves the recognition of race and racism, whereas the literature on double-loop learning is silent on this issue.

References

Argyris, C. (1977). Double loop learning in organization. *Harvard Business Review,* 115–125.

Argyris, C. (1982, Autumn). The executive mind and double-loop learning. *Organizational Dynamics.* 5–22.

Argyris, C. (1991). Teaching smart people how to learn. *Harvard Business Review, 69*(3), 99–109.

Argyris, C., & Schön, D. A. (1996). *Organizational learning II: Theory, method, and practice.* Reading, PA: Addison-Wesley.

Bartlett, L., & Brayboy, B. (2005). Race and schooling: Theories and ethnographies. *The Urban Review, 37*(5), 361–374.

Bauman, G. L. (2005). Promoting organizational learning in higher education to achieve equity in educational outcomes. In A. Kezar (Ed.), *Organizational learning in higher education* (Vol. 131). San Francisco: Jossey-Bass.

Bensimon, E. M. (2005). Closing the achievement gap in higher education: An organizational learning perspective. In A. Kezar (Ed.), *Organizational learning in higher education* (Vol. 131). San Francisco: Jossey-Bass.

Bensimon, E. M. (2006). Learning equity-mindedness: Equality in educational outcomes. *The Academic Workplace, 1*(17), 2–21.

Bensimon, E. M. (2007). The underestimated significance of practitioner knowledge in the scholarship of student success. *The Review of Higher Education, 30*(4), 441–469.

Bensimon, E. M., Dowd, A. C., Alford, H., & Trapp, F. (2007). *The Missing 87: A study of the "transfer gap" and "choice gap."* Long Beach and Los Angeles: Long Beach City College and the Center for Urban Education, University of Southern California.

Bensimon, E. M., Rueda, R., Dowd, A. C., & Harris, F., III. (2007). Accountability, equity, and practitioner learning and change. *Metropolitan, 18*(3), 28–45.

Birnbaum, R. (1988). *How colleges work: The cybernetics of academic organization and leadership.* San Francisco: Jossey-Bass.

Boudett, K. P., City, E. A., & Murnane, R. J. (Eds.). (2005). *Data wise: A step-by-step guide to using assessment results to improve teaching and learning.* Cambridge, MA: Harvard Education Press.

Dewey, J. (1900). Some stages of logical thought. *The Philosophical Review, 9*(5), 465–489.

Dewey, J. (1938). *Logic: The theory of inquiry.* New York: Henry Holt.

Dill, D. D. (1999). Academic accountability and university adaptation: The architecture of an academic learning organization. *Higher Education, 38*(2), 127–154.

Dowd, A. C., & Korn, R. (2005). *Students as cultural workers and the measurement of cultural effort.* Paper presented at the Council for the Study of Community Colleges, Boston, MA.

Garvin, D. A. (1993, July–August). Building a learning organization. *Harvard Business Review.*

Gillborn, D. (2005). Education policy as an act of White supremacy: Whiteness, critical race theory and education reform. *Journal of Education Policy, 20*(4), 485–505.

González, N., Moll, L. C., & Amanti, C. (Eds.). (2005). *Funds of knowledge: Theorizing practices in households, communities, and classrooms.* Mahwah, NJ: Lawrence Erlbaum Associates.

Greenwood, D. J., & Levin, M. (2000). Reconstructing the relationships between universities and society through action research. In N. K. Denzin & Y. S. Lincoln (Eds.), *Handbook of qualitative research* (2nd ed., pp. 85–106). Thousand Oaks, CA: Sage.

Hacker, A. (2003). *Two nations: Black and White, separate, hostile, unequal.* New York: Touchstone.

Harper, S. R., Patton, L. D., & Wooden, O. S. (2009). Access and equity for African American students in higher education: A critical race historical analysis of policy efforts. *The Journal of Higher Education, 80*(4), 289–414.

Horvat, E., & O'Connor, C. (2006). *Beyond acting White: Reframing the debate on Black student achievement.* Lanham, MD: Rowman & Littlefield.

Kuh, G. D. (2003, March/April). What we're learning about student engagement from NSSE. *Change, 35*(2), 24–32.

Ladson-Billings, G. (2006). From the achievement gap to the education debt: Understanding achievement in U.S. schools. *Educational Researcher, 35*(7), 3–12.

Lave, J., & Wenger, E. (1991). *Situated learning: Legitimate peripheral participation.* New York, NY: Cambridge University Press.

Matsuda, M. J., Lawrence, C. R., III, Delgado, R., & Crenshaw, K. W. (1993). *Words that wound: Critical race theory, assaultive speech, and the first amendment.* Boulder, CO: Westview Press.

McLaughlin, M. W., & Mitra, D. (2001). Theory-based change and change-based theory: Going deeper, going broader. *Journal of Educational Change, 2,* 301–323.

Moll, L. C., Amanti, C., Neff, D., & Gonzalez, N. (1992). Funds of knowledge for teaching: Using qualitative research to connect homes and classrooms. *Theory Into Practice, 31*(2), 132–141.

Nasir, N. S., & Hand, V. M. (2006). Exploring sociocultural perspectives on race, culture, and learning. *Review of Educational Research, 76*(4), 449–475.

National Center for Higher Education Management Systems. (2010). *Closing the college attainment gap between the U.S. and most education countries, and the contributions to be made by the states.* Boulder, CO: Author.

Ogbu, J. U. (1990). Minority education in comparative perspective. *Journal of Negro Education, 59*(1), 45–57.

Peña, E. V., Bensimon, E. M., & Colyar, J. (2006). Contextual problem defining: Learning to think and act. *Liberal Education, 92*(2), 48–55.

Perakyla, A. (2005). Analyzing talk and text. In N. Denzin & Y. S. Lincoln (Eds.), *The Sage handbook of qualitative research* (3rd ed., pp. 869–886). Thousand Oaks, CA: Sage.

Polkinghorne, D. E. (2004). *Practice and the human sciences: The case for a judgment-based practice of care.* Albany: State University of New York Press.

Pollock, M. (2004). *Colormute: Race talk dilemmas in an American school.* Princeton, NJ: Princeton University Press.

Rogoff, B., Baker-Sennett, J., Lacasa, P., & Goldsmith, D. (1995). Development through participation in sociocultural activity. *Cultural Practices as Contexts for Development,*(67), 45–65.

Roth, W.-M., & Lee, Y.-L. (2007). "Vygotsky's neglected legacy": Cultural-historical activity theory. *Review of Educational Research, 77*(2), 186–232.

Rueda, R. (2006). *A sociocultural perspective on individual and institutional change: The Equity for All project.* Los Angeles: Center for Urban Education, University of Southern California.

Solórzano, D. G., Villalpando, O., & Oseguera, L. (2005). Educational inequities and Latina/o undergraduate students in the United States: A critical race analysis of their educational progress. *Journal of Hispanic Higher Education, 4*(3), 272–294.

Tanaka, G. (2002). Higher education's self-reflexive turn: Toward an intercultural theory of student development. *The Journal of Higher Education, 73*(2), 263–296.

Tharp, R. G. (1993). Institutional and social context of educational practice and reform. In E. A. Forman, N. Minick, & C. A. Stone (Eds.), *Contexts for learning: Sociocultural dynamics in children's development.* New York, NY: Oxford University Press.

Tharp, R. G., & Gallimore, R. (1988). *Rousing minds to life: Teaching, learning, and schooling in social context.* New York, NY: Cambridge University Press.

Tinto, V. (1987). *Leaving college: Rethinking the causes and cures of student attrition* (2nd ed.). Chicago, IL: University of Chicago Press.

Valencia, R. R. (1997). Conceptualizing the notion of deficit thinking. In R. R. Valencia (Ed.), *The evolution of deficit thinking: Educational thought and practice.* Washington, DC: Falmer Press.

Vygotsky, L. S. (1978). *Mind in society: The development of higher psychological processes.* (M. Cole, V. John-Steiner, S. Scribner, & E. Souberman, Eds.). Cambridge, MA: Harvard University Press.

Vygotsky, L. S. (1987). *L. S. Vygotsky, collected works Vol. I.* (R. Rieber & A. Carton, Eds.; N. Minick, Trans.). New York, NY: Plenum. (Original work published 1934).

Weick, K. E. (1976). Educational organizations as loosely coupled systems. *Administrative Science Quarterly, 21*(1), 1–19.

Weick, K. E. (1979). *The social psychology of organizing* (2nd ed.). Reading, MA: Addison-Wesley.

Wenger, E. (1998). *Communities of practice: Learning, meaning, and identity.* Cambridge, UK: Cambridge University Press.

Wenger, E., McDermott, R., & Snyder, W. M. (2002). *Cultivating communities of practice: A guide to managing knowledge.* Boston, MA: Harvard Business School Press.

Yosso, T. J., Parker, L., Solórzano, D. G., & Lynn, M. (2004). From Jim Crow to affirmative action and back again: A critical race discussion of racialized rationales and access to higher education. *Review of Research in Education, 28,* 1–25.

2

SCORECARD TEAMS AS HIGH LEARNING GROUPS

Group Learning and the Value of Group Learning

Georgia L. Lorenz

I n the theory of change underlying the Equity Scorecard process, the first principle is that joint-productive activity produces learning, which in turn can bring about change in individual and institutional practices to produce equity in educational outcomes. Central to the Equity Scorecard process is the examination and discussion of institutional data regarding student outcomes by evidence teams. The premise of the project is that institutional data acts as a powerful trigger for group learning about inequities in educational outcomes. Essentially, it is through the examination of institutional data on inequity in educational outcomes that participants realize they have encountered an indeterminate situation. In this chapter, I present the findings of textual analysis of field notes documenting the Equity Scorecard process of evidence teams from the original fourteen participating institutions made up of private and public four-year institutions and community colleges in the Southern California region. I describe three types of Scorecard teams: *High Learning, Middle Learning,* and *Low Learning* groups. The High Learning groups experienced the highest levels of group learning and gave precedence to the information revealed through examination of the data over their collective experiential knowledge of the institution and its students. These teams were also in the best position to develop agendas for change at their institutions because they had engaged in a deeper level of inquiry, looked at qualitative evidence (e.g., student interviews) in the educational process for students rather than only performance indicators of educational outcomes, and sustained their examination of the data outside the boundaries of the project. As a result, these teams identified potential points for intervention to make progress toward narrowing the gap in educational outcomes for African American and Latino students.

Learning has been deemed a critical skill for organizations to adapt, remain viable, and compete in a fast-paced, changing, and volatile environment. Organizational learning involves a variety of activities, including studying the organization's own history, studying the best practices of other organizations, and systematic problem solving (Garvin, 1993). Three conditions highlighted in the literature as those that can promote organizational learning are (a) the presence of new ideas, (b) the cultivation of doubt in existing knowledge and practices, and (c) the transfer of knowledge among institutional actors. The examination by working groups of data related to institutional performance on given indicators in novel ways, in this case disaggregated by race and ethnicity, can provide all three of these conditions, and, in turn, trigger episodes of group learning.

Learning as the Solution: Reframing the Problem of Inequity in Educational Outcomes

As discussed in the chapter on the theory of change (chapter 1), the Equity Scorecard takes a different approach in that we consider the continued existence of inequitable educational outcomes as a problem in institutional performance. Rather than focusing on the deficits of minority group students that prevent them from being successful, the Equity Scorecard employs the use of routine data by institutional actors that, when disaggregated on the basis of race and ethnicity, bring to light patterns of inequitable educational outcomes. Through careful analysis of field notes documenting each Scorecard team's process, I aim to find the ways in which the inequities revealed by examination of data might lead institutional actors to recognize that inequities exist. The difference between studies that focus on students and this study is the recognition that the factors that have been found to contribute to low educational attainment for minority students are sometimes within the control of faculty and staff. For example, a common finding is that having taken two years of advanced math courses in high school is one of the strongest predictors of bachelor's degree completion (Adelman, 1999). Once a student enrolls in college, nothing can be done about what courses he or she took in high school. However, I contend that once institutional actors understand the nature of the problem there is greater likelihood that they will implement corrective actions and preventive measures, and they will be more capable of producing success.

Organizational Learning as a Means of Increasing Institutional Performance

One answer to ameliorating problems in institutional performance is provided in the literature on organizational learning. Organizational learning has been identified as a critical process by which organizations make sense of their environment, understand their relationship with it, and adapt and adjust to changes in the environment in order to remain competitive in the marketplace (Argyris & Schön, 1978; Daft & Huber, 1987; Fiol & Lyles, 1985; Garvin, 1993; Harvey & Denton, 1999; Huber, 1991; Levitt & March, 1988; Marsick & Watkins, 1999; Popper & Lipshitz, 1998; Weick & Westley, 1996). Organizational learning has been defined and conceptualized in various ways, but essentially it represents change in awareness or practice among organizational actors for the purpose of improving organizational performance (Daft & Huber, 1987; Fiol & Lyles, 1985; Huber, 1991). It involves promoting the variety of ideas present in the organization by studying lessons learned from past experiences, seeking out best practices of other organizations, engaging in experimentation, and exploring for new ideas (Garvin, 1993; Huber, 1991; Levitt & March, 1988; March, 1991). Authors assert (Dill, 1999; Garvin, 1993; Weick, 1979; Weick & Westley, 1996) that the presence of new ideas and the promotion of doubt in an organization's existing knowledge and practices, as well as transfer of knowledge among institutional actors, facilitate organizational learning. The examination of institutional data in novel ways within the context of working groups can create these conditions. For example, in the context of the project under study, even if the collection and use of particular institutional data, like passing rates in mathematics courses, are considered routine, new ideas can be generated by asking new questions of these data or examining them in new ways, such as disaggregated by ethnicity. Also, by disaggregating data by ethnicity, an institutional actor may be given cause to doubt that the institution is serving all students equally well—if African Americans are failing math at higher rates than any other group, this is evidence that may raise questions in people's minds. By examining data in the context of working groups, transfer of knowledge is immediate. Actors interact and communicate, sharing their understandings of, thoughts about, and reactions to the evidence they study.

There is a body of literature that addresses the use and transfer of information and knowledge within organizations in order to maximize institutional performance (Cutcher-Gershenfeld et al., 1998; Huber, 1991; Levitt & March, 1988; Sormunen-Jones, Chalupa, & Charles, 2000; Wenger & Snyder, 2000). And recently working groups (also referred to as *teams, communities of practice, committees,* etc.) have begun to gain recognition as constituting an important forum for knowledge sharing and knowledge generation to take place.

Colleges and universities have been used as an example of a type of organization that does not engage in organizational learning effectively (Dill, 1999; Garvin, 1993). While learning is the central work of colleges and universities, the institutions themselves are believed to lack the attributes needed for organizational learning. David Garvin (1993) asserts that to be a learning organization the entity must acquire new ideas that trigger improvements in the way the organization does business, and "many universities fail to qualify [because] . . . these organizations have been effective at creating or acquiring new knowledge but notably less successful in applying that knowledge to their own activities" (p. 80). However, as explained previously, the use of institutional data by committees in colleges and universities can provide new ideas that might trigger improvements in organizational problems. While the involvement of outsiders in the work of these campus committees makes them atypical of the way institutional committees normally function, they provide a situation that is ideal for an empirical examination of Garvin's assumption that institutions of higher education are unable to effectively engage in organizational learning.

The Joint Examination of Data as a Catalyst for Learning

Organizational learning is facilitated by (a) the presence of new ideas (Garvin, 1993), (b) the cultivation of doubt in existing knowledge and practices (Weick, 1979; Weick & Westley, 1996), and (c) the transfer of knowledge among institutional actors in groups (Dixon, 2000; Wenger & Snyder, 2000). The use of institutional data can provide these conditions in higher education institutions.

Data as a Source for New Ideas

Examining existing institutional data in novel ways and asking new questions of routine data can provide new ideas and information. As documented in the database of field notes, the evidence teams at the fourteen institutions participating in the Equity Scorecard gained new insight regarding educational outcomes by looking at the data disaggregated by ethnicity for the first time; for example, teams may have realized that African American and Latino students graduate at lower rates than students from other groups. These realizations (some of which are described in the institutional case studies in Part Two of this volume) result from the joint examination of existing institutional data and represent new ideas. By looking at institutional data in this new way, new information became visible. The same would be true for examining grade point average (GPA) disaggregated by ethnicity. This also represents asking new questions of the data. Rather than asking only, "What is the GPA of our graduating class?" institutional actors asked, "What is the GPA of our graduating African Americans?" Garvin (1993) asserts that colleges and universities do not apply the research skills used for other purposes to institutional self-study and improvement. This may be true to the extent that institutional actors do not typically ask questions of institutional data that might provide new ideas as they might for research projects in other areas. The Knight Higher Education Collaborative (2000), made up of educational leaders and researchers, asserts that many questions can be answered through the use of data, such as "Who starts but does not finish and why? What is being learned, and for what purpose?" (p. 8). Answers to such questions through the exploration of institutional data would provide new ideas and knowledge about institutional effectiveness and performance.

Using Data to Promote Doubt in Existing Knowledge and Practices

Weick (1979) developed a model of how groups (or organizations) reduce the multiple meanings that members may hold about a phenomenon to a shared, common understanding such that the group can act on the understanding in the future—in this case equity is our goal for shared understanding. Weick did not label this learning; he called it the "organizing" process. This process is dependent upon communication and interaction among group members. Weick theorized that something in the environment triggers the organizing process—some event or piece of information catches the group's attention. The group then engages in cycles of communication, restricted by rules and norms embedded in the culture of the group (or the organization within which it operates), and eventually the group reaches some sort of common understanding, which is then stored in some manner for future use by the group or organization. For example, most colleges and universities include phrases about the importance of diversity in their institutional mission statements. This might lead institutional actors to believe that they serve all members of their diverse student community equally well, in spite of the existence of educational inequity. That common understanding has been "stored" in a sense in the culture of the college.

Weick (1979), like other organizational theorists (Argyris & Schön, 1978; March, 1991), suggests that organizations learn when the stored understandings and information are called into question. When organizational actors doubt what they have traditionally believed, an opportunity for learning arises. To learn is to doubt and discredit the retained understanding that resulted from the organizing process. Organizations should treat the "past as a pest" (Weick, p. 221) and question the retained information such as routines, norms, rules, and other elements of the organization's culture and operations, which are often considered sacred and unchangeable in organizations. Unfortunately, "the thick layering of routines in most organizations, coupled with the fact that departures from routine increase vulnerability, mean that discrediting is rare" (Weick, p. 225).

In terms of the problem of educational inequity, the joint examination of institutional data can promote doubt in the existing knowledge and practices of institutional actors—an indeterminate situation. First, during the Equity Scorecard process, faculty members, administrators, and other personnel examine and make sense of data that reflect the true state of equity at the institution, itself a novel concept. Because this data is disaggregated by race and ethnicity, team members are confronted by any "gaps" that might exist between student groups. Rather than be able to hold on to personal beliefs and experiential knowledge, the examination of data forces team members to question their beliefs as they seek to reconcile what the data say with what they might have previously believed. Second, the types of new questions that arise during the Scorecard process promote dialogue among team members that might urge them to reflect upon institutional practices or their own instructional practices. At many of the institutions, team members might attribute inequities to some deficit in the students. In many cases, another team member, or a facilitator from CUE, might ask a question to reframe the discussion; for example, if a math faculty member says that students delay taking a certain mathematics course because they hate math, another team member or facilitator from CUE might respond by proposing another explanation (e.g., the oversubscription, or limited number of seats, in that mathematics course). In this situation, the examination of data and resulting discussion of that data promote doubt in existing knowledge and practices.

Data as a Means to Transfer Knowledge Among Institutional Actors in Groups

Both information, or data, and knowledge play important roles in organizational learning. Daft and Huber (1987) see organizational learning occurring along two dimensions: the systems-structural dimension, which focuses upon the acquisition and distribution of information, and the interpretive dimension, which involves the interpretation of that information. Interpretation and understanding of information by institutional actors is associated with knowledge. Daft and Huber assert that "organizations undertake both types of activity" (p. 10), and that both activities contribute to organizational learning.

Davenport and Prusak (1998) provide definitions for data and information. Data are "a set of discrete, objective facts about events" (p. 2). Kock (1999) refers to data as "carriers" of information and knowledge and asserts that data are distinct from information because "an ocean of data may contain only a small amount of information that is of any value to us" (p. 30). Information is described as a message that intends to change the way in which its receiver perceives something, "to make some difference in his outlook or insight" (Davenport & Prusak, 1998, p. 3). Brown and Duguid (2000) distinguish data and information as distinct and different from knowledge because they are independent of people, existing as self-contained in documents or databases. Having data or information does not imply understanding or knowledge; they are repositories of unprocessed facts available for interpretation. In most institutions of higher education the various information repositories—on students, faculty, programs, finances, and accountability—offer a wellspring of knowledge that, for the most part, is untapped.

Knowledge is "broader, deeper, and richer than data or information" (Davenport & Prusak, 1998, p. 5). Knowledge is contained within the minds of knowers and results from an amalgamation of experiences, personal values, personal characteristics, and interactions with others and is used to interpret, evaluate, and incorporate new experiences and interactions. Kock (1999) labels knowledge "associative." He states that knowledge "allows us to 'associate' different world states and respective mental representations, which are typically linked to or described by means of pieces of information" (p. 35). In organizations knowledge often becomes embedded in "organizational routines, processes, practices, and norms" (Davenport & Prusak, 1998, p. 5). Knowledge has been delineated into various types. For example, Dixon (2000) defines "common knowledge" as "the knowledge that employees learn from doing the organization's tasks" (p. 11). Davenport and Prusak define this same type of knowledge as "working knowledge" that is put into action within the organizational context.

Because knowledge is dependent upon knowers, the exchange and creation of knowledge take place within and between humans. The field of knowledge management is concerned with managing, transferring, and maximizing the knowledge held in organizational actors' minds for improvement of the organization as a whole. Many organizations lament that they don't know what the sum of their members know; Hewlett-Packard's (HP's) former chairman, Lew Platt, has been quoted as saying, "If only we knew what we know at HP" (Brown & Duguid, 2000, p. 123). To find out what members know, organizations set up interactions such as job transfers where employees are moved from department to department with the intention of picking up new practices and other important knowledge along the way. In other cases experts float from department to department sharing their knowledge and spreading it throughout the organization. Each of these examples is structured to promote social interaction between actors for the purposes of knowledge sharing and creation. Authors who study organizations consider this transfer of knowledge one of the essential ingredients for organizational learning (Daft & Huber, 1987; Garvin, 1993; Huber, 1991; Levitt & March, 1988).

Groups are becoming a highly valued structure within organizations for the purposes of promoting knowledge sharing and creation. In fact, "companies in every industry are striving to create team-based work systems" (Cutcher-Gershenfeld et al., 1998, p. 59). There is a boom of literature focused upon the characteristics and qualities that lead to effective teams in organizations: "Books and articles have been written about how to design empowered or self-directed work teams . . . executive teams . . . and team-based organizations" (Cohen & Bailey, 1997, p. 116). For example, Bensimon and Neumann (1993) differentiated between "real" and "illusory" college executive teams on the basis of the groups' functions and the diversity of thinking displayed by the members of the groups.

An innovative and newly recognized organizational strategy that is gaining some attention is the "community of practice." Communities of practice are typically small groups within larger organizations who congregate due to "expertise and passion" (Wenger & Snyder, 2000, p. 139) in a particular area, such as issues related to retention and student success, and meet on a regular basis over an extended period of time. Those who engage in communities of practice "share their experiences and knowledge in free-flowing, creative ways that foster new approaches to problems" (p. 140).

What Stands in the Way?

As the Knight Higher Education Collaborative (2000) advocates, colleges and universities must use data strategically "as a gauge of capacity and prospects" (p. 2). Data can help institutional actors to gain understanding of where the college has been as well as the potential for the ways in which it might grow and improve. But actors within higher education resist using data in order to protect the status quo and prevent airing of dirty laundry. The collaborative explains that "data are not collected for two reasons: 'We really don't want to know because it will make us change our minds' or 'We don't want someone else to know'" (p. 3). These orientations toward the use of data are unproductive and lead to single-loop learning, which often reflects a deficit perspective toward inequities and to the detriment of double-loop learning, which reflects the capacity to view inequity as a problem of institutional values and lack of knowledge about the ways in which structures create disadvantage.

I have attempted to argue here that data that have not previously been collected or examined can provide new ideas and understandings about the institution, its members, its operations, and the associated educational outcomes. Committees could be formed to further investigate what the data reveal and raise fundamental questions like: What have we learned from these data? Is this knowledge consistent with how we think things are? How does this new information fit with the mission, vision, and goals for the institution? What should be our collective response to this new information?

By providing this new information, the data also promote doubt and questioning of retained organizational understandings, practices, and norms. Before examining the Scorecard data, Leland College prided itself on the diversity of its student body and the achievements of all students, operating under the assumption that all students, regardless of ethnicity or race, experienced the same educational processes and outcomes. Viewing data that show that African Americans and Latinos graduate at significantly lower rates and with significantly lower GPAs than their White peers called these operating assumptions into doubt. This doubt has the potential to trigger both the organizing process and an episode of organizational learning.

The Equity Scorecard Project and Group Learning

In the following section, I describe the methods of data collection and analysis that guided my investigation of learning among the Equity Scorecard teams.

Description of the Study

As explained previously, I chose to use a database of field notes derived from the meetings during the first year of the three-year Equity Scorecard project, which focused on engaging institutional actors in examination of the educational outcomes for African American and Latino students in order to identify areas in which institutional data might reveal inequities. The project addressed the effectiveness of institutions in serving the educational needs of a changing student population—one that is becoming less and less White. For example, the committees were encouraged to ask themselves questions like: Are African American and Latino students graduating at the same rates as other students? Are they proportionately represented on the Dean's List? Are they *over*represented in some majors while *under*represented in majors that lead to careers that are in high demand?

The project involved a partnership of fourteen institutions of higher education in the Southern California region. Community colleges, public universities, and independent colleges were represented among the fourteen partner institutions. At each institution the president appointed a small group to work together on this project, including at least three members and no more than seven members. The groups were composed of a mix of faculty and administrators who came from departments across campus and held positions of varying levels within the institution, from transfer counselors to the executive assistant to the president. The charge for these groups was to identify racially stratified patterns of educational achievement and report back to the president with recommendations about what areas the institution might address to reduce these disparities—areas in which the institution might change. The project staff members who worked with and facilitated these fourteen groups strongly recommended that each group use existing institutional data to identify these problem areas. One of the operating assumptions of the project was that there were a lot of data available in each of the participating institutions, but that much of it went unused.

The features of the project under study facilitated the three conditions listed previously that are assumed to promote organizational learning: (a) the presence of new ideas, (b) the cultivation of doubt in existing knowledge and practices, and (c) the transfer of knowledge among institutional actors. Because institutional data were examined disaggregated by ethnicity, in most cases for the first time, new information and ideas were present. Seeing the disaggregated data caused the committee members to doubt their own knowledge about the given indicators as well as the performance of their institutions in serving the educational needs of African American and Latino students. Finally, because the examination of data happened in the context of working committees, committee members had the opportunity to interact and communicate about these findings, test their own understandings, and discuss how their own understandings had been contradicted or confirmed. The variety of interpretations and understandings of the data being examined juxtaposed with the members' experiences in the institution created learning opportunities.

Defining Group Learning

Using the organizational learning literature as a point for departure, I began the first stage of my analysis of the text by looking for instances in which it was recorded that a group member acknowledged that he or she had learned, or newly recognized, a piece of information that he or she either had not known before or had suspected to be true but had now been confirmed by the institutional data under examination. In the literature, such a learning moment may be categorized under the umbrella term of *organizational learning*. For the purposes of this study I refer to what may typically be labeled "organizational learning" as "group learning" because the groups, not the organizations of which they are a part, are the unit of analysis. *Group learning* is defined as the new recognition that results from the introduction of new information. It is the change in understanding that takes place between the understanding held by the committee before the introduction of new information (precondition) and the understanding held by the committee after the introduction of new information (postcondition) (see Figure 2.1). For example, a committee may have held a common understanding that African American women graduated at the lowest rates of all student groups in their institution. However, upon examining the data, the committee learned that Latinos actually graduated at the lowest rate of all groups for the past three years and that African American women's graduation rates have been rising

FIGURE 2.1
Group learning.

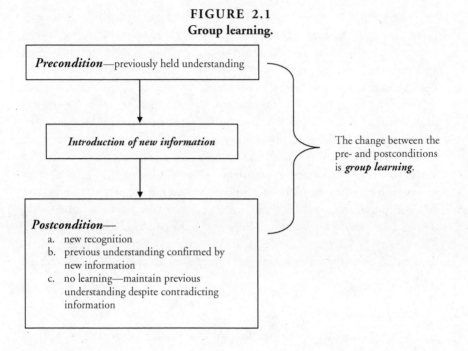

steadily for the past five years. As a result of examining the data, the committee's understanding of graduation rates among ethnic groups was changed.

The group learning, or new recognition of inequities in student outcomes, that results from examining data may be characterized in two ways: (a) a new understanding is developed, as in the example given previously, or (b) the committee's previously held understanding (precondition) is confirmed by the new information that is introduced. In fact, the committee members may have discovered that the data verified their previously held perception that African American women graduated at the lowest rates of all ethnic groups. Both of these types of learning were labeled "new recognition" for the purposes of analysis.

Learning has not taken place when the previously held understanding is maintained by committee members despite the introduction of new information that may contradict or disconfirm it, or introduce a potentially new understanding to the committee. If the committee described previously ignored or justified the data that contradicted their understanding showing that Latinos graduated at lower rates than African American women and resisted changing their understanding, no learning would have taken place.

Learning Group Types

In the following section, I present the findings of the study and describe each of the three group types identified through the analysis: (a) High Learning, (b) Medium Learning, and (c) Low Learning groups. Within each of these types, the role of *data focus,* the role of *experiential knowledge,* and what was learned by groups of that type are explained. Within the role of data focus, the group type's level of inquiry, orientation toward the data, and engagement with the data are explored and described. High Learning committees were those that experienced the highest levels of group learning and those for whom prioritization of the data was a critical factor.

High Learning Groups

The committees of the High Learning type experienced the highest level of group learning; they considered their own experiential knowledge as hypotheses to be proven, and they made judgments about inequities based on data. The data took precedence over experiential knowledge. The important feature of what was learned by the High Learning groups was that they identified potential points for intervention to impact the identified inequitable educational outcomes.

Evidence teams that experienced high levels of group learning in which the role of the data was dominant and experiential knowledge facilitated the committee's inquiry are classified as High Learning groups. There were several characteristics that defined evidence teams of this type. First, for the most part these committees seemed to begin with a sense of the problem of inequities in educational outcomes for African American and Latino students, and many also had a sense of the institution's responsibility in resolving this problem. This seemed to already be part of their experiential knowledge and beliefs about the institution, and, as a result, there seemed to be little resistance to the idea of inequities in educational outcomes. Of course this varied across the five committees who were High Learning groups. The committees used their experiential knowledge of the institution, its students, and its priorities to facilitate their inquiry into the data. Committee members seemed to have a fairly good sense of where inequities existed in the institution and were not generally shocked by what the data revealed, although they did learn new things by examining the data. These committees prioritized the data over other sources of information, like their own experiential knowledge, and used the data as the foci of their meetings and work together.

New ideas were generated from examining and talking about the data. And in some cases, doubt about existing experiential knowledge and the practices of the institution was raised as a result of examining data. For example, mythologies—the campus lore that was considered common campus knowledge—were contradicted or called into question. What is noteworthy about this in High Learning groups is that the committee members were willing to question such campus mythologies and give precedence to the data over their experiential knowledge, even when that knowledge was contradicted.

Experiential knowledge also played a role in the development of new recognitions. Committees of this type were characterized by using their experiential knowledge of known problem areas and institutional priorities in order to facilitate and shape their examination of the data. This knowledge helped them to choose which data to examine out of the abundance of institutional data available. Being cognizant of institutional interests and priorities helped to prevent the committees from pursuing what may be deemed lost causes. For example, a committee might intentionally study an area of interest to the president and strategic planning committee in order to maximize the likelihood that the committee would see results from their hard work.

The High Learning groups experienced more group learning than did committees of other types. However, what was important about the learning of these groups was not necessarily that they focused on more important or unique areas of inequity—committees in both the High Learning and Medium Learning groups identified quantitative reasoning and gateway courses[1] as problem areas, for example. High Learning groups learned about areas of inequitable educational outcomes at a different level by approaching the data with a second-order level of inquiry, digging deeper into the data rather than maintaining a telescopic perspective, and attending to indicators within the educational process rather than only indicators of outcomes. As a result, High Learning groups identified potential points for intervention rather than only indicators of inequitable educational outcomes.

Medium Learning Groups

Those committees that were of the Medium Learning type consulted institutional data but relied more heavily upon their experiential knowledge. Medium Learning groups identified areas in which there were inequitable educational outcomes, but unlike the High Learning groups, they did not identify potential points for intervention.

In contrast to High Learning groups, the Medium Learning groups experienced medium levels of learning, and data focus and experiential knowledge played different roles. The data were not considered preeminent sources of information. Experiential knowledge was relied upon to a greater extent than data. Medium Learning groups consulted data, but they seemed to operate under the assumption that the data would confirm their experiential knowledge—as though they already knew what the state of inequity was at their institutions. When they did examine data, these groups stayed at a fairly broad level, used telescopic measures, tended to look primarily at outcomes indicators, and maintained limited engagement with the data. Because these groups did not delve deeply into the data and tended to look at more traditional, broad measures, they seemed to maintain the status quo and learned less about inequitable educational outcomes than High Learning groups. As a result of the first year of the project they might have learned that African Americans had lower GPAs than any other group at the point of graduation, but they didn't know more than that. For example, they didn't know if the GPA gap was worse than when the students started college or at what point the GPA gap began to widen in a student's career. There was no implied point for intervention without digging deeper into the data.

Experiential knowledge was prioritized over the data. These groups treated statements made about inequitable outcomes based on personal experiences as fact, as if this knowledge were data. The members of these committees held on to their own assumptions and explanations of inequitable educational outcomes despite a lack of supporting evidence and even when there was disconfirming evidence presented. Although the High Learning groups seemed to begin the project with a sense of the inequitable educational outcomes for African American and Latino students and seemed to accept, at least to some extent, that the institution should take some responsibility for resolving these inequities, the Medium Learning groups seemed to resist the notion of institutional responsibility. They did not necessarily resist the idea that inequitable educational outcomes existed, but when explaining and rationalizing the inequities found in the data, the members of Medium Learning groups tended to attribute the problem to students and their lack of motivation, poor academic preparation in the K–12 education system, competing demands from family and job responsibilities, and family structures that tended to inhibit them academically—all of which the college or university had no control over, and therefore no responsibility for. Members of these committees also wanted to avoid examining or sharing data that might make their institution "look bad."

There were fewer new ideas presented and less cultivation of doubt because these groups tended to rely on what they already "knew" to be true about the institution and its students. Relying so heavily upon existing experiential knowledge actually gave more credence to this knowledge, rather than calling it into question or creating doubt in it. The Medium Learning groups based their work primarily on experiential knowledge, which is the very knowledge that High Learning groups tended to doubt. Ultimately, committees of this type functioned to maintain the status quo by relying upon existing experiential knowledge and explaining away or rationalizing data that might introduce new ideas or cast doubt upon experiential knowledge and the practices of the institution.

Low Learning Groups

The committees classified as Low Learning groups experienced very little, if any, group learning about inequities in educational outcomes. These committees operated without examining data and relied primarily on experiential knowledge. Unlike High and Medium Learning groups, Low Learning groups never examined data as a group during the first year of the project. Experiential knowledge far outweighed data focus because it was really the only source of information that they utilized when discussing inequitable educational outcomes. What is particularly noteworthy is that even the experiential knowledge that was shared among committee members did not have any real focus or direction.

In reading the text associated with one of the two committees of this type, it seemed as though the same meeting occurred again and again. The committee members consistently revisited the same topics, describing and discussing other diversity-related programs that were being developed on campus. No connections were made to their work on this project; they just seemed to be spinning their wheels. The second committee followed a similar pattern; the members simply discussed whatever problems came to mind, whether they were diversity related or not.

Experiential knowledge played the dominant role in groups of this type. Low Learning evidence teams tended to rely exclusively on experiential knowledge as the only source of information or knowledge used in the group. Like the Medium Learning groups, the members of evidence teams classified as Low Learning made assertions based on their experiential knowledge that were accepted as fact and, therefore, inhibited further inquiry.

There were no recorded instances in which members of Low Learning groups developed new recognitions of inequitable educational outcomes for African American and Latino students at their institutions. The committee members had ideas about where problems might exist, based on their experiential knowledge, but these areas were never explored or confirmed by examining institutional data. Although these groups may have learned about other things through their conversations and interactions with one another, they did not engage in group learning about inequitable educational outcomes. They may have learned what fellow group members thought about the gaps in educational outcomes and where those gaps might lie, but they never used data to confirm or disconfirm these notions.

Conclusion

The treatment of and approach to the data were the critical factors in promoting group learning. The High Learning groups treated the data as preeminent and approached them with a second-order level of inquiry; examined indicators of educational process, not just educational outcomes; and sustained their engagement with the data even outside the work of their committees. As a result, the High Learning groups learned more than where inequities in educational outcomes exist—they also discovered where institutional actors could make a difference. They learned about the building blocks within their institutions that might cumulatively contribute to inequitable educational outcomes. For example, they did not learn only that African American and Latino students were underrepresented in math-related majors but that these students had high failure rates in courses that lead to such majors. So if these students were given the tools and support to succeed in gateway math courses, the inequitable representation in math-related majors might be diminished.

The experiential knowledge of High Learning groups acted as a guide for inquiry, a starting point. The groups resolved their own questions and curiosities by examining data rather than relying primarily on their own past experiences and understandings. When their own experiential knowledge was disconfirmed by the data, they were willing to trust and believe what the data revealed. Because of this, the data were able to provide new ideas and cast doubt on existing knowledge and institutional practices.

This stands in contrast to the practices of Medium Learning groups and Low Learning groups in which experiential knowledge was dominant. Medium Learning groups held fast to their own understandings and found ways to rationalize or justify data that disconfirmed or challenged their own views. They learned less because they relied so heavily upon already existing knowledge. Low Learning groups learned the least of all of the committees in the study, which seems related to the fact that they never examined data during the first year of the project. Thus, it seems that instances of new recognition were most likely to occur when experiential knowledge was the ground and data became the figure (Weick, 1979)—experiential knowledge served as the context or background, but the data were what the committee really paid attention to. These two were not held in balance; a productive tension between the two was developed and maintained in which data were prioritized but experiential knowledge served to guide the inquiry.

In sum, High Learning groups were in a better position to develop agendas for change at their institutions. They had identified potential intervention points in the educational processes of their students that preceded inequitable educational outcomes, and therefore could change those outcomes. For example, by identifying which courses contribute to the tendency for African Americans and Latinos to switch from majors that lead to careers in high demand to majors that do not, the committee has identified where extra support might be needed for those students. These committees have learned more about these problems to a finer level of detail and can communicate to campus community members where their attention, resources, and energy should be allocated.

Note

1. A gateway course is one that acts as a prerequisite for particular majors or programs or a generally required course for graduation, and a student's success or failure in such a course might limit his or her options and the ability to graduate. For example, calculus is a prerequisite for engineering. If a student does not pass calculus, he or she cannot declare engineering as his or her major.

References

Adelman, C. (1999). *Answers in the tool box: Academic intensity, attendance patterns, and bachelor's degree attainment.* Washington, DC: U.S. Department of Education.

Argyris, C., & Schön, D. A. (1978). Organizational learning. In D. S. Pugh (Ed.), *Organization theory* (pp. 416–429). New York: Penguin Books.

Bensimon, E. M., & Neumann, A. (1993). *Redesigning collegiate leadership: Teams and teamwork in higher education.* Baltimore, MD: Johns Hopkins University Press.

Brown, J. S., & Duguid, P. (2000). *The social life of information.* Boston, MA: Harvard Business School Press.

Cohen, S. G., & Bailey, D. E. (1997). What makes teams work: Group effectiveness research from the shop floor to the executive suite. *Journal of Management, 23*(3), 239–290.

Cutcher-Gershenfeld, J., Nitta, M., Barrett, B. J., Belhedi, N., Sai-Chung Chow, S., Inaba, T., . . ., Wheaton, A. C. (1998). *Knowledge-driven work: Unexpected lessons from Japanese and United States work practices.* New York, NY: Oxford University Press.

Daft, R. L., & Huber, G. P. (1987). How organizations learn: A communication framework. *Research in the Sociology of Organizations, 5,* 1–36.

Davenport, T. H., & Prusak, L. (1998). *Working knowledge: How organizations manage what they know.* Boston, MA: Harvard Business School Press.

Dill, D. D. (1999). Academic accountability and university adaptation: The architecture of an academic learning organization. *Higher Education, 38,* 127–154.

Dixon, N. M. (2000). *Common knowledge: How companies thrive by sharing what they know.* Boston, MA: Harvard Business School Press.

Fiol, C. M., & Lyles, M. A. (1985). Organizational learning. *Academy of Management Review, 10*(4), 803–813.

Garvin, D. A. (1993, July–August). Building a learning organization. *Harvard Business Review, 71*(4), 78–90.

Harvey, C., & Denton, J. (1999). To come of age: The antecedents of organizational learning. *Journal of Management Studies, 36*(7), 897–918.

Huber, G. P. (1991). Organizational learning: The contributing processes and the literatures. *Organization Science, 2*(1), 88–115.

Knight Higher Education Collaborative. (2000). The data made me do it. *Policy Perspectives, 9*(2), 1–12.

Kock, N. (1999). *Process improvement and organizational learning: The role of collaboration technologies.* Hershey, PA: Idea Group Publishing.

Levitt, B., & March, J. G. (1988). Organizational learning. *Annual Review of Sociology, 14,* 319–340.

March, J. G. (1991). Exploration and exploitation in organizational learning. *Organization Science, 2*(1), 71–87.

Marsick, V. J., & Watkins, K. E. (1999). *Facilitating learning organizations: Making learning count.* Burlington, VT: Ashgate.

Popper, M., & Lipshitz, R. (1998). Organizational learning mechanisms: A structural and cultural approach to organizational learning. *Journal of Applied Behavioral Science, 34*(2), 161–179.

Sormunen-Jones, C., Chalupa, M. R., & Charles, T. A. (2000). The dynamics of gender impact on group achievement. *Delta Pi Epsilon Journal, 42*(3), 154–170.

Weick, K. E. (1979). *The social psychology of organizing* (2nd ed.). New York: McGraw-Hill.

Weick, K. E., & Westley, F. (1996). Organizational learning: Affirming an oxymoron. In S. R. Clegg, C. Hardy, & W. R. Nord (Eds.), *Managing organizations.* Thousand Oaks, CA: Sage.

Wenger, E., & Snyder, W. M. (2000). Communities of practice: An organizational frontier. *Harvard Business Review, 78*(1), 139–145.

3

THE EQUITY SCORECARD PROCESS

Tools, Practices, and Methods

Estela Mara Bensimon and Debbie Ann Hanson

C ompleting the Equity Scorecard involves a cycle of action inquiry, including identification of gaps in educational outcomes, inquiry into instructional and academic support practices, purposeful changes in practices based on the results of systematic inquiry, and evaluations of the effectiveness of changes.

The completion of the Equity Scorecard is assisted by practical tools, such as the vital signs data template, and other protocols for inquiry, benchmarking, and assessment. For additional information visit http://cue.usc .edu. These tools guide teams of faculty members, staff, and administrators through fine-grained data analyses with a focus on curriculum, programs, and learning outcomes. This chapter describes the essential features of the Equity Scorecard process and tools.

The Equity Scorecard Process: Evidence Teams, Data Tools, and Data Practices

The framework of the main data tool—the Equity Scorecard—is structured after the Balanced Scorecard for business (Kaplan & Norton, 1993), and the Academic Scorecard for higher education (O'Neil, Bensimon, Diamond, & Moore, 1999). It provides four concurrent perspectives on institutional performance in terms of equity in educational outcomes. For four-year colleges the perspectives are access, retention, institutional receptivity, and excellence.

For community colleges the perspectives are academic pathways, retention, transfer readiness, and excellence.

Evidence Teams

The first step in initiating action inquiry is to create a campus evidence team of about ten individuals. The Center for Urban Education (CUE) then trains these individuals to take on a role of "practitioner-researcher" and conduct inquiry into existing institutional data to identify and address gaps in student outcomes by race and ethnicity. Essentially, this team of practitioner researchers collaborates to transform numerical data into knowledge about how everyday and taken-for-granted practices and policies unknowingly disadvantage students of color. The teams also function to bring together individuals from across the infamous "silos" of higher education—faculty, administration, student affairs, and institutional research—and coordinate their actions to improve disadvantaging policies and practices and, ultimately, student outcomes.

Team members are selected for specific criteria: their dedication to improving student outcomes, knowledge, and leadership attributes, as well as involvement in decision making, academic governance, and administrative structures. Choosing members who are dedicated to improving outcomes bolsters the team's overall ability to examine, ask questions about, and address inequities. Selecting team members who are knowledgeable and "cognitively complex" (Bensimon & Neumann, 1993) allows the team to structure a more multifaceted understanding of their institutional context and to design more encompassing interventions. Finally, choosing team members who are leaders and integrated into decision-making bodies better ensures that the team's findings and recommendations are widely distributed and acted upon.

Team Leaders

Evidence teams include one or more team leaders, preferably faculty members, as well as a member of the institutional research office. Effective team leaders serve in a threefold capacity: They facilitate data discussion, coordinate the logistical needs of the team, and serve as advocates for the Equity Scorecard process.

As facilitators of data discussion, team leaders

- Help create a safe and friendly culture of inquiry.
- Support questioning of taken-for-granted knowledge.

- Encourage a collaborative learning experience and do not allow others to dominate.
- Guide dialogue that demonstrates the institution's role and responsibility in attaining equity, and reframe language that hinders action, such as language that focuses on perceived student deficits.
- Assist in managing tense dialogue and conflict that arises in the team. The goal is not to avoid these discussions, but to understand how and why the data lead to different interpretations.

As the director of team logistics, team leaders:

- Define the agenda and keep it focused on problem defining rather than on jumping to solutions.
- Prepare for team meetings and share materials with all team members beforehand.
- Serve as task monitors to help remove obstacles for the team, facilitating the team's work and remaining mindful of the process.
- Ensure the team meets regularly and completes the Equity Scorecard.
- Support and coordinate the dissemination of the team's findings.

As advocates for the Equity Scorecard process, team leaders:

- Keep their provost informed and engaged in the project.
- Communicate or publicize the project and connect to other campus initiatives.
- Anticipate and address team challenges.

Institutional Researchers

The functional role of the institutional researcher is to collect existing institutional data and share it with team members using the Scorecard's templates, as well as prepare new reports to address questions the team members pose during inquiry. The institutional researcher's role is also as a teacher who:

- Organizes raw data into user-friendly formats and walks the team through, approaching the explanation as if they were teaching a foreign language.
- Is willing to suspend judgment and adapt to data practices and presentation methods that are tailored for nondata people. They will not

get stuck on technical statistical issues and will understand that the team's learning takes precedence over the purity of methods.
- Creates an environment that allows nondata people to feel safe in asking seemingly "dumb" questions.
- Does not assume people can read and interpret a data table in the same way he or she does.

The Equity Scorecard Framework

The Equity Scorecard provides four concurrent perspectives on institutional effectiveness in terms of equity in educational outcomes: access, retention, institutional receptivity, and excellence.

Access Perspective

Equity indicators of access show the extent to which underrepresented students have access to programs and resources that can significantly improve their ability to compete for economic advancement. Indicators in the access perspective are concerned with such questions as (a) To what programs and majors do underrepresented students have access? (b) Do the programs and majors to which underrepresented students have access lead to high-demand and high-paying career opportunities? (c) Do underrepresented students have access to select academic and socialization programs, such as special internships or fellowships? (d) What access do underrepresented students have to financial support? (e) What access do community college students have to four-year colleges? (f) What access do community college students have to programs with the highest starting salaries? (g) What access do underrepresented students have to postbaccalaureate graduate and professional schools?

Retention Perspective

Equity indicators within the retention perspective provide answers to questions such as (a) What are the retention rates for underrepresented students by program type? (b) What are enrollment and drop-out patterns for underrepresented students in particular "hot" programs—(e.g., engineering and computer sciences)? (c) What are the retention rates of underrepresented students in basic skills courses? (d) What are retention rates in the associate degree, bachelor degree, and credential and certificate programs?

Institutional Receptivity Perspective

The institutional receptivity perspective includes indicators of responsiveness to underrepresented students and answer questions such as (a) Do new appointments enhance the racial and ethnic diversity of faculty, administrators, and staff? (b) Does the composition of the faculty represent the racial and ethnic composition of the student body? (c) How are new faculty and staff trained and what does this say about the institution's values? (d) What metrics are included or not included in evaluation efforts?

Excellence Perspective

The excellence perspective indicators depict underrepresented students' access to exclusive advantages, benefits, elite programs, and exceptional achievement. This perspective responds to questions such as (a) What are the completion rates of underrepresented students in highly competitive programs? (b) What percentage of underrepresented students graduate from college with a GPA of 3.5 or higher? (c) What is the size of the pool of high-achieving, underrepresented students who are eligible for graduate study in the full range of academic disciplines? (d) What percentage of underrepresented students graduate in the top 10 percent of their class? (e) What percentage of community college underrepresented students transfer to highly selective four-year colleges?

The Vital Signs

A unique feature of the Equity Scorecard approach is that it does not require the collection of new data. Colleges and universities have a wealth of data, and most use only a small fraction of it. Worse still, much of the data that are stored in the computer files of institutional research offices rarely get into the hands of the individuals who are closest to the students. The common belief that there is a lack of data is misleading. The problem is that higher education organizations, despite being dedicated to the production and transmission of knowledge, often lack the structures, know-how, and experience that are necessary to transform data into actionable knowledge.

Data are only as good as the questions that are posed of them. To initiate the process of raising critical questions we provide a data template called the *vital signs*. The vital signs consist of data that are routinely collected on most campuses, disaggregated by race and ethnicity. We call them *vital signs* because they provide insight into the "health" and "status" of an institution with respect to equity in student outcomes. For example, "the number and percentage of students who earn an associate degree within six years" is a vital sign for the retention and persistence perspective in the two-year college version of the Equity Scorecard. Likewise, "the number and percentage of community college transfers admitted and enrolled" is a vital sign in the access perspective in the four-year college version of the Equity Scorecard. In sum, the vital signs provide a starting point for the team's examination of data, by highlighting potential gaps and inequities in student outcomes. The format of the vital signs is specifically tailored for people who are not accustomed to examining data. For each of the Scorecard's four perspectives there is a set of vital signs.

As team members review and discuss the vital signs data, they are encouraged to notice unequal outcomes by race and ethnicity, and then to ask questions to unpack the inequalities identified. The purpose of "unpacking" or "breaking down" the inequalities that are made visible by the vital signs is to trace them to their origins. Unpacking inequalities makes it possible to define them more precisely and create solutions that target the causes of the problem. The process of "unpacking" inequalities is essential for learning and change and is the means of transforming data into actionable knowledge.

Constructing the Equity Scorecard

Once the team has gone through the cycle of reviewing vital signs data, discovering potential areas of inequity, asking questions about the data, and reviewing subsequent data, the members work collectively to agree upon indicators that will be included in the Equity Scorecard. For example, if the team members find that Latino and Latina students are disproportionately enrolled in basic skills English and math courses that are not applicable to the associate degree, they may decide to include "successful progression from basic skills to college-level English" and "successful progression from basic skills to college-level math" as indicators in the "academic pathways" perspective of their Equity Scorecard. They may also discover that many Latino and Latina students do not persist beyond a critical "gateway course" within the sequence, "English 100," for example. Gateway courses are those that serve as entry or exit points to graduation, transfer, or completion of basic skills requirements. Thus, students who are not successful in these courses are disadvantaged in several respects, notably time to degree completion. As such, the team may decide to include "successful completion of English 100" as one of its Equity Scorecard indicators. The team members continue this type of analysis and collaborative sensemaking until they have developed indicators for all four of the Equity Scorecard perspectives. Once the Equity Scorecard has been fully constructed by the team, the members' next task is to disseminate their findings to stakeholders who can use the knowledge to mobilize change.

Communicating the Equity Scorecard Findings to Stakeholders

The teams disseminate their learning and findings by way of a comprehensive written report to the president of the institution. In the report, the team discusses the data that served as the focal points of its analysis, the gaps and inequities it discovered within each perspective, and recommendations for action and further inquiry. Although the Equity Scorecard culminates with a report to the president and campus community, teams do not wait until the report is completed to spread knowledge. Throughout the process team members make presentations to stakeholder groups that shape and influence campus policies and practices that can have a direct effect on equity in student outcomes. The academic senate, strategic planning committee, academic deans, and academic departments in which the most significant inequities exist (e.g., math and English) are examples of some of the groups to which teams present their findings.

Lastly, team members, all of whom have been selected strategically because of their capacity to pass on their learning to others, take their newfound knowledge and awareness of inequities in student outcomes to the other formal and informal groups of which they are a part. These may include other committees, tasks forces, departments, and collegial circles.

Data Inquiry

The data inquiry process used in the Equity Scorecard is different from conventional approaches to data use. These differences are outlined in Table 3.1.

In the Equity Scorecard approach, evidence teams composed of faculty, staff, and administrators examine educational outcome data, disaggregated by race and ethnicity, to assess the nature of inequities on their campus and delve deeper into finer- and finer-grained measures to understand *where* and *when* these inequities occur. Guided by the thoughtful facilitation of team leaders and institutional researchers, teams select three to five of these fine-grained measures, or indicators, to continually monitor. In doing so, they

TABLE 3.1
Contrasting the Equity Scorecard Approach With Typical Approaches to Assessment and Data Inquiry

Typical Approaches to Data Inquiry	*Scorecard Approach to Data Inquiry*
Objectives:	
• To enhance productivity and efficiency • To ensure the excellent management of resources	• To enhance service to students • To ensure each student achieves desired learning and educational objectives • To demonstrate accountability to stakeholders
Types of Measures and Data:	
• Input/output, process, and productivity-oriented • Transactional, financial, and procedural • Primarily administrative • Aggregated data (totals and subtotals)	• Results, outcome-oriented • Measures of student progression from admission to graduate • Both administrative and academic • Problem-, issue-, or opportunity-focused • Disaggregated data by target populations and other factors
Examples of Measures:	
• Number of general education sections per thirty students needing requirement • Five-year graduation rate • Average turnaround (in days) for processing financial aid • Classroom and lab occupancy rates • Revenue $ per full-time equivalent student/expenditure $ per full-time equivalent student • Debt service to expenditure ratio • Expendable assets and amount of long-term debt • Turnover rate due to resignations	• The percentage of students, by target group, who achieve a C grade or better in "gateway" courses • The percentage of target group students enrolled in science programs or selected technical majors • The percentage of "early drops" from transfer courses by target group students • The pass rates in remedial English and math courses for target group students • The frequency with which target group students "stop out" of school for one semester or more
Methods of Analysis:	
• Variance between planned and actual • Increase or decrease from year to year in percentage, number, ratio, or rate	• Variance between target groups of students to ascertain differential outcomes • Rate of change from within semester, from semester to semester, from year to year • Gaps in progression by target groups • Problem or opportunity areas

(continued)

TABLE 3.1 (Continued)

Typical Approaches to Data Inquiry	Scorecard Approach to Data Inquiry
People Involved in Data Analysis and Interventions:	
• Finance director	• Teams of experts or constituents including:
• Institutional researcher	• Faculty
• President, vice presidents, deans, directors	• Students
• Planning and budgeting council/ committee	• Administrators and staff
	• Provost, vice president for instruction, academic vice president
	• Deans, directors, department chairs
	• Assessment director
Findings Used For:	
• Monitoring general operations	• Monitoring progress and success of interventions
• Making utilization decisions (managing the relationship between inputs and outputs)	• Making strategic decisions to enhance student achievement
• Examining specific or limited operational issues	• Recognizing problems or issues pertaining to differential student outcomes
	• Recognizing early indicators or warning signs of problems and issues

inquire more deeply into their institution's progress in producing equitable educational outcomes for underrepresented and underserved minority students. The findings that emerge are distributed along both formal and informal channels to the larger campus community. This ongoing focus on the institution's responsibility to students differs from the traditional data focus on topics of efficiency and allows for greater campus ownership of student outcomes data.

References

Bensimon, E. M., & Neumann, A. (1993). *Redesigning collegiate leadership: Teams and teamwork in higher education.* Baltimore, MD: Johns Hopkins University Press.

Kaplan, R. S., & Norton, D. P. (1993). Putting the balanced scorecard to work. *Harvard Business Review, 71*(5), 134–142.

O'Neil, H. F., Jr., Bensimon, E. M., Diamond, M. A., and Moore, M. R. (1999). Designing and implementing an academic scorecard. *Change, 31*(6), 32–41.

PART TWO

PRACTITIONER EXPERIENCES OF THE EQUITY SCORECARD

4

THE DIVERSITY SCORECARD AT LOYOLA MARYMOUNT UNIVERSITY

An Exemplary Model of Dissemination

Abbie Robinson-Armstrong, Andrea Clemons,
Matthew Fissinger, and Marshall Sauceda

The following chapter was written by the Equity Scorecard Team at Loyola Marymount University (LMU). Not only did this team develop an effective Scorecard, it also successfully disseminated its findings such that ten academic units and programs subsequently engaged in developing their own Equity Scorecards. The team identifies the power of evidence, the importance of supportive institutional leadership, and engaging practitioners doing the work in organizational learning as its keys to success. LMU stands out as an institution that turned its commitment to structural diversity into a commitment to equity in educational outcomes—from the classroom to the president's office.

Institutional change in higher education is a subject of great import. As student demographics and circumstances continue to evolve (Upcraft, 1996), postsecondary institutions face new challenges that will require measured change (Kezar, 2001). Particularly in urban areas, the "traditional" college student is quickly becoming the exception rather than the rule: A greater proportion of students attending urban colleges and universities commute, are employed, and come from diverse racial, cultural, and economic backgrounds compared with students attending campuses in suburban areas

(Rantz, 2002). This influx of "nontraditional" students has left colleges and universities scrambling to adapt to these changes. The new reality in higher education is that "nontraditional" is the now the norm. As a result, colleges and universities are increasingly finding themselves confronted with issues of equity and diversity. Although changes in policies (e.g., affirmative action, targeted recruitment) may increase the numbers of underrepresented students on an institution's campus and diversify the student body, these policies cannot ensure academic equity. This is evidenced by the ever-present and often widening achievement gaps between racialized students and White students in higher education (Bowen & Bok, 1998). Academic equity is more complex than representational diversity, because equity is highly dependent on what happens *inside* the classroom and subsequently is dependent on each individual faculty member or instructor (Bensimon, 2004). Faculty members' practices, assumptions, beliefs, and values have great implications for academic equity. Thus, institutional change efforts that seek to address issues of equity must take into account the role of the individual and tailor strategies to not only change teachers' practices, but their beliefs and assumptions as well.

This chapter details the implementation of the Equity Scorecard at Loyola Marymount University (LMU) and chronicles the change process that occurred among the members of the LMU Equity Scorecard Team. The dissemination strategies employed by the evidence team and university leadership to institutionalize the Scorecard are also explored.

Shifting the Focus from Diversity to Equity

Prior to its involvement with the Equity Scorecard Project in 2000, LMU had been addressing diversity issues for many years. Indeed, diversity is a central tenet in the university's mission, goals, and ten-year strategic plan. The university's ten-year strategic plan, for instance, states, "Diversity is critical to academic excellence and the promotion of a civil society. . . . LMU will seek to create a more vibrant student culture through an enhanced intellectual environment, a strong intercultural curriculum, and improved student services" (Loyola Marymount University, 2006). The emphasis on interculturalism reflects the value placed on diversity in its broadest sense and the fostering of intergroup interactions for the purposes of learning.

Like many other postsecondary institutions, the university recognized the value of a diverse student body and faculty and took active steps to become more inclusive. LMU was awarded several grants to target women and scholars from racialized groups for faculty positions, offer fellowships to doctoral students, and develop professional development courses on pedagogy and curriculum transformation. New academic major offerings in African American, Asian American, and Chicana/o Studies were established, and all undergraduates were required to fulfill a diversity course requirement. The university also established a Multicultural Affairs office within the Student Affairs division to provide support to students of color. However, many of these good-faith and often effective efforts to increase diversity were compartmentalized, or contingent on grant funding. For example, the hiring program and graduate fellowships ended after the grants expired. Additionally, efforts to bring attention to and improve diversity on campus were confined to those offices designated as "diversity offices." Diversity and interculturalism were not recognized as institutional values in practice across the campus.

Recognizing this disconnect between diversity as an espoused value and as a driving force behind the structure, planning, and practices of the institution, the resident and academic vice president created a new senior-level position, assistant to the president for intercultural affairs. This position was designed to create a "point person" to lead the university's efforts to increase diversity. Shortly after this position was created, LMU was invited to participate in the Equity Scorecard Project by the Center for Urban Education (CUE) at the University of Southern California (USC).

Although the Equity Scorecard framework fed into a preexisting "culture of evidence" around mission-based outcomes assessment and student learning outcomes at LMU, the CUE facilitators, by introducing the Scorecard framework, reoriented the institutional research paradigm at LMU from an intercultural focus to an equity focus. Our previous approach to institutional assessment was to analyze data sets in comparison with national and local university measures. With students of color at LMU composing 35 to 40 percent of the student body, the university had historically appeared as a model of diversity compared with the national and local averages of other institutions.

However, the Equity Scorecard Project reoriented the institutional research lens at LMU to the "accountability side of diversity." Bauman, Bustillos, Bensimon, Brown, and Bartee (2005) explain, "Essentially an institution takes inclusive excellence seriously if it (1) accepts the responsibility for producing equitable educational outcomes for students from historically disenfranchised groups and (2) monitors the development of high achievement among historically underrepresented students" (p. 9).

"Academic equity" refers to equality in educational outcomes for all students, including students from historically disenfranchised groups. For example, if African Americans constitute 25 percent of a college's student population, achieving academic equity would mean that 25 percent of students on the Dean's List are also African American. Equity goes several steps further than the goal of diversity. Even on diverse campuses, intrainstitutional stratification based on race and ethnicity is a reality (Bensimon, Hao, & Bustillos, 2006). Currently, few higher education institutions recognize the difference between diversity and equity, and thus they are not capable of rectifying academic inequities (Bensimon, Polkinghorne, Bauman, & Vallejo, 2004). In order to produce equitable educational outcomes, institutions need to (a) understand the concept of equity, (b) recognize equity as a desirable goal and a matter of institutional responsibility, (c) monitor the educational outcomes of students from historically disenfranchised groups, and (d) enact effective strategies to produce equitable outcomes.

After accepting the invitation to participate in the Equity Scorecard, the president along with other key faculty and administrators began to understand the distinction between diversity and equity and recognized that although diversity is indeed necessary and desirable, more work would be needed to ensure that LMU produced equitable educational outcomes for all students. As Estela Bensimon and other researchers from CUE communicated to us, we, as an institution, would not be able to achieve academic equity through a "quick fix." Instead, the achievement of equity in educational outcomes would require a shift in institutional culture and practices, as well as changes in the values, beliefs, and assumptions of practitioners at LMU. In short, the realization of academic equity would require institutional change.

In the following sections of this chapter, we detail the implementation of the Equity Scorecard at LMU and the efforts to disseminate our findings and institutionalize equity as a performance measure at the university. We also highlight key factors that contributed to the successful implementation of the Scorecard at LMU and discuss difficulties encountered throughout the process.

The Implementation of the Equity Scorecard at Loyola Marymount University

We begin our description of the implementation of the Equity Scorecard at LMU by detailing the institutional context at the time of our participation.

We then discuss the composition of our evidence team, and then describe the Scorecard process as experienced by the team members and other institutional actors. As we highlight in the following section, learning and change among the team members and the broader campus community was facilitated by the strong support of institutional leadership.

Loyola Marymount University: Institutional Context

Founded in the early twentieth century and located in Los Angeles, California, Loyola Marymount University is one of twenty-eight Jesuit universities in the country. In 2005, the student body consisted of 5,465 undergraduates, 1,639 graduate students, and 1,377 law students. Students of color constituted 37 percent of the undergraduate population, with the following breakdown: 19 percent Latinos and Latinas, 11 percent Asian and Pacific Americans, 6 percent African Americans, and 1 percent American Indians. Caucasian students composed about 50 percent of the student population, and the remaining students declined to state their racial or ethnic background.

LMU is structured into four colleges—Liberal Arts, Business Administration, Communication and Fine Arts, and Science and Engineering—and two schools—the School of Education and the School of Film and Television. The university's institutional mission states, "Loyola Marymount University understands and declares its purpose to be: the encouragement of learning, the education of the whole person, the service of faith and the promotion of justice."

LMU Equity Scorecard Team

The first step in establishing the project at LMU required the development of an "evidence team," led by the Special Assistant to the President for Intercultural Affairs. The evidence team's role was to initiate and oversee the gathering of existing data to assess the educational equity status of underrepresented students university-wide. Appreciating the importance of history, tradition, and culture for facilitating change on campus (Kezar & Eckel, 2002), the president of the university appointed an ethnically and professionally diverse initial Equity Scorecard Team, including established and well-respected members of the campus community. This initial team served the function of an "evidence team" and consisted of male and female faculty and staff of African American, Asian, Latino, and Anglo descent, including the assistant to the president for intercultural affairs, the associate dean of ethnic and intercultural services, the director of institutional research, and a senior faculty member from the English department.

The LMU Equity Scorecard Team met sixteen times from January 1, 2001, through January 28, 2003. The team attended four meetings at USC, which also included teams from all of the fourteen colleges and universities participating in this project. The initial meetings centered on building a sense of shared responsibility by focusing the LMU Scorecard so that it complemented the university's mission, intercultural definition, vision statement and principles, and the new ten-year strategic plan.

Garnering Support for Evidence-Based Change Through Inquiry

At the outset of the Equity Scorecard Project at LMU, the university president took an active role in its implementation. He supported a diversity-focused investigation, he appointed a broadly representative Scorecard Team, and he asked for annual public reports from the team. Visible and ongoing support from LMU's institutional leadership gave the project legitimacy. Importantly, the context in which the president cast the Scorecard was tied to mission, not to performance. The Scorecard, while evidence driven and likely to reveal shortcomings, was not presented as punitive or critical, but as an opportunity to work collaboratively toward shared goals.

In the initial stages of the Equity Scorecard Project, though all of the members of the evidence team were solidly behind the goals of the project, some were dubious that their efforts would spark institution-wide change. Much of this initial skepticism stemmed from the team members' previous experiences with evaluative and assessment projects that had never made any difference on the campus. Several months after the project began, one team member revealed his initial doubts:

> I don't know whether I was ever a disbeliever in assessment [but] you would do it, then they would throw it away and things would go on; and when changes occurred, it was because somebody intuited that change was needed, not because they had a lot of evidence for it.

The Scorecard project stood in contrast to these previous efforts as it emphasized inquiry rather than intuition as the guide to change. The team examined institutional data regarding student enrollment, retention, graduation rates, and achievement (i.e., grade point average) in order to understand where LMU stood as an institution, and to determine where we were falling short. The Scorecard process required that the team take a long, hard look at the data and make sense of inequities in educational outcomes among different racial and ethnic groups. However, the members of the Equity Scorecard Team realized that it would be their duty to, in a sense, break the news regarding inequity to the campus community. The apprehension of this responsibility weighed heavily on much of the team as it expected some degree of "fallout" from the results of the Equity Scorecard project.

One of the primary duties of the special assistant to the president for intercultural affairs was to be involved in the Equity Scorecard project. She was appointed soon after the advent of the project and was named the team leader. Her responsibilities would necessitate frequent contact with the president of LMU in the form of regularly scheduled one-on-one meetings. Her background (doctorate in higher education) uniquely qualified her to take on this role of team leader. She was knowledgeable regarding issues of equity and was committed to achieving academic equity at the institution. Due to her academic work, she was familiar with the literature and was able to effectively disseminate her knowledge to the team members and the wider campus community.

The team was certainly more empowered after the arrival of the special assistant to the president. As one team member noted, "Now that people know that she has the ear of the president, she's permanent, and she has a lot of guts, people stand up and take notice." The special assistant's presence on the team served as an explicit endorsement of the team's work by the leadership of the university. Earlier concerns that the Scorecard would fail to bring about change faded from the team's dialogue. The new team leader's contact with the president strengthened the team's perceived value of the project. The team members felt that their findings would be communicated to the president and that he would be receptive to them. The team's new-found confidence and sense of agency directly affected the remainder of the project. As the team members continued to progress and became more immersed in the actual analysis of institutional data, their initial hesitance diminished, allowing them to coalesce as an effective team.

Examining Vital Signs and Disaggregating Data

The first step of the data analysis involved collecting and examining "vital signs" data. As Bauman and colleagues (2005) explain, "Like blood pressure and temperature, these are particular indicators that every institution uses and reports as baseline measures of institutional health and/or status" (p. 18). It was critically important that these data be disaggregated by race and ethnicity and, in some cases, gender. The goal of this activity was to determine if academic inequities existed, and to prompt team members to ask questions that arose from the vital signs data.

At LMU, the initial vital signs indicators included enrollment by race and ethnicity, enrollment in major or college by race and ethnicity, retention from freshman to sophomore year by race and ethnicity, retention to graduation by race and ethnicity, and the number of tenured and tenure-track faculty by race and ethnicity. For many of these indicators, the team examined data from multiple years in order to detect trends. This initial data analysis allowed the team to raise questions and request new data from the director of institutional research.

While reviewing the vital signs, the team learned that the percentages of African American and Latino and Latina students had decreased in the previous five years despite a 21 percent increase in total undergraduate enrollment in the same period. Between 1997 and 2001, the African American population decreased from 7.8 to 6.4 percent, and the Latino and Latina population decreased from 20.6 to 18.5 percent. European American students represented 67 percent of the increase in undergraduates.

This newly acquired knowledge regarding the decline in African American and Latino and Latina enrollment prompted the team to further inquire into the data. For example, one team member asked, "Has the proportion of male versus female minority students changed over time?" This led the team to further disaggregate enrollment data by gender. The analysis of the enrollment by race and ethnicity and gender revealed that more than 60 percent of the African American and Latino and Latina students on campus were women, whereas other groups had a more balanced gender distribution.

The team then examined the distribution of undergraduate degrees conferred across the four academic colleges. The data revealed that African Americans and Latinos and Latinas were severely underrepresented in science and engineering. Among the questions raised from this data were, "How do minority students end up concentrated in particular colleges" and "Are these students migrating out of their original majors or applying to particular majors upon entry to LMU?" These inquiries led to the development of fine-grained measures and the collection of additional data. As Bauman and colleagues (2005) explain, these "[fine-grained] measures go beyond the traditional indicators used by institutions and enables [the team] to identify problem areas more specifically" (p. 22). In the words of a team member, the data were "eye-opening," and convinced team members, including the skeptics, of the importance of academic equity.

The LMU team members identified access to different majors as a potential area of inquiry. They wanted to know whether African American and Latino and Latina students were proportionally represented in majors that were pathways to careers in high-demand fields, such as engineering and computer science. In addition to identifying areas of underrepresentation, the team also wanted to find out if minority students were overrepresented in other majors.

In order to answer these questions, the team looked at graduation rates by major, disaggregated by ethnicity. From these data, they learned that African Americans and Latinos and Latinas were underrepresented in science and engineering. However, this first-order analysis did not reveal the reasons behind the underrepresentation. The team decided to examine longitudinal data that tracked cohorts of students from their originally proposed major to the major in which they graduated.

The longitudinal analysis revealed that 42 percent of the 1997 cohort of African American students who had enrolled in the College of Science and Engineering had left that college, and the African American enrollment in the College of Liberal Arts had increased by 31 percent. By tracking the specific majors that African American and Latino and Latina students who left science and engineering migrated to, the team identified particular prerequisites and courses, known as "gateway courses," that act as obstacles to these students' academic advancement. This higher level of inquiry not only enabled the LMU team members to identify inequities in educational outcomes, but it also allowed them to understand some of the specific contributors to the perpetuation of these inequities. Armed with this knowledge, the LMU team members could formulate recommendations to present to the president and campus community in order to resolve inequitable educational outcomes.

Report to President and Campus Community

At the completion of the Equity Scorecard, the team was required to submit a final report to the president that described the findings on the state of equity at LMU. The team had to decide which of the many equity indicators it examined to include in the report. These choices had to be made with careful consideration because there was a large potential for political fallout from the report. Because the findings would also be shared with the larger community, the compilation of the report was a delicate and deliberate process. Although it is true that a major purpose of the report was to raise awareness of academic inequities, this had to be done in a way that encouraged faculty, administrators, and other institutional actors to take action to eliminate these inequities—not to react defensively. The report also included recommendations for action, such as volunteering to continue their data analysis, involving other departments, and using institutional resources to eliminate inequitable educational outcomes.

The president of LMU called for a town hall–style meeting to discuss the Equity Scorecard findings and the resulting recommendations. At the meeting, copies of the report were provided for attending campus community members and the report was posted on LMU's internal website. Many faculty, administrators, and staff attended the meeting, which was opened by the provost. Each team member used PowerPoint to present a section of the report, using data to display the inequities the team had discovered. At the conclusion of the presentation, the special assistant to the president for intercultural affairs, who served as the Equity Scorecard Team leader told the audience, "Everyone has to commit to being evidence monitors," and emphasized that "equal access does not guarantee equity in success."

The team felt that it was important to involve faculty and administrators from all academic units in the project. Although the team members were able to uncover educational inequities across disciplines, they felt that they did not have the expertise to develop action plans to meet the demonstrated needs and establish assessment measures for the various units of the university. In the final report, they wrote:

> If we wanted the best results, we need to rely on the experts who worked in these areas. We further realized we needed their commitment. The Scorecard had to be their project. They needed to be part of the team, and we had to work to facilitate their efforts on behalf of [LMU's] underrepresented students.

Later in the report the team wrote:

> We assumed responsibility for raising awareness of the current situation at LMU by providing statistical evidence. We saw ourselves as both "evidence monitors" and a group that could provide resources and facilitate continuing work in this area. Now it is time for broader campus involvement in the work of being "evidence monitors."

One of the recommendations, which was agreed upon by the president, stated that each college within the university ought to create its own Equity Scorecard, using the LMU team's report as a foundation. Thus, in order to connect the change process to individual and institutional identity, the initial Scorecard Team evolved into a larger University Scorecard Team, which consisted of representatives from across the campus and particularly from Academic Affairs.

Spreading the Scorecard

In this stage of the project dissemination, the creation of a new university-wide Scorecard Team helped develop a greater campus-wide perspective on the issues of equity central to the project's goals, shifting focus from a centralized Equity Scorecard Team to individual departments or programs. When the broader Scorecard Team was assembled, the membership included representatives from ten units, across the academic divisions as well as from Student Affairs. The Student Affairs group included the Admission Office, the Honors Program, all the colleges and schools, and the Student Affairs offices providing ethnic and intercultural services. This breadth of participation gave the impression and, in fact, created the consciousness of community-wide responsibility for access and equity, for which the Scorecard was an assessment tool.

To promote organizational self-discovery about equity on a unit-by-unit basis (Morgan, 1986), the initial evidence team, in consultation with the president, decided that each of the ten units composing the new Equity Scorecard Teams would tackle their own data and determine their own goals, outcomes, and assessment gauges to create a unit-specific Scorecard to be added to a comprehensive Scorecard for the university. Deans appointed associate deans and directors of key programs to participate in the project so that they would all be represented.

The original members of the LMU Equity Scorecard Team coached the academic units on how to construct their scorecards. Each college's team used the findings from the initial Scorecard Team in the report as a starting point to identify one measure to investigate more thoroughly. Involving each academic unit diminished the opportunity for faculty and staff to say that the responsibility for creating equity in educational outcomes lay elsewhere, as might have been likely had this project been conceived and constructed differently. The creation of evidence teams in these various departments placed the concept of accountability front and center, which was reinforced by the monitored progress of the various Scorecard Teams as they prepared for their presentations to the president.

The findings and recommendations from the ten new teams were presented to the president at another town hall meeting thirteen months after the presentation of the original report. Rather than calling for the creation of new programs, most of the recommendations made for addressing inequities involved changes in internal practices and policies. The manageable and "no-cost" nature of each team's recommendations increased the likelihood that they would be enacted. The president lauded the efforts of the ten teams and closed the meeting by saying:

> I want to talk about temptations. First, there is the temptation to be over-whelmed by data. I am very happy to see that you have avoided it. Second, is the temptation to relish knowledge but not allow it to lead to action. Here you're all taking action, which is great. Third, is the temptation to do too much and therefore make your efforts too diffuse. I am happy that you are taking manageable actions. I applaud you and your commitment.

After the March meeting, the president decided to post the university Scorecards on the LMU website. This step in the dissemination process was followed soon after by the president's decision, in consultation with the special assistant to the president for intercultural affairs, to promote the Scorecard initiative in the Fall 2003 edition of the LMU alumni magazine, *Vistas,* and to publish a press release announcing the Equity Scorecard as a benchmark initiative for the university. By taking the Scorecard "public" in this way, the work of the initial Equity Scorecard Team, as well as that of the teams in each academic unit, was shared with an even broader audience of students, faculty, and alumni.

Institutionalizing Change: Examples from Department Scorecard Teams

The transition of responsibility from centralized to decentralized research teams helped people to feel that they were in control of the process as it pertained to them. Regular team meetings allowed participants a forum in which to provide insight and background to illustrate their equity issues more clearly. This was not an agenda imposed upon them but rather this was an opportunity to share valuable information that could help their departments improve and from which other departments could learn.

The LMU Graduate School of Education was the only graduate pro-gram to participate in the Scorecard project, for instance, and interpreted its unique Scorecard data in a way that offered direction for all graduate pro-grams. Through the Scorecard data compilation process, the School of Edu-cation found that, although its numbers of Latino and Latina and African

American students exceeded or matched those of the larger university, the school had no way to measure retention or excellence of these students because these data at the graduate level were not readily available. The Scorecard for the School of Education argued,

> The absence of a database of diversity measures in graduate programs requires a reevaluation of how the university collects and interprets these data. For instance, when many graduate students do not follow a prescribed timeline, as is typical in graduate programs, we need to determine how to measure retention in a meaningful way. Moreover, excellence indicators need reconsideration in light of the unique trends in graduate coursework. Since graduate programs require a minimum 3.0 grade point average by participating students, we need to ask what excellence measures are meaningful for graduate programs. (Clemons & Martin, 2003, p. 5)

As we learned more about the unique diversity circumstances of each unit, the departmental Equity Scorecard Teams found that we had to rely on each other for the data and for support of our individual efforts to be successful. For example, each of the colleges required admission data and support to assess their own unique circumstances, and they, in turn, assisted the admissions office with tracking information and evidence of strengthened access to LMU. The experience of the College of Communication and Fine Arts is a clear example of how a unit, through monitored progress, disseminated and solidified awareness of Scorecard efforts and goals.

The dean of the College of Communication and Fine Arts instituted a diversity task force to monitor project progress. Task force members from the dance, music, theater, and art departments studied the college's Scorecard data and agreed that there were two major equity issues: (a) underrepresented students not enrolling in the arts at LMU and (b) lack of scholarships available for students of color who are interested in the arts. With this understanding of institutional viability challenges, college task force members met with counselors in admissions and financial aid to brainstorm interventions. As a result, task force members were invited to participate in a "Latino/a Overnight" event sponsored by the admissions office. These faculty met with parents and students at the event and even extended open invitations to their classes to Latino and Latina students interested in knowing more about classes in the arts.

This type of collaboration cemented the dissemination of the Scorecard project to the campus community level, and sharpened the understanding that these efforts were critical to our understanding of our mission and identity.

Challenges to Dissemination and Integration

Arguably, it was inevitable that some segments of the LMU community did, in fact, feel that an agenda was being imposed, and that desired outcomes were presumed. At the very least, there was some defensiveness in response to the early data, most often as this related to equity, as measured by persistence, in some undergraduate programs. Although the departmental teams appreciated the public attention their work was getting, there continued to be skepticism to overcome. At the initial meetings, the participants and key campus leaders wondered whether their efforts would really lead to programmatic change, much less campus culture change. As time passed after the initial presentation of the scorecards and meetings continued, certain departmental Scorecard Team members became frustrated that funding was not forthcoming once data demonstrated inequities.

In one instance, data revealed minority students were migrating from a certain school's programs. The Scorecard Team representative of the school expressed his concern about the underpreparedness of minority students in this area of study and proposed a Bridge Program for these students as a remedy for the problem. At Scorecard Team meetings, other team members challenged this deficit view of the students as the problem. We dialogued about the need for more qualitative input on the issue, in order to understand the reasons for student migration from the students' perspective. Here, the initial evidence team and the CUE facilitators played a very important role. They emphasized the positive, mission-related nature of the project and the need for a deeper examination of the causes behind the migration of students. Despite this dialogue and the offers of support for further investigation, frustration over the lack of financial support for what was assumed to be a viable intervention for student migration was not resolved.

As this example demonstrates, the focus on equity and the openness of the team to the disorderly process of addressing how equity is best achieved by each unit diminished but did not eliminate disagreements based on paradigms and politics. The Equity Scorecard Project at LMU demonstrated that change in higher education is political. Some individuals were apprehensive about others using the Scorecard to advance personal and political agendas. Certain individuals expressed concerns about "outsiders" having access to internal information for fear of looking bad and possible negative ramifications. They felt that the Scorecard might reveal issues that a department feels are beyond its ability to resolve. Some individuals did not believe that a Scorecard was necessary because students of color already composed 35 to 40 percent of the student body at LMU. The uncompromising positions of certain faculty and administrators, who resisted the push to investigate equity issues, were the biggest challenge to disseminating and integrating the Scorecard.

Even though the Equity Scorecard Team and committee unit representatives articulated core characteristics for the project while maintaining different change strategies for each unit's initiatives in order to reduce the potential for disagreements based on politics, certain units refused to engage in the dialogue under the assumption that "diversity" was a nonissue for their units. For example, the Scorecard of one of the largest university colleges notes equity issues pertaining to representation of diverse faculty and representation of its African American students in the honors program. Yet the causes of these equity issues are not identified in the Scorecard as connected to the college in any way. The conclusions of this Scorecard placed the blame of faculty underrepresentation on housing costs in Los Angeles and blamed student underperformance on financial aid. Specifically, the Scorecard stated, "Discussion among College . . . administrators and faculty has often disintegrated into reliance on assumptions ('Clearly, the problem is one of inadequate financial aid.') and anecdotal evidence." Because of the initial presentation of this college's data, it has reported no progress on the equity issues identified in its Scorecard.

This example illustrates that although active resistance to change for developing and implementing programs to improve access and outcomes has never existed at LMU and still doesn't, such passive resistance can become an obstacle when an institution or a unit fails to take responsibility for equity. Passive resistance characterized the most challenging factors to institutional change throughout the Equity Scorecard Project.

Lessons Learned

LMU's experiences with the Equity Scorecard project reveal many themes about the nature of equity-driven institutional change in higher education. Among these are the power of evidence, the importance of supportive institutional leadership, and the importance of fostering institutional change through individual learning so that change occurs from the bottom up, not just from the top down.

The Power of Evidence

Evidence is essential to the Equity Scorecard's conceptualization of institutional change. Factual data related to educational outcomes serve many purposes in the Equity Scorecard Project. First, it is used to raise awareness of academic inequity. The LMU team members needed to look at data in order to gain awareness of educational inequities on their campus. Without these data, team members tended to rely on anecdotes or their own experiences. Pauline Lipman's (1997) account of a change effort in which teachers jointly discussed the state of equity at an elementary school revealed the difficulties that can arise when individuals rely on anecdotal information. Because teachers made decisions based on their personal experiences and perceptions, the beliefs of the majority ruled instead of factual information. For example, the opinions of African American teachers at the elementary school in Lipman's (1997) study were ignored because they were outnumbered, not because their opinions were invalid or inaccurate. Without factual data, change is more difficult to create because anecdotes are given the same epistemic status as fact. Although it may be difficult for individuals to set aside their own experiences in favor of data, it is critical that they do so. Institutional policy should not be based on anecdotes. After all, for every story that one faculty member relates, another will likely have a different account. A consensus cannot be reached when individuals attempt to reconcile their subjective interpretations of reality. In contrast, data are more objective and provide a snapshot of the current reality with respect to equity on campus.

Along these same lines, evidence also has the power to convert skeptics into "believers." It is difficult for individuals to hold on to the belief that their institution is equitable when confronted with data that disprove that belief. Evidence is capable of creating cognitive dissonance, which leads to learning (Argyris, 1982; Kezar, 2001). Milbrey W. McLaughlin (1990) refers to this process as "belief following practice" (p. 13). This occurred with at least one of the LMU team members. Although he was initially skeptical of the project and appeared "antagonistic," by the project's conclusion he understood the importance of taking action to eliminate inequities in educational outcomes and was an active participant in "spreading the word." The success of this evidence-based approach to change is capable of overcoming individuals' socially constructed knowledge. As Oakes, Wells, Jones, and Datnow (1997) illustrate, teachers' socially constructed understanding of concepts like intelligence and ability can significantly affect, and sometimes derail, equity-driven change efforts. Incorporating evidence into the change process can overcome the barriers posed by individuals' socially constructed understandings of the world.

The second purpose of data in the Equity Scorecard project is to empower the campus team members. Evidence of educational inequities revealed by factual data provides team members with a foundation upon which to base campus conversations about equity. As one LMU team member said, "Doing [the Equity Scorecard] gives [us] a good opportunity to have dialogue. Now we can raise issues." Through the project, team members were armed with data that backed up what they were saying about the importance of equity and the need for the institution to take action. Instead of yielding when encountering resistance, the teams were able to refute cynics with evidence. Because the team members had this knowledge, they were more apt to stay committed to the fight for equity.

Lastly, data are an effective tool with which to institutionalize equity-driven change. Evidence legitimized the team's change efforts and gave it credibility in the eyes of the larger community. One LMU team member talked about his newfound credibility:

> I, myself, am a minority. I could not generate [the Scorecard] on my own. People might have asked why or would have been suspicious of my data. Now I can say, look at this report I did for the [Equity Scorecard].

Although some individuals on the LMU campus reacted negatively to the team's findings, these individuals could not effectively argue against the Equity Scorecard report. These individuals' resistance stemmed from their own discomfort rather than from the facts presented. Much of the campus reacted positively, because the process of the Scorecard was transparent, credible, and replicable.

The Importance of Supportive Institutional Leadership

During the Scorecard process, the LMU team members came to understand that institutional change around equity and perspectives on diversity are political phenomena. As such it was vital that the team had the support of institutional leadership and was directed by an influential and enthusiastic team leader. The president of LMU and the special assistant to the president for intercultural affairs played a major role in the success of the Equity Scorecard project. The team leader was able to change the trajectory of the LMU team. The team's initial sense of powerlessness disappeared once the special assistant to the president arrived on campus and was placed in charge of the team. Much of this change can be attributed to her contact with the president. Through her regularly scheduled meetings, the team leader was able to bypass many levels of bureaucracy and work directly with the president. As a result, the president became deeply interested in the work that the Equity Scorecard Team members were doing. His sustained interest was vital to the success of the project at LMU. Because he was familiar with the work conducted by the team, he made it an institutional priority and provided the team with the platform it needed to effectively disseminate its findings. The president's "buy-in" bolstered the team's efforts to increase campus-wide involvement in matters related to equity in educational outcomes. For example, when the president accepted the recommendation to create new Scorecard Teams in each academic area, the deans and directors of each division followed his lead and became involved in the efforts.

Change From the Bottom Up: Engaging Practitioners in Learning

The dissemination efforts detailed in this chapter illustrate how engaging faculty and staff from a variety of disciplines and departments can effectively drive institutional change. Although support from external facilitators and institutional leaders was motivational, it was not sufficient to ensure long-term, institution-wide commitment. The opportunity for organizational self-discovery on a unit-by-unit basis was essential to help formulate a campus-wide perspective on the issues of equity central to the project goals.

Importantly for the dissemination and institutionalization of the project, the Scorecard allowed individual departments to frame the issues within their own contexts. When faculty within a department examined the data and then determined how it affected them, it reinforced the benefit of departmental autonomy as a motivating factor in institutional research and institutional change. As such, the Equity Scorecard allowed us to implement institutional change from the bottom up as well as from the top down. By taking a multidirectional, rather than unidirectional, approach, we sought to facilitate learning among leadership, administrators, and faculty.

Conclusion: Outcomes From the Scorecard

The Equity Scorecard project and the establishment of departmental Scorecard Teams at LMU has led to many positive changes in terms of student access to the institution, student participation rates in the special programs, faculty representation, and course curricula. For example, the number of students of color invited to the University Honors Program increased since the implementation of the Scorecard. In 2002, African Americans represented 1.9 percent of students in the program; by 2005, this figure rose to 2.4 percent. Latino and Latina students' share rose from 6.7 to 8.3 percent in the same period. The Scorecard also led to the establishment of a new faculty professional development program that focuses on inclusive instruction and changes in some course curricula to engage more students of color (Robinson-Armstrong et al., 2007).

Though university leadership, faculty, and staff attribute these positive outcomes to the Equity Scorecard project, the work of the campus regarding equity in educational outcomes remains unfinished. The Equity Scorecard project and the spreading of the process to each of LMU's ten academic units have helped to promote equity as an institutional goal and frame equity in educational outcomes as a measurable and desirable goal. Through the process of benchmarking, academic units will continue to monitor their progress in creating equitable outcomes for all students, particularly underrepresented minorities. However, as with all institutional change efforts, there is a concern regarding the sustainability of the change brought about by the Scorecard project. Dean Fink (2000) discusses the attrition of change in his article detailing "lighthouse" schools in a district in Canada. His study revealed that when the individuals associated with a reform left the school, the change diminished over time, so that "lighthouse" schools eventually resembled traditional schools in the district. It is possible that in spite of the best efforts of the LMU president and Scorecard Team members to institutionalize the Scorecard and equity as an institutional priority, the change brought about by the project could wane. Universities, even more so than other organizations, are often rigid to change in the first place and may revert back to the "old ways" of doing things as soon as the change agent, be it an individual, a grant-funded project, a special initiative, or a process, is removed from the environment. Other times, change erodes when new priorities supersede those behind the initial change efforts. LMU's Scorecard Team continues to take steps to prevent the attrition of change by incorporating equity into new faculty training programs, using equity as a basis for new external funding, and forming communities of practice across disciplines with equity as a common focus.

References

Argyris, C. (1982). How learning and reasoning processes affect organizational change. In P. S. Goodman (Ed.), *Change in organizations.* San Francisco, CA: Jossey-Bass.

Bauman, G. L., Bustillos, L. T., Bensimon, E. M., Brown, M. C., & Bartee, R. D. (2005). *Achieving equitable educational outcomes with all students: The institution's roles and responsibilities.* Washington, DC: Association of American Colleges and Universities.

Bensimon, E. M. (2004). The diversity scorecard: A learning approach to institutional change. *Change, 36*(1), 45–52.

Bensimon, E. M., Hao, L., & Bustillos, L. (2006). Measuring the state of equity in higher education. In G. Orfield, P. Gandara, & C. Horn (Eds.), *Expanding opportunity in higher education: Leveraging promise* (pp. 143–164). Albany, NY: SUNY Press.

Bensimon, E. M., Polkinghorne, D. E., Bauman, G. L., & Vallejo, E. (2004). Doing research that makes a difference. *The Journal of Higher Education, 75*(1), 104–126.

Bowen, W. G., & Bok, D. (1998). *The shape of the river.* Princeton, NJ: Princeton University Press.

Clemons, A., & Martin, S. (2003). *Diversity Scorecard report: School of education.* Los Angeles, CA: Loyola Marymount University.

Fink, D. (2000). The attrition of educational change over time: The case of innovative, model, lighthouse schools. In N. Bascia & A. Hargreaves (Eds.), *The sharp edge of change: Teaching, leading, and the realities of reform* (pp. 29–51). London: Falmer Press.

Kezar, A. (2001). Understanding and facilitating organizational change in the 21st century: Recent research and conceptualizations. *ASHE-ERIC Higher Education Reports, 28*(4).

Kezar, A., & Eckel, P. (2002). The effect of institutional culture on change strategies in higher education: Universal principles or culturally responsive concepts? *The Journal of Higher Education, 73*(4), 435–460.

Lipman, P. (1997). Restructuring in context: A case study of teacher participation and the dynamics of ideology, race, and power. *American Educational Research Journal, 34*(1), 3–37.

Loyola Marymount University. (2006, January). *The strategic plan for Loyola Marymount University.* Office of the President. Retrieved from http://www .lmu.edu/Assets/President$!27s+Division/LMU+Strategic+Plan.pdf

McLaughlin, M. W. (1990). The Rand change agent study revisited: Macro perspectives and micro realities. *Educational Researcher, 19*(9), 11–16.

Morgan, G. (1986). *Images of organization.* Beverly Hills, CA: Sage.

Oakes, J., Wells, A. S., Jones, M., & Datnow, A. (1997). Detracking: The social construction of ability, cultural politics, and resistance to reform. *Teachers College Record, 98*(3), 482–510.

Rantz, R. (2002). Leading urban institutions of higher education in the new millennium. *Leadership and Organizational Development Journal, 23*(8), 456–466.

Robinson-Armstrong, A., King, D., Killoran, D., Ward, H., Fissinger, M. X., & Harrison, L. (2007). Creating institutional transformation using the Equity Scorecard. *Diversity Digest, 10*(2), 7–8.

Upcraft, M. L. (1996). Teaching and today's college students. In R. J. Menges, M. Weimer, & Associates (Eds.), *Teaching on solid group: Using scholarship to improve practice* (pp. 21–42). San Francisco, CA: Jossey-Bass.

5

FACULTY LEARNING AND REFLECTION FROM STUDENT INTERVIEWS

Laura Palucki Blake, Edlyn Vallejo Peña, Diana Akiyama,
Elizabeth Braker, Donna Kay Maeda, Michael A. McDonald,
Gretchen North, John Swift, Michael Tamada, and Karen Yoshino

Based on the results of its Equity Scorecard, Occidental College decided to under-
take a qualitative interview project to gain more in-depth knowledge of the inequi-
ties that exist among our students. This chapter focuses on that project's effect on
participating faculty members and administrators. First, the authors discuss the
rationale for employing an empirical approach to structuring the interview project.
Next, the authors discuss how the knowledge generated from the interviews contrib-
uted to their understanding of inequities on campus. Specifically, they address
how the information learned from students affected them in their roles as faculty,
administrators, and campus leaders. The authors also discuss how an awareness of
double consciousness has shaped new practices inside and outside the classroom.
Lastly, they discuss the effect of the interview project on students.[1]

Occidental College is a private four-year independent college that throughout much of its history has acted under the assertion that a quality academic experience occurs within a diverse community of scholars and students. In the late 1980s, this small private liberal arts college located in Los Angeles, with a student body of just over 1,500 students, made a strong commitment to creating an academic community that was both diverse and talented. On many fronts it has succeeded—most notably increasing the percentage of students of color to 37.7 percent in 2001. At the time this project began, the student body was just over 1,800; the student/faculty ratio was 12:1, students came to Occidental from forty-four states and twenty-six countries, and the ethnic composition of the student body was as displayed in Table 5.1.

Regularly ranked as one of the most diverse undergraduate liberal arts colleges in the country, Occidental prides itself on its ability to create an educational environment where diverse thoughts, ideas, cultures, and people intermingle freely. Our involvement in the Equity Scorecard Project allowed us to measure the effect of the college's diversity initiatives and to establish indicators that would enable us to examine and improve student outcomes for historically underserved students with an eye toward equity. Having achieved some measure of structural diversity, the time had come for Occidental to examine the influence of its educational programs on diverse students' educational experiences.

The results of Occidental's first Equity Scorecard in 2002 revealed that, given our diverse student body, we were not doing as well as expected in providing equitable educational outcomes for all our students. On the eleven measures we investigated to examine student success, White and Asian students were at or above equity on nine, whereas African American and Latino students were below equity on ten (Occidental College, 2002). Particularly worrisome to us were the findings that indicated that African American students had the lowest first-year retention rates and four-year graduation rates, the lowest participation in calculus—a gateway course into many majors, including the sciences—and the fewest students graduating with grade point averages above 3.5. Latino students had the lowest attainment of advanced degrees after graduation, and the lowest participation rates in study abroad.

TABLE 5.1
Ethnicity of the Student Body, Fall 2001

Ethnicity	Percentage
African American	7.4
Asian	15.1
Latino/a	14.0
Native American	1.2
White	54.6
Declined to State/Other	4.3
International	3.5
Total	**100**

Subsequent to the president reviewing the data, the complete findings were presented for discussion at a faculty retreat. Many possible ways the educational outcomes for African American and Latino students could be improved were actively discussed and debated. After the retreat, the recommendations were compiled and discussed by the Scorecard team, which consisted of four faculty members and four administrative staff members from Occidental as well as members of the Center for Urban Education (CUE) research team. Many of the recommendations were worthy of exploration, and the team reaffirmed its commitment to closing the gap between White and Asian students and African American and Latino students. However, we felt we were not ready to make formal recommendations and plans to implement change without a deeper understanding of the factors that might be contributing to the differences in educational outcomes. In short, we felt that in order to be more effective in closing the achievement gap between our students, we first must have a deeper understanding of why those gaps exist.

In collaboration with the CUE team, we decided to undertake a second more in-depth phase of the Equity Scorecard. A qualitative interview project was designed involving volunteer interviewers from the faculty and administration who conducted interviews with those students more susceptible to the negative student outcomes we observed in the Equity Scorecard. The team intentionally chose to frame the research question as, "Under what conditions do African American and Latino students succeed?" in order to signal to interviewers, students, and the Occidental community the desire to focus this inquiry on institutional structures and policies as opposed to student deficits.

This chapter focuses on the changes the faculty and administrators underwent as they listened to the students interviewed. We hope to illustrate what faculty and administrators can learn from an in-depth qualitative approach, and how that can translate into institutional change. Lastly, we speak briefly regarding the changes in the students who took part in the project.

A Practitioner-Researcher Approach

The qualitative inquiry project we participated in represented a novel approach to bringing about institutional change. Typically, practitioners develop understandings about educational problems that exist on their campuses through past experiences and daily interactions with others (Polkinghorne, 2004). Conversations and experiences with colleagues and students, for instance, influence the ways in which practitioners make sense of particular issues that affect students. The limitation to developing knowledge about an educational problem in this manner is that the information is not usually collected and evaluated in a purposeful and meaningful way. Practitioners do not typically inquire into students' experiences using structured and collaborative inquiry activities with the purpose of bringing about a richer understanding of the complexity of students' academic and social lives. Without structure, purpose, and institutional collaboration, listening to students' stories may not result in informed practices that successfully address the educational problem of interest.

The theory underpinning our inquiry project is that institutional change can occur through individual members of a community who are practitioner-researchers (Bensimon, Polkinghorne, Bauman, & Vallejo, 2004; Peña, Bensimon, & Colyar, 2006). In the practitioner-researcher approach, practitioners work together to investigate student problems in their own educational settings. They can collect information and data by conducting interviews, observations, and focus groups of students on their campus. Then practitioner-researchers hold meetings to discuss the students' experiences, make sense of them, and reflect on their implications. The stories that emerge from students individually and collectively can be a powerful way of inspiring change among practitioner-researchers as instructors and advisors. By becoming more knowledgeable about the problem they engage, practitioner-researchers come to change their own beliefs and practices, which in turn can spread through an institution. The aspirational goal of the Equity Scorecard process is to develop practitioners' funds of knowledge to increase their capacity to raise awareness about equity among others, and serve as models of equity advocates within their own departments and campus.

Logistics of the Project

Eight faculty members[2] and administrators took part as interviewers. After a brief training in interview methodology and protocol development, each interviewer was assigned between three and five students to interview. Care was taken so that no faculty members were assigned to interview students currently enrolled in their respective classes. Two administrators who left the college after the spring 2004 semester were replaced on the team with two additional faculty members.

Students were recruited to take part in the study by e-mail. College ethnicity records were used to send a message to all eighty-seven African American, Latino and Latina, or mixed-heritage first-year students, inviting them to a pizza party. A total of twenty-six students responded, for a response rate of 30% of the African American and Latino first years. For more information on the ethnic breakdown of the participants, see Table 5.2. Students were given $100 gift certificates to the bookstore upon completion of each round of two interviews. They were told this was an interview study designed to follow them through their time at Occidental to help Occidental better understand what made minority students successful.

As of spring 2005, each student had interviewed three times: once at the beginning of the spring 2004 semester, then again at the end. The third interview took place in the spring of 2005. The interviews were informal and semistructured. There was a protocol developed for each interview, and each protocol consisted of several questions around a general theme (e.g., adjustment to college, classroom environment, campus climate). Each interview lasted approximately forty minutes. Each interview was taped and transcribed. The interviewers, along with researchers from CUE, met after each round of interviews to process and bring order to the data. In addition, the meetings allowed the faculty and administrators to begin developing the next interview protocol based on information and impressions from the interviews.

The benefits of semistructured interviews are many. By allowing our interviewers and interviewees some degree of freedom to explore topics of interest in the interview, we hoped that the students would be more willing to provide insights into their lived experiences. It also allowed the interviewers as a team to gather a great deal of data quickly—talking with a cross-section of African American and Latino students as we did gave us a variety of voices and experiences to be heard.

TABLE 5.2
Participant Demographics

	African American	Latino	Total
Female	4	13	17
Male	4	5	9
Total	**8**	**18**	**26**

Data meetings, facilitated by the CUE team, were held at the end of each round of interviews. They were vital to this project for several reasons. They gave the interviewers the chance to listen to each other and begin to organize the data and their experiences into themes. They also provided an opportunity to develop further questions that could be explored in the data or in follow-up interviews. They offered a chance to interpret the findings—to provide meaning and context for the findings. Perhaps most importantly, they gave the interviewers a chance to reflect back with each other on personal and institutional practices that influence student experience. Together, the interviews and data meetings provided the structure needed for us to develop intimate knowledge about minority students' challenges and successes. What we learned as practitioner-researchers was invaluable in mobilizing changes in how we think about our students and the ways in which we approach them in our teaching and advising practices. Moreover, our commitment toward redressing inequitable outcomes by way of institutional changes was deepened.

The next sections are devoted to discussion of the knowledge generated from participation in the interviews and the changes made as a result of participation in the project. The quotes reported in the following sections were audiorecorded and transcribed by a CUE researcher who served as a participant observer during data meetings.

Knowledge Gained From Interviews

At the beginning of this project we had some fairly concrete notions of the kinds of information we were likely to get from students—revealing the importance of academic advisors—about what constituted good teaching, about the importance of finding peer and study groups, and about the role extracurricular and cocurricular activities played in their academic and social development. The importance of many of these did indeed come through in the interviews, but not necessarily in the ways in which we thought they would. In addition, we heard many students talk about themes we did not think about in advance.

The Role of Peers

We believed that the importance of peers would be a theme that would emerge from interviews, especially with respect to cocurricular life, but many interviewers also heard about the prominence of relationships with peers as a source for advice about academic issues. The following revelations were made by several team members who interviewed students:

> One knows you rely on your peers for academic advice. But I didn't realize to what extent they rely on their peers to the exclusion of their academic advisor. My students saw their academic advisor as where you go to get the signature . . . but they are not the person you ask the questions. . . . They are asking other students the questions about choosing a major, what course to take to fulfill a requirement, whether and where to study abroad, going to graduate school. It is not the reliability of advice that is important, it is the availability of advice. Having someone in the dorm to ask casually is easier and quicker and less threatening than an advisor.

> We had questions about . . . where do you get your information and advice about classes and academic issues and this was not news, but it reinforced for us . . . their answers were always their fellow students and . . . advisors were way down on the list.

Importance of "Fitting In" to the Occidental Community

One theme that the interviewers noted to be of particular significance to the students was the disparity between Occidental's mission and the way they were treated during the admissions process, as well as the reality students experienced after they enrolled:

> Two of my interviewees focused on the element of how the community here was not as multicultural as they painted it out to them prior to arriving. They arrived when they had a big multicultural admit day when you come and check out the campus. They had all these different students from various cultural backgrounds and the campus was alive. Once they got here, to them it was as though those people had disappeared.

Besides the apparent disconnect, faculty were interested to hear from students about the intraracial conflict that often arose as part of fitting in on campus:

> What I found most remarkable in the interviews I conducted had to do with identity conflict within a race group. How it is that generalized identified race groups have their own idea about what it means to belong and what it means to be considered someone who is part of the inner circle or someone who is on the margins of that group and how that creates stress for students as well.

Interviewers did note that the stress of being a minority student at Occidental was clearly an issue to be addressed by the community, but it was also important to put the issue into a larger context. For some students, feelings of unease were indeed temporary and as the interviews continued, many students reported finding a place within the Occidental community:

> The first round of interviews, you'd hear this sort of uncertainty about whether they thought they fit at Occidental College or not. Gone by the second interview. They liked being here. You hear about this in the literature and so forth, and anecdotally as well, that the students have this "adjustment period." But I really heard it in the voices of these students.

> [The student I interviewed] saw himself as entering a kind of ethnic cultural mainstream. He saw Occidental as part of the process of doing that. He felt optimistic about it. He was pleased with the fact that there were many others much like him at Occidental doing the same kind of thing.

Racial Dynamics

Interviewers were interested to learn that much of the discomfort surrounding race that was reported to us had to deal with negotiating relationships with other students:

> My students did report sometimes tension or strangeness with Latino or Black students. And students perhaps not viewing them or viewing them as being different or as not what was expected. When I asked these students where they were getting these reactions from . . . in all cases they were talking about interactions with fellow students.

When students discussed the importance of racial dynamics with faculty, having relationships with faculty of color was an important anchor for students:

> It was quite clear that dealing with faculty of color . . . there was a kind of comfort zone that was established in classes when the faculty member clearly belonged to an underrepresented minority group, or had experience as a member of such a group.

Interestingly, interviewers often reflected that as they asked students to talk about racial dynamics, one of the results for them was an increase in their perception of the diversity that exists within minority students:

One thing I have learned is that I would never generalize about someone's experience based on the three people I spoke with because they have very different experiences here.

I had a certain narrow image or stereotype of these students. . . . Two of them are Latina and neither of them fit that stereotype. They were conscious of it. My stereotype was someone born outside the U.S. or someone who was first generation. They had much wider, differing backgrounds than that.

Classroom and Learning Styles

Not surprisingly, interviews reinforced the importance of small classes and personal contact with instructors. These are aspects of our curriculum that we value, and the forcefulness with which students conveyed their importance to the faculty was noted:

I'd never seen quite so convincing an anecdotal demonstration of the, the real superiority, in the eyes of students, of small classes. . . . I know this is sort of conventional wisdom, but we tell our students that we value the small class situations, but it was interesting to see it mirrored back to me quite as forcefully as it was. . . . Their experiences in large classes were pretty much uniformly alienating. . . . It's not even as though the student hated the lectures, they just felt as if they weren't learning as effectively in them, and that they weren't a part of them in the valuable ways that they were finding in the smaller classes.

Another one was personal contact with instructors. But again it was interesting to see it as dramatically and forcefully laid out as it was by all three of [the students I interviewed].

Other interviewers brought up the importance of making use of multiple learning styles or the acceptance of difference in learning styles among students, and how reliance on one particular style in a classroom can be alienating for students:

One message that I got very strongly . . . was they'd both had experiences of feeling for themselves or on behalf of friends in their class that there was not an acceptance of difference. . . . Either difference in learning style, difference in background, different cultural differences from their professors. That really shocked me because that is not what we are supposed to be about.

As a result of this knowledge about how minority students construct their academic and social world at Occidental, we began to focus our attention on the root causes of the inequity on student outcomes. Initial discussions localized the problem outside of the sphere of the interviewers (e.g., "If only department X could hear these students talk about advising in their department, then they would have to change") and were often designed to correct what the team perceived as problems. With the facilitation of the CUE team, the discussions shifted focus rather quickly and began to move toward the interviewers' reflections on how their own beliefs and expectations about students, as well as practices at the institutional level, may serve to perpetuate the inequalities they heard described to them.

Double Consciousness and Stereotype Vulnerability

One important theme that emerged from the student interviews that resonated with the interviewers was the notion of double consciousness. Double consciousness (DuBois, 1903/1993) describes what it feels like to always see oneself through the eyes of Whites:

> It is a peculiar sensation, this double consciousness, this sense of always looking at one's self through the eyes of others, of measuring one's soul by the tape of a world that looks on in amused contempt or pity. One ever feels his twoness—an American, a Negro; two souls, two thoughts, two unreconciled strivings; two warring ideals in one dark body, whose dogged strength alone keeps it from being torn asunder. (p. 179)

During interviews, many of the students described the sensation of monitoring themselves or their behavior while at Occidental (Colyar, Peña, & Bensimon, 2004). This notion resonated strongly with the interviewers. One faculty member described the effect of hearing an interviewee talk about the stress she felt when monitoring her language choices. She was fearful of being stereotyped or viewed as less intelligent by her professors and peers:

> I found out how one student whose first language is not English has struggled to find her place and her voice in this community. I have learned how she struggles with participation in class with the added burden of thinking about how she will be perceived every time she opens her mouth. And I've heard about her development of her sense of identity and about her intellectual and personal passions. This project has been invaluable to me

as I weave the personal stories of three of our students of color, their perceptions on the institution, with my perceptions of the institution, our
policies, and our structures. It helps me gain a deeper sense of the difficult
questions about equity that must be asked and must be addressed. It helps
me think about how I bring my own experiences and, yes, prejudices to
the shaping of my teaching and the other work I do at the institution and
how this may or may not resonate with all of our students.

As this quote suggests, an awareness of the extent to which minority
students are monitoring themselves in and outside the classroom and the
effect it can have on their academic and other development has allowed
interviewers to begin to think about the relationship between individual
students and the institution, and in turn to become more reflective about
student's behaviors. Rather than simply viewing unequal outcomes for
minority students as a matter of preparation, motivation, or self-discipline,
interviewers became aware of the pressures double consciousness can place
on a student, which can negatively affect their success in college:

I'm going to have to think in terms of the tremendous variety of experiences, including ethnic experiences, these students are bringing to bear on
their academic situations. . . . To think about one student, for example,
and his relationship to his choice of major, how he studies, where he
studies . . . I'm going to have to think a lot more about the fact that he
defines himself as Hispanic.

In addition to being more reflective about students, the awareness of
double consciousness has led interviewers to consider the negative implications that help-seeking behaviors such as attending tutoring sessions or taking papers to the writing center for critique may have for minority students.
It is possible that these help-seeking behaviors might be seen as drawing
attention to their lack of ability, or as a sign of weakness, and therefore
something of which to be ashamed or to be avoided.

A relevant concept related to the idea of double consciousness is stereotype vulnerability (Steele & Aronson, 1995), which suggests that certain students are at risk of confirming, as a self-characteristic, a negative stereotype
about their own group. Briefly, this suggests that when a student is asked to
perform a challenging task, and she is aware that her ability is being assessed
in a domain in which members of her group are generally thought to perform poorly, she feels anxious about confirming or being judged by the
stereotype, and her anxiety interferes with her performance. For example,

when a student who is aware that members of his racial group are not generally seen as good at math is asked to take a math exam that he believes measures his mathematical ability, he becomes anxious that he will confirm the negative stereotype. His anxiety interferes with his ability to perform on the exam. Whereas Steele, Spencer, and Aronson (2002) do point out that stereotype vulnerability is a universal phenomenon and is not associated with any particular group, they argue that students who are stereotype vulnerable tend to disengage from work in the anxiety-provoking domain to avoid ego assaults that may cause them to feel helpless or incapable, resulting in this case in diminished academic success.

As the interviewers became familiar with the effect that phenomena such as double consciousness and stereotype threat may have on students, specifically with respect to help-seeking behaviors, they began thinking about and implementing alternative approaches to reach out to students. For example, one interviewer noted the importance this has with regard to advising:

> What I got out of it, the main thing is, I'm a much better advisor. I have some advisees who I pay so much more attention to now that I have some idea of all the things they must bring with them to school. . . . I think that's the one practical repercussion from these [interviews] that has really made me see that the advisor has a pretty powerful role. And it has made me realize I have to be—to take this advising seriously and I should take it even more seriously with students of color. . . . I shouldn't look at it as they need extra help, but I should continue to pay extra attention. . . . I do think that I try just a little bit harder. . . . Just making eye contact and making sure that my office door is open and these are my office hours and I really like to talk to you. . . . And e-mail, it works really nicely too. So I bet I send just slightly . . . one or two more e-mails to my African American students than to others, perhaps.

Changes in Perceptions and Interactions With Students

Faculty and administrators spoke often about how the interviews led to changes—both small and large—in the way they thought about and in the way they interacted with their students. Some responses dealt with the way they structured the class and how students behaved in the classroom:

> That was one thing I learned from this, I don't have to be embarrassed about how much I like my subject matter, even though not everybody does. I can just be excited about it and that rubs off a little bit.

I actually thought about it a great deal in the classroom about making eye contact, making certain that I call on quiet people. I think it's true. . . . I think I gathered it from our talking together as a group. But it is something that I knew before, but the group is reinforcing and that is I think particularly students of color might respond to a kind of personal interest, particularly when they don't expect one from say a large biology class. So I am making an effort to really make sure that everyone knows that I know who they are personally and I'm personally interested in what they have to say. I know it is making me more attuned to what an individual student might need.

In doing this project and being engaged and talking about diversity and support for all students, it reminds me sort of continually that when I'm in class that I want to try to make connections with everybody and make sure everybody feels represented in the class.

I think it gives us hints about how all of us at Occidental can alter our behavior, even if just slightly, in ways that make Occidental more welcoming to students, for example, interacting with students more in the classroom by asking more questions, active learning exercises, etc.

Others spoke about how the interviews changed their approach to advising:

The way it affected my behavior most, this procedure, was as an advisor. I e-mailed my advisees particularly hoping for them to respond. One student came to me and cried every time we met. The student ended up with a 3.96 and got an award. I had seen the student grow like this and I am not saying it was anything I did as an advisor, but I took particular care in making sure the student was in the right classes after the first round of interviews. This student was not an interview student, but is a Latino advisee. I realized after the first interview, personal involvement is a big component about how they feel about school, how they feel about themselves. I bent over backwards to keep in touch with this student and the African American student. . . . It changed the way I advised.

The more I meet with students now, just to have the interview questions that we used in the back of my mind in terms of engaging. The way that I've used it and I think is a little bit different now in terms of the type of information I'm trying to get from a student. Most of the time we are attempting to avoid conflict. The student wants to come into my office and get the information they need and move on, but maybe they need to be challenged a little bit and look at things that maybe they are purposely not trying to.

One interviewer spoke about changes in how he thinks about students with respect to himself:

> I think I have a selfish point of view in the kinds of conversations I've had over the years here and most recently with this group, with the students who I am talking to who remind me of how important their lives are and in a way how important my life is as well.

Moving Toward Institutional Change

In addition to changing the way the interviewers interacted with students, they also spoke about ways in which the interviews served an instrumental purpose in the way they construed their roles at the college:

> It's been a self-reflective process for me, too. Who am I in relation to the students, and what is my purpose and role in light of their educational journey?

> [S]everal observations are that we have a lot of students of color hoping to major in the field . . . and we lose them. . . . We are restructuring the major but I don't think that's the whole answer. I think part of the answer is the large introductory courses. I think one strong predictor of success is math comfort within the field. So to what extent do I need to pay attention to all of my advisees to see what their math comfort is if they are interested in a career in the field?

One aspect of promoting institutional change has been the use of knowledge gained from the interview project across campus. Many interviewers spoke of bringing up data from the interview project in other committees and settings, and about how they thought about how to disseminate the information from student interviews to relevant committees and discussions that could serve to inform decision making at the institution:

> We can start to talk about what we're hearing from students with others and [the] possibilities that may contribute to retention issues, high GPA, low GPA. We are starting to develop a sort of framework around the meaning that is coming out of this data. The interview project gives me concrete

information to be able to urge others that this is the basis on which I'm saying this and they can take action on the basis of this.

One interviewer summed up attempts to engage others not currently involved in the interview project in the type of double-loop learning (see chapter 1 of this book) that has occurred among the interviewers this way:

The way I take all of this stuff is it's good information to help us ask good questions, to help us analyze a little bit deeper and think about what we do. The challenge I face in my department . . . is sometimes people feel like data is there to blame or data is there to point out deficiencies or something like that. I don't think that's the idea of this. So, what I try to do particularly with my department is get them focused on what else do we want to find out because this has been raised and how can it help us ask questions internally about what we do and how we do it better as opposed to saying the methodology is flawed or it didn't ask the right people the right questions.

Another interviewer spoke about the notion of institutional change happening first on an individual level:

I am interested in this idea of changing one professor at a time. It (the project) changed the way I think about my classroom and it's changed the way I think about my own education. And I think having these kinds of conversations can have a powerful effect on these relationships. . . . I guess one thing that interested me was that there was a moment for me where there was a kind of safety in the conversation that I was having with the students I was talking to. I am specifically talking about a student coming to me outside of our sessions. The student said, "Actually you need to make some changes in the curriculum here." The student wanted to talk beyond . . . personal experiences and . . . wanted to talk about the way Occidental sets itself up.

In general, faculty and administrators involved in this project were already knowledgeable and sympathetic to issues of diversity on campus. One of the biggest effects the project had was to keep issues of diversity in the forefront of their thoughts and reflect the desire for other faculty and administrators to be able to have this kind of sustained and personal interaction with students in order to gain a deeper perspective on the role diversity plays in a college like Occidental.

It [this project] also gave me a year-and-a-half long contact with diversity issues that served to keep my attention on this part of being an Occidental faculty member.

Impact on Students

Although the goal of this chapter has been to document the changes faculty and administrators underwent as a result of the interview project, it is nevertheless important to mention briefly the effect participation in this project had on the students who were interviewed. Of the twenty-six students who began the project twenty-two still remained involved two years later.[3] The students were asked to reflect on their participation in the project in a large group setting, where they could interact with one another and all eight of the interviewers. Their responses were overwhelmingly positive and centered around three major themes: feelings of importance and comfort, the value of a nonacademic relationship with a faculty member, and a desire to see the interviews used as a source of change on campus.

Feelings of Importance and Comfort

Students discussed the importance they felt at being included in the project. In most cases, they talked about the fact that their experiences were heard by faculty members and expressed hope that they would make a difference in the lives of other faculty and students:

> She said she would keep asking me questions so she can hear my story. And someone else is going to hear it, and it is going to get written up into results, so we are going to be represented in some way and I guess that made me feel kinda good. That at least I am going to make some kind of difference.

> What you were saying about personal experience to political action—what's really good about the Equity Scorecard Interview Project is that I get to share my personal story and other people get to share their personal story. So when all the students get together and people say "All these students are just complaining" it's like "No, you have a record of me saying this and this and this happened," and so I think that's really important. It's like there is evidence that we are not just complaining about our professors.

These quotes speak not only to the importance the students felt about telling their stories, but also of the validating aspect being heard by a member of the faculty or administration has had on them. By taking part in these interviews, the students clearly felt that they were being taken seriously, and that their unique experiences and voices were heard and validated.

Many students addressed the topic of comfort with their interviewers, and how they were able to raise issues with them that they would not be at ease talking about with other students, or faculty:

> There were lots of things that I found I was very angry and frustrated about that I couldn't articulate with other students. But for some reason there was a safe place created by the interviews that allowed me to voice these frustrations. And I thought that was very valuable.

> I definitely think that we felt safe and you weren't going to judge us on anything. And that definitely helped us bring up issues for me personally that I didn't feel comfortable talking about.

Interview projects like this one present opportunities for connection and unity, and this was one of the outcomes we were hoping for in the project. We wanted the students to feel comfortable talking with their interviewers and to be able to express their thoughts not only about Occidental and diversity, but about their own personal and academic development. We hoped that over time, the students would come to view the interviewers as an additional resource to help them navigate Occidental and beyond, and as the next section suggests, this was in fact one of the greatest outcomes of the project for students.

Relationships With Faculty

It is clear from the students that over the course of this project, they were able to move beyond the power differential that characterizes the relationships between most students and faculty-administrators during the interviews. Some students talked about making a connection with a faculty member they might not have come in contact with during the course of their education and being able to speak with that person in ways that they would not ordinarily speak with a professor:

> For me, it was that she was unassuming when I first met her. For us to just sit down and talk about issues that are, maybe you don't talk about with professors. It's not usually something you do with a professor, especially a science professor. And for me, it was like you can be free with a person who wasn't going to judge me, wasn't assuming I was a certain way because

of how I looked. She was just talking to me as a person and about issues that she thought were important to me.

[B]eing able to be an individual along with my racial identity [was] something that I valued when I talked to my interviewer.

Several students also expressed a hesitancy to engage in conversations with faculty, so being approached to be in this project by a faculty member was important to them:

I always had, still have, a difficult time approaching Profs [*sic*]. I always wished that . . . I was happy that a faculty approached me. And that I was able to build a connection with him and it was also like therapy.

Other students reflected on the importance of their interviewers following up with them on important aspects of their lives they may have mentioned in previous interviews and of interviewers allowing them to express themselves freely and in ways that were important to them:

I enjoyed sharing my story and also building a relationship with my interviewer. She is the one who advised me about the . . . program. I appreciate her not just being an interviewer but actually following up with me on different things that I told her about in the interview. So that was important. I'm not in science so I wouldn't have had a reason to have a relationship with her. That was really important . . . and they would be able to recognize that I do carry a lot of baggage with me because of my race. Because of my experience as an African American, period. I think that recognizing that is really important.

It was good to sit down with a faculty member and express ourselves and have someone listen to us. I didn't have that my freshman year—not until we had interviews. It was like therapy.

Using Interviews for Change

It became clear that, much like the faculty and administrators involved, the students reflected on their interviews and learned about themselves, and in some cases made changes in their behavior as a result:

I came to realize many things. I got to know more about myself as a student. . . . I learned a lot and felt important too, which I never feel. So it was like "Yay!" I was able to express my voice.

And in replying to this thing, I thought OK, well people are going to think "OK. She is White" you know, I'm Cuban, so I had all of that to deal with. So I was really questioning whether I should do it or not. I really think it helps a lot. I mean it helped how I view things. It helped me to clarify things and helped me to figure things out about diversity.

Before this semester, I never even thought to voice to a professor that I'm not at the starting point, that I don't have the same [academic] foundation. The only thing I have ever voiced is "I'm having trouble. I need help right now." But I guess I never, before this semester, really looked to the root of the problem, to where the problems are actually coming from.

Lastly, the students expressed the importance of using the data and information gained from the interviews to bring about change both in individuals and on campus:

I just hope that my own interview and everybody else's here makes a difference. Even if it only touched one person. Even if it touched my interviewer and all of you, then that's good enough for me.

Thank you so much for starting this up. It's just amazing to be a part of it, part of something that will hopefully branch off into bigger change here at the school.

The research from this data, once it's presented, unless people flat out ignore it, something has to be done with it. Whether there are programs instituted or, at the very least, it allows professors . . . like you said, to have your eyes opened. That's something right there. That's the first step of making changes.

It is apparent that these students, like the faculty and administrators involved, are committed not only to examining their own lives, but to leaving Occidental a better place for minority students and using their experience to foster change.

Conclusion

Occidental College is a leader in higher education in terms of access for minority students and for valuing diversity; interviewing minority students about their experiences provided important information for the practitioner-researchers involved as well as the larger campus community. The project is seen by the practitioner-researchers and by the administration as an exceptional and promising method with which to address inequities among our students, but additionally as a professional development experience that changes faculty practices, policies, and structures at the institution. These changes transpired as we dug deeper into our research findings and held productive and sometimes difficult conversations about the implications of students' experiences at Occidental College. What we learned from students inspired us to think about supporting students in ways we had never thought of before. Our enthusiasm for the project became contagious, spreading across the institution as Occidental College leadership took notice of the deep and meaningful changes experienced by our team. This is why the practitioner-research approach is so powerful.

The recommendations for the project included continuing involvement with interviewees through their time at Occidental. As these students continue their education at Occidental and beyond, we hope to learn more about their academic and social development.

Because one advantage that was mentioned by each and every interviewer was the positive nature of establishing a nonacademic relationship with several minority students, another step that the team has taken is to involve more faculty so that they too can get to know the students the way the interviewers have gotten to know their students. Currently, two similar interview projects are under way at the departmental level as a way for faculty to gain a better understanding of student life and perceptions of Occidental.

The value in interviewing students in a project such as this can be summarized as providing the opportunity to (a) gain knowledge that serves to inform individual practices, (b) allow interviewers to be critically reflective about their roles as faculty and administrators, and (c) challenge interviewers to reexamine their beliefs about how to engage minority students.

We believe that the reduction of inequalities in the educational outcomes seen at Occidental depends on faculty members who are committed to collectively examining the issue in depth and reflecting on the extent to which they and the institution play a role in promoting learning and change. In addition, the institution bears responsibility for its leadership, culture, and practices. The Equity Scorecard Interview Project has shown that individuals, who in their roles as professors, administrators, advisors, and leaders, are willing to examine their beliefs, actions, and motivations toward becoming agents of change on campus.

Notes

1. Laura Palucki Blake is listed as primary author for writing this chapter. Edlyn Vallejo Peña is listed as second author for data collection on faculty experiences and written contributions. Each of the subsequent authors contributed equally to the interview project, and thus are listed in alphabetical order.

2. Occidental had a full-time faculty of 135 in 2003 and four of the interviewers had combined faculty-administrative roles.

3. The four students who were no longer participating were no longer enrolled at Occidental.

References

Bensimon, E. M., Polkinghorne, D. E., Bauman, G. L., & Vallejo, E. (2004). Research that makes a difference. *The Journal of Higher Education, 75*(1), 10–126.

Colyar, J., Peña, E. V., & Bensimon, E. M. (2004). *Interviewing African American and Latino/a students to understand the creation of unequal educational outcomes.* Unpublished manuscript, University of Southern California, Los Angeles, CA.

DuBois, W. E. B. (1903/1993). Double-consciousness and the veil. In Charles Lemert (Ed.), *Social theory: The multicultural and classic readings* (pp. 177–182). Boulder, CO: Westview Press.

Occidental College. (2002). *The Occidental College diversity scorecard: A report to president Theodore R. Mitchell.* Los Angeles CA: Author.

Peña, E. V., Bensimon, E. M., & Colyar, J. (2006). Contextual problem defining: Learning to think and act. *Liberal Education, 92*(2), 48–55.

Polkinghorne, D. E. (2004). *Practice and the human sciences: The case for a judgment-based practice of care.* Albany: State University of New York Press.

Steele, C. M., & Aronson, J. (1995). Stereotype threat and the intellectual performance of African Americans. *The Journal of Personality and Social Psychology, 69* (5), 797–811.

Steele, C. M., Spencer, S. J., & Aronson, J. (2002). Contending with group image: The psychology of stereotype and social identity threat. In M. P. Zanna (Ed.), *Advances in experimental social psychology* (Vol. 34, pp. 379–440). San Diego, CA: Academic Press.

6

THE MATH PROJECT AT LOS ANGELES CITY COLLEGE

Leticia Tomas Bustillos and Robert Rueda with Don Hentschel, Daryl Kinney, Janice Love, Iris Magee, Naeemah Payne, Hector Plotquin, and Roger Wolf

Faculty members from Los Angeles City College's (LACC's) mathematics department embarked on a fifteen-month action research project after completing the Diversity Scorecard Project. Team members involved in the "Math Project" sought to understand why African American and Latino students enrolled in remedial mathematics courses were performing at lower levels than their White and Asian peers. To do so they studied routinely collected institutional data, administered the Learning and Study Strategies Inventory survey to students enrolled in remedial math courses, and conducted individual interviews with students. The results of their efforts led them to have a greater awareness of their students, from their perceptions of mathematics to the resources they need to succeed at LACC. This chapter details the efforts of this group, offers their recommendations to help improve the educational outcomes of their students, and articulates their individual reflections in regard to their involvement with the Math Project.

L arge-scale demographic changes and social movements within the last forty years have radically changed the postsecondary institutional environment, particularly that of the community college. This country's emphasis on access to greater postsecondary educational opportunities has paved the way for more racialized students with diverse racial and ethnic backgrounds to enroll in large numbers in institutions of higher education.

As a result, the face of higher education has changed and now sports a more diverse hue. LACC is no exception to the changes and it is an institution characterized by its diversity. Students who enroll at LACC are a reflection of the large, urban metropolis in which the college is located: 11 percent of students are African American, 20 percent are Asian,[1] 38 percent are Latino, 24 percent are White, and 7 percent include Native Americans and students of unknown ethnic designations. Figure 6.1 shows the enrollment percentages for LACC disaggregated by race and ethnicity for the 2004 fall term.

The mission of LACC is to foster an environment that develops within all students the knowledge, skills, and attitudes necessary to lead successful personal and professional lives. Data examined in 2000, however, suggested African American and Latino students were not meeting the goals of LACC's mission. This was particularly evident in mathematics as African American and Latino students were not attaining a level of success commensurate with that of their Asian and White peers in critical pathway mathematics courses. Institutional policies and structures at the time were not in place to enable

FIGURE 6.1
Enrollment by race and ethnicity at LACC, fall 2004.

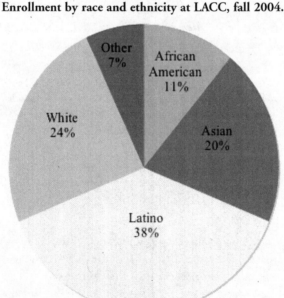

Source: Los Angeles City College, 2004.

decision makers to undertake a systemic investigation into the persistent disparities between ethnic and racial groups in these courses. To explore the unknown factors that yielded these inequities, LACC became involved with the Diversity Scorecard Project in December 2000.

The purpose of this chapter is to describe the activities and findings of the "Math Project," an endeavor that evolved from LACC's participation in the Diversity Scorecard Project. This chapter begins by briefly describing LACC's partnership with the Center for Urban Education (CUE) and the findings that led to the formation of the Math Project. The activities of the Math Project are subsequently summarized, detailing the results from the team members' administration and analysis of the *Learning and Study Strategies Inventory* (LASSI) assessment in addition to the findings from individual student interviews conducted by math faculty members. This chapter concludes with the team members' recommendations for future action and their reflections in regard to their involvement in the Math Project.

Partnership Between CUE and LACC

LACC was invited to become one of the partner institutions in December 2000. Then-president Mary Spangler accepted CUE's invitation and appointed three individuals who would compose the Diversity Scorecard Project Evidence Team: Dr. Daniel Seymour (executive dean, Institutional Planning and Analysis), Tammy Robinson (instructor, English/ESL) and Rebecca Tillberg (dean, Planning and Research). In summer 2001, Janice Love (research analyst) joined the team while Tammy Robinson left the team due to time constraints.

The examination of routinely collected institutional data by this group of individuals revealed that retention and success rates in mathematics courses required further study. What they in fact found were considerable gaps in achievement by African American and Latino students enrolled in mathematics courses between 1997 and 2001. Two statistics stood out:

1. The high enrollments of African American and Latino students in remedial mathematics courses, accompanied by below-average passing rates
2. Students' low passing rates in college algebra (a course required to graduate from LACC and a prerequisite for courses that are transferable to a four-year college or university)

With an approximate enrollment of 6,000 students per semester, "[T]he size of the department meant that mathematics has a significant impact on the overall course success rates for the college" (Love, Bauman, & Bensimon, 2004, p. 7).

The Math Project

Mathematics is one of the most important subject areas for all students irrespective of long-term educational goals. Mathematics is a requisite component for transfer, degree, and certificate attainment, and completion of basic skills prerequisites. Most importantly, mathematics becomes the critical pathway to specific majors and future employment opportunities. The goals of the Math Project were (a) to examine inequities in African American and Latino and Latina students' educational outcomes through the collection of qualitative data to supplement the quantitative data made available from the Scorecard findings, and (b) to develop a plan for intervention to help improve the outcomes of racialized students enrolled in remedial mathematics courses.

The Math Project involved eight faculty members and administrators from LACC and two researchers from the CUE. They met monthly from May 2004 through December 2005, typically after the monthly math department meeting. During this time, team members engaged in the following activities:

- Discussed and analyzed institutional data specific to educational outcomes within the mathematics department, disaggregated by race and ethnicity
- Administered the LASSI (Weinstein, Palmer, & Schulte, 2002), an instrument that allows students to self-report their learning strategies and study habits, to more than one hundred students enrolled in four remedial mathematics courses and two calculus courses
- Analyzed and discussed the results of the LASSI
- Developed an interview protocol based on the LASSI results and other issues raised during the monthly meetings
- Conducted individual interviews (one to two students per team member) with eleven students who took the LASSI
- Read and analyzed the student interview transcripts

- Wrote and presented a report to LACC's president in which the team detailed its findings and offered its recommendations for future action

The following sections discuss the results of the LASSI administration and the findings gathered from the team members' interviews with students enrolled in both remedial and advanced mathematics courses.

LASSI Administration

Initial discussion between project team members revealed uncertainty about the primary factors affecting learning in remedial courses. Many team members raised numerous questions regarding the students' aptitude and desire to achieve in mathematics, focusing on such issues as study skills, motivation, and self-efficacy. Unfortunately, the evidence collected had no bearing on the questions raised by the team. The only "evidence" available was anecdotal in nature, hardly a basis for shaping future action. Moreover, there were no data on factors other than those related to presumed student deficits. Recognizing the importance of data, but understanding the weaknesses of the data available from traditional database sources, the group agreed to administer the LASSI to all students enrolled in four remedial math courses and to students enrolled in two advanced calculus courses. The LASSI administration took place in late February 2005.

The LASSI is an inventory created to help students develop a better awareness of how they learn so that they can become more successful in college. There is good evidence that these factors are not only critical for school success but that they can be learned. The inventory identifies students' strengths and weaknesses in ten different areas as a means to help students become more strategic and successful students: anxiety, attitude, concentration, information processing, motivation, self-testing, selecting main ideas, use of support techniques and materials, time management, test strategies and preparation for tests. The LASSI focuses on both the covert and the overt to guide practitioners in developing educational interventions that will yield greater success for students in postsecondary educational environments. Utilizing a ten-scale, eighty-item assessment, the LASSI provides standardized scores and national norms that allow students to compare their strengths and weaknesses relative to those of their peers.

Over two hundred[2] students enrolled in courses taught by the Math Project team members took the LASSI assessment. Additionally, students were given a two-page survey that provided project team members with a demographic profile of the participating individuals. Of the students who participated, over two thirds of the students surveyed were of Latino or Hispanic descent. Forty-five percent of students reported their primary language to be English, and nearly 30 percent reported Spanish to be their primary language. Most students surveyed were enrolled in Math 115, the second course in the remedial math sequence. Students were concentrated within three age groups—younger than twenty, twenty to twenty-five, and twenty-five to thirty-five—with the largest percentage found in the latter group.

In addition to demographic data, students were asked questions that provided team members with a more in-depth profile, such as language proficiency, place of birth, number of hours studied, and highest level of math achieved. Students were evenly distributed between those born in the United States (46 percent) and those born abroad (50 percent). The majority of students reported having a high level of proficiency in English speaking (60 percent) and reading (61 percent). Students were evenly split between those with a high level of proficiency in English writing (45 percent) and a medium level of proficiency (42 percent). Over half the students surveyed reported having to work (57 percent) outside of class, 34 percent of whom worked in excess of twenty hours per week. Twenty-three percent of students reported having children, with 19 percent serving as their children's primary caregiver. The data that were perhaps most surprising to the team members concerned students' highest level of math taken, grades received, and the number of hours students typically studied outside of class. Tables 6.1 and 6.2 provide more detailed information.

The data illustrate the fact that many of the students enrolled at LACC had a fair amount of success in their high school mathematics courses. Nearly 19 percent of students surveyed completed Algebra II and 15 percent completed Calculus. Most students reported having received between a B and a C in their math courses. What was striking, however, was that many of these students were enrolled in remedial math courses irrespective of the relative success they had prior to their enrollment at LACC.

Figure 6.2 shows the number of hours students spent studying for their math courses. As can be seen, over 60 percent of students reported studying less than four hours a week for their math classes, a number that the math faculty believe to be insufficient to be successful in college math courses. Faculty members involved in the project recommend that students study at least two hours for every unit per course. Based on the self-reported data by

TABLE 6.1
Highest Level of Math Achieved in HS

	#	%
Arithmetic	4	2.8
Pre-Algebra	20	13.8
Algebra I	14	9.7
Geometry	12	8.3
Algebra II	27	18.6
Trigonometry	9	6.2
Pre-Calculus	14	9.7
Calculus	22	15.2
Missing	23	15.9
Total	**145**	**100.0**

the students surveyed, only 25 percent of students were meeting the time required *outside* of class to review critical mathematical concepts that team members believe equate success in class.

Equally significant to the amount of time students spend studying are the data showing that a very small percentage of students seek tutoring for help with their math courses. Only 26 percent of students surveyed reported utilizing the services of an outside tutor. This was particularly disturbing, given the numerous resources available to students at LACC. The Pi Shop is a math and computer tutoring center that is available to students enrolled

TABLE 6.2
Average Grade Received in High School

	#	%
A	16	11.0
B	42	29.0
C	45	31.0
D	16	11.0
F	1	0.7
H	1	0.7
N	1	0.7
Missing	23	15.9
Total	**145**	**100.0**

FIGURE 6.2
Hours studied per student enrolled in math courses at LACC.

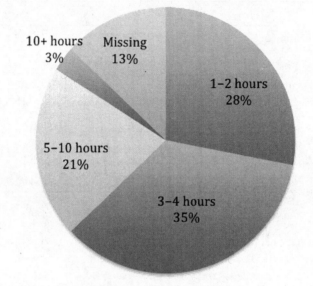

Source: LASSI Survey Data, 2005.

in remedial mathematics courses. According to the survey, however, only 6 percent of students reported using the Pi Shop. A small percentage of students (6 percent) indicated they worked with private tutors, and a slightly larger percentage of students (30 percent) reported working with some form of online tutoring. A few students, 12 percent, stated they were part of a mathematics study group.

Results from the LASSI provided equally important information previously unknown to the Math Project team members. As previously noted, the LASSI provides a diagnostic assessment of students' strengths and weaknesses in ten areas of proficiency. Scoring above the seventy-fifth percentile indicates an area of relative strength. Scores between the fiftieth and seventy-fifth percentiles suggest room for improvement. Scores below the fiftieth percentile identify areas of weakness requiring priority attention for both the student and the instructor.

To better understand the individual needs of students, the LASSI sub-scale scores were graphed to provide each of the team members with a visual representation of the students' strengths and weaknesses. In addition, each of the subscales was disaggregated according to race and ethnicity to see how each group fared individually and in comparison to others. To begin, Figure 6.3 presents a comparative graph that illustrates the differences between students enrolled in remedial math courses and students enrolled in advanced math courses.

As can be seen in Figure 6.3, students predominantly enrolled in the advanced math courses had scale scores between the fiftieth and seventieth percentiles. Students in these courses, for the most part, demonstrated relative strengths in each of the subscales with a few areas in need of improvement. Students enrolled in remedial math courses mostly scored below the fiftieth percentile in seven of the ten subscales. Notable exceptions were in the areas of concentration, information processing, and self-testing. Similar to their math counterparts, these students scored below the thirtieth percentile with respect to attitude, suggesting a lack of clarity regarding educational goals and the value of school. The apparent weakness in attitude by students in both course sequences gave rise to numerous questions from the team, particularly regarding how students understood the role of school broadly, and mathematics specifically. Given the low scores in regard to attitude, the

FIGURE 6.3
LASSI subscale scores for remedial math courses versus advanced math courses.

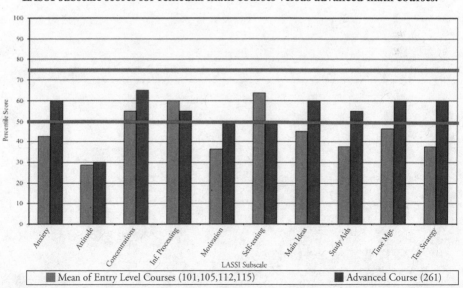

graph in Figure 6.4 depicts the attitude subscale disaggregated by race and ethnicity.

According to the authors of the LASSI, students' attitudes toward school and their general motivation for success greatly influence the degree of diligence they apply to their study habits, both when in class and while studying alone. The authors contend if students' life goals and school goals are not clear, they find it difficult to maintain "a mind-set that promotes good work habits, concentration, and attention to school and its related tasks" (Weinstein & Palmer, 2002, p. 9). Students' general attitudes and motivation for success in school and performing tasks that will yield success are critical for academic success. The graphic representation of the attitude subscale in Figure 6.4 demonstrates an overall low average score among all groups. Pacific Islanders appear to have a higher self-reported score on attitude (fortieth percentile), with Asian and African American students not too far behind. Lowest of all students are White and Latino students, with a percentile score of twenty.

Project team members devoted several meetings to reviewing and digesting the results of both the subscale and the overall results of the LASSI administration. There was some concern with respect to the accuracy of

FIGURE 6.4
LASSI Attitude subscale by race and ethnicity.

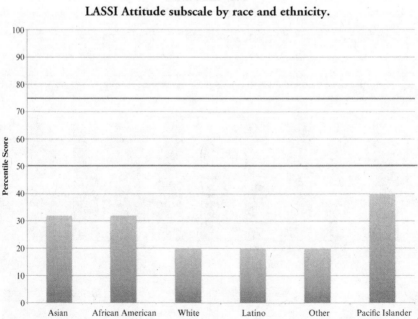

"self-reported" data, given the tendency of individuals to report higher scores. The consensus among team members, therefore, was that more information was needed from students to get to the crux of the issue of math achievement, specifically what prompts success among certain individuals and what does not. To gain a deeper understanding into students' experiences both inside and outside the classroom, team members decided to interview students to obtain their individual perspectives as to what they believed they needed to become successful learners of math.

Student Interviews

Team members interviewed a total of eleven students for this project. Students were selected from across the spectrum of math courses—from those enrolled in remedial courses to those enrolled in advanced calculus—to furnish a comparative sampling of experiences. This provided team members with a unique view into the lives of students, as illustrated by the following two case studies.

Student 1: Ana

Ana is a young Latina in her early twenties. At the time of her interview, she was near completion of her first year at LACC. She attends school part-time because she is the mother of two young boys and works full-time as a waitress during the graveyard shift at a local restaurant.

During her interview, Ana shared some of her experiences as a high school student and the degree to which she felt that her education prepared her for a postsecondary career. Ana shared she was a "straight-A" student while attending junior high. She loved to go to school and enjoyed learning. Unfortunately, while attending high school, she encountered difficult circumstances with her classmates that led her to develop a sense of detachment from school. She said,

> I got discriminated, I got hit and everything and I didn't want to get
> involved in nothing so, like, I started losing interest in school. As a result,
> I started getting bad grades because I didn't even want to [go to school]. I
> started making up excuses, like "Oh, my head hurts."

Ana attended a high school in which she was a minority within the student population. This, she felt, contributed to the discrimination and violence she experienced.

Ana's father, recognizing the difficult circumstances affecting his daughter, opted to move her and her older brother to another high school with the hope that they would receive a better education in a safe environment that was more conducive to learning. Unfortunately, this initial move led to three other moves—all before Ana was seventeen. At her second high school, Ana felt that the sheer size of the high school prevented her from receiving the proper counseling that would help her rediscover her love for learning. So, as she recounted, "I just totally lost interest when I went through all this phase." At the age of seventeen, Ana became pregnant with her first child and opted to drop out of school. Although she did complete her GED, it would be six years before she would return to school.

Ana took her first courses at LACC in fall 2004. At the time she started, she had an interest in law enforcement so she opted to take courses in administration of justice. Perhaps as a result of her negative experiences while growing up, she likewise chose to take courses in Chinese, a way for her to learn about and appreciate new cultures. She remarked,

> I'm the kind of person that tries to see the positive side to negative things. And through experience I've gained a lot of, well, experience through all these things, like, for example, I like to learn about different cultures.

For her, LACC provided numerous opportunities to "expand [her] mind" and reconnect with school. She recognizes that her absence of six years from school makes her work extra hard, as does balancing school with her responsibilities at home. As noted before, she is responsible for the care of her two young children. With the help of her mother, she was able to attend school and carve out some time to do her homework. To accommodate her school schedule, she worked the graveyard shift at a local restaurant. She said, "The hardest part for me is just finding time. Time to sit down and go through [my school stuff] without being bothered."

Because she dropped out of school at an early age, her exposure to mathematics was limited; she did not go beyond algebra. Therefore, upon taking the placement test at LACC, she was assigned to Math 112, the second course in the basic skills sequence. By all accounts, she takes her studies seriously, often using what little time she has between her children's naps or between classes to do homework and study for class. She takes advantage of both the Pi Shop and the learning skills center. In the Pi Shop, she is able to use the computer to do her work because, as she explained,

> It [provides you with] enough time for you to work out your homework, for you to go to tutorials, and that's, I think, that makes it easy because going through the tutorials is like having a second instructor at home.

At the learning skills center she was introduced to the use of a calculator. This was new to her because, as she admits, "I am not a calculator person."

In fall 2004, Ana received a B in her Math 112 course. Unfortunately, at the completion of her second semester at LACC, she was enrolled in Math 115 and received a D for a final grade and thus finished the term with a 2.6 GPA. Overall, Ana comments that she is pleased with her experience at LACC and believes her instructors have been helpful as she once again adapts to being a student. If she has any complaints, they are reserved for the course schedule. Often, her available hours prevent her from taking the courses she needs at a time when she is most able to attend. Nonetheless, she is pleased to be back in school and relishes the opportunities that attaining a degree will provide her. Ana, a self-described "go-getter," does not feel that anything can stop her even when times get tough. As she said,

> There's been situations when I feel like I think I need to work more than school because of the issues. [Other times], like [I feel] the need to spend time with my kids, you know? I feel like I don't really spend time with them. But then again, it'll pay off in the long run.

Throughout her interview, Ana demonstrated that she is a self-disciplined, motivated individual returning to school with the hope of improving her life circumstances and those of her children.

Student 2: Alex

Alex is perhaps the direct opposite of the first case study in the sense that he resembles the more "traditional" college student. Alex is a twenty-two-year-old White male who is originally from Victorville, California. At the time of his interview, Alex was taking a course load that included English, math, and computers for a total of twenty units. He was enrolled at LACC as a full-time student and received monetary support from his family. Thus, he did not have to work to maintain his apartment or to purchase his school materials, likely making him atypical from other students attending LACC.

Based on his school grades, Alex is doing very well. He has a 3.5 GPA and in his two math classes he has received As. This is perhaps not surprising given that he reports he was a good student in high school with a 4.0 GPA. He believes his high school prepared him well for his postsecondary career, particularly in mathematics. He reported that he went through the entire math sequence, completing Calculus 1 and 2 by the time he graduated.

What is very interesting, or perhaps perplexing, is that despite his high marks in high school, Alex started not by taking college-level mathematics, but by taking Math 105, the first course in the remedial math sequence. He took Math 105 in fall 2004, Math 112 in the winter (three-week course), and at the time of his interview was taking Math 115. In his interview, he mentioned his plan to take Math 125 in the summer. According to Alex, math isn't difficult, but rather it is learning how to "play the game" that facilitates success. He said, "[In math], the name of the game is practice. Time is practice. Math is not hard, it's just logic. It is logic. I mean, you know, if there is a problem, there is a solution." He devotes a significant amount of his time to studying and practicing. He spends a good portion of his days ("24 hours!") at the Pi Shop, where he is able to ask questions on problems he doesn't understand and receives immediate assistance from the tutors.

On the whole, Alex is complimentary of LACC and, like Ana, believes that LACC is a good school and is providing him with a wealth of opportunities. He is a biology major and hopes to transfer to one of the schools in the University of California system. One of the concerns Alex expressed was focused on the delivery of instruction by some of his instructors. He commented that his most difficult math class was conducted by a professor whose teaching style made him feel as if he was not learning and simply "wasting his time." When asked to articulate what would make a good math class, Alex responded by talking about his Math 115 professor and describing his teaching style. He said,

> The way he's explaining [makes] you understand everything. He is very simple to understand. You know with [examples] or with stories or whatever. But with others, there are professors that don't care—they just put the problem on the board and that's it.

For Alex, a professor who provides numerous examples and tries to apply the concept to other situations constitutes what he feels are the hallmarks of a good professor. Those who merely lecture and spend little time on explanation are the ones he is unable to learn from. As a result, he feels that this is why students typically don't enjoy math and shy away from taking math courses. He said,

That's why people [don't] like math and people think that it's a really hard subject, but not really. It's just practice, you can do it, you know, there's a problem, there's a solutions. And definitely, you have to love your teacher. If you love your teacher, then you are going to do the subject.

Without the benefit of a good professor who can explain the concepts in numerous ways and connect with students, Alex believes that learning math will present significant challenges for students.

Common Themes

In conducting student interviews, the team got an in-depth look into the lives of the students who participated. What the group found throughout the interviews was that no two students were alike, and all came to LACC with varying experiences. The interviews showed the team the extent to which their personal lives outside of the school environment either facilitates or hinders their success as college students and learners of mathematics. Throughout the interviews, some important themes resonated with the team, leading to intense discussions into what the department and the individual faculty members can do to facilitate learning and improve the success rates of these students and others like them in their classrooms.

Some of the more salient themes that cut across all of the interviews are as follows:

- Access to good professors is paramount. Good professors are described by the students as those who do not spend an inordinate amount of time lecturing, but rather take extraordinary steps to explain concepts and apply them to situations that make them more comprehensible. Thus, the need to study "good" professors.
- Many of the students commented on the benefits of using the Pi Shop and other tutoring services provided by the department, including the learning skills center. Yet at the same time, not all students were familiar with the outreach services available to them. As such, only a handful of students were fully able to take advantage of the resources made available to LACC students.
- A running theme throughout the interviews was the issue of time. Many of the students interviewed had outside obligations, whether they were familial responsibilities or work requirements. All of these external responsibilities and scheduling issues often diminished the amount of time they could devote to their studies outside of the

classroom. Additionally, these time restrictions further prevented students from taking courses that were offered only during certain periods of the day.

- Many of the basic skills math courses are conducted via computer. In some interviews, students commented that learning via computer was helpful and facilitated the completion of their work because they could log on at any time of the day. Students conversely commented that the use of computers also posed a challenge if they did not have access to computers at home or did not have up-to-date computers that would allow them to use the most recent software tutorials that often accompany textbooks. It is clear that not all students have adequate access to the Internet and, because of time restrictions, do not or cannot take advantage of the resources available on campus.

Based on the team's analysis of the findings presented in this chapter, the following recommendations were offered for consideration and future action.

Recommendations

The team members' recommendations presented here aim to build upon existing academic resources and activities of math faculty members. The first recommendation pertains to the existing tutoring center, and the second proposes a workshop for students enrolled in the developmental math course sequence.

The Pi Shop

The Pi Shop is LACC's mathematics and computer science tutoring center. Opened in fall 1998, the Pi Shop helps students to succeed in math by providing them with the assistance and requisite skill development that makes learning math easier and more enjoyable. The goals of the Pi Shop are as follows: (a) increase retention, success, and enrollment rates; (b) help students improve performance and grades in the math classes they are taking; (c) help students understand the concepts needed to solve their math homework and in-class assignments; (d) provide different ways for learning math concepts in order to increase the degree of student understanding; (e) provide a friendly and helpful environment that is conducive to student learning; (f) help students overcome their math anxiety; and (g) provide students with the math skills and competency for the technical workplace. To date, the Pi Shop has expanded services to include 15 tutors (from 6 in 1998) who assist well over 700 students (from 100 in 1998).

The success of the Pi Shop is well documented and is evidenced by the data. Data compiled by team member Robert Madirosian shows that 85 percent of the students who use the Pi Shop pass their courses compared with 76 percent of students who do not use the Pi Shop. As a result of its success with LACC students, the Pi Shop has been recognized by the State Academic Senate as an "Honorable Mention" in its *Exemplary Program Award* competition. Given the success of this unique tutoring program, team members recommended expanding the program so that it can reach an even greater number of students enrolled in the remedial math courses.

Mathematics Developmental Workshop

The second recommendation consists of a pilot workshop, which will be geared toward students enrolled in the remedial mathematics courses (Math 105, Math 112, and Math 115). Students enrolled in these courses will be required to register for the workshop and meet twice a week throughout the semester. The purpose is not to focus on specific course assignments, but rather on more general mathematical problem solving and reasoning in small-group settings.

The workshops will be led by math faculty members who are also teaching in the remedial math courses. Throughout the workshops, faculty members will serve in the capacity of facilitator in a classroom structured around student groups. Workshops will meet twice a week for sixty- or seventy-five-minute sessions. Workshops will be offered during morning and evening hours to accommodate all students.

Workshops will focus on the following: (a) teaching math study skills; (b) working on subject material related to what was discussed during class; (c) working in a collaborative, group environment; and (d) providing students with practice exams to prepare them for in-class examinations.

Because this is a pilot program, data will need to be collected to track the progress of students, disaggregated by race and ethnicity, to see the overall effectiveness of this new approach to working with students. The Accuplacer Test will be given to all students at the conclusion of the course. The results of each student's test will be compiled and compared to the end-of-term results (grades) of students enrolled in similar courses but not participating in the workshops.

Additional Recommendations

These additional recommendations likewise emerged from the discussion among the team members and were also offered for consideration for future action.

- Given the LASSI data, expand more current efforts that focus on learning and study strategies, and integrate these efforts more closely with the math department. Although a course exists that specifically targets the critical learning and motivational factors assessed by the LASSI, this resource is not generally familiar nor heavily used by math students. Exploratory efforts have been made to integrate these efforts more closely with the math department, expanded and more systematic development of this option is a promising direction to increase student outcomes.
- Given the complexities of students' lives (including work schedules, child care, transportation, etc.), investigate more flexible scheduling options to accommodate students—extending hours of tutoring and of the Pi Shop, and offering weekend courses are examples.
- Given students' financial and other constraints involved in equitable access to technology that would assist academic progress, explore options to ensure that students have access to required technology (e.g., seek grants or other funding sources to facilitate low-cost loans to permit purchase of computers, or make technology available in other ways such as increased lab space).
- Given the importance students attach to teaching, engage in focused study of "excellent" or "successful" teachers both within the LACC faculty and in other institutions serving similar populations. How can the techniques, practices, and approaches be incorporated into the current math courses? What are the best ways of teaching specific content to specific kinds of students? How do these compare with existing teaching practices? How can "flextime" be used to provide faculty members with opportunities to engage in this learning?
- Provide institutional recognition and support for continuing and expanding the work of the team.

Team Member Responses

The six mathematics faculty members involved in the project participated in individual, one-hour interviews in August 2005 to offer their reflections on their involvement with the Math Project. The common denominator among all six was their hope to reach some understanding into why their students, particularly African Americans and Latinos and Latinas, were not succeeding and transitioning out of remedial math courses with a level of success similar to that of students from other groups. One faculty member best expresses the feelings of the group when she states,

> So with this project is allowing me to do . . . is more . . . get more of the student perspective opposed to our assumption 'cause there's a very big difference. [I want to know] what can we do differently to—to make them more successful, and that's one of the reasons why I wanted to participate in this . . . this group because I think just like technology, we're changing as well.

For her, as well as for the other team members, involvement in the project is giving them an opportunity to view the issues from the other side. They recognize, as the faculty member indicated previously, that they have their own assumptions as to why students are succeeding (or failing). Yet those assumptions may not be in alignment with the everyday reality of the students. Another faculty member commented,

> I don't have a feeling that I know what is going on with people. I can point out the people that know how to study, yes. I can point out that. I can point out that the way we are teaching math could be greatly improved, and not because we are not good enough teachers. We are good teachers, but we need to teach it differently.

So while they understand that changes need to be made to facilitate success among all students, the strategies they use and the interventions they implement may not be as effective because they do not have a comprehensive picture into the lives of their students. The LASSI assessment provided them with a first step in illuminating this picture; however, it was the student interviews that brought this picture into focus. One faculty member in particular was in awe of what he discovered because he did not realize the extent to which students had to make sacrifices in order to be able to attend school. As he said,

> [Interviewing students] was awesome . . . because of the crap that they had in their lives. . . . Two kids, one in preschool, one in grade school. Working at night, going to school full time during the day. Sleeping three hours. . . .

Throughout the conversations that took place during project team meetings, the faculty members shared stories of students facing challenges in high school ("I had somebody in jail") to more current challenges that ranged from family issues, to employment difficulties, and for some, language barriers that they've had to overcome. One faculty member said, "I mean all their stories and their fears, they're all the same, you know, it's difficult to hear." For the team members, engaging in conversations with the students and their overall participation in the project allowed them to see into the inner workings of their students—what motivates them and what prevents them from attaining success in math.

Conclusion

The Math Project team members are to be commended for engaging in this project. They have devoted a significant number of hours of their own time and resources to thinking about and acting on these issues and have sustained their commitment over time. They are united by a common desire to maximize the outcomes of their students. As is the case in most institutions of higher education, routine "everyday" demands are overwhelming, and there is little "space" to think about the ways to improve. Therefore, perhaps the biggest contribution of this project has been to help provide this "space," specifically the opportunity to engage in systematic, long-term, and focused consideration of how to improve student success. Unfortunately, in most universities and colleges, this opportunity is all too rare, in part due to the competing demands for time and attention. However, the focus of the Math Project was based on the assumption that such work is necessary to improve educational outcomes for all students, including those who do not traditionally perform well.

One of the hardest lessons, but the most basic, is that there is no easily packaged approach; rather, progress depends on the day-to-day hard (and sometimes uncomfortable or even painful) work such as that carried out by this team. Although the Math Project has provided the initial foundation for these efforts, long-term success depends on "ownership" of the process by both the institution and the faculty and staff. Therefore, this chapter is presented not in the spirit of having the answer to all of the issues identified, but as the initial steps in creating a process and institutional commitment to continuing the work described here.

Notes

1. This descriptor includes Filipino and Pacific Islander students.
2. The results of 145 students are discussed in this chapter.

References

Love, J., Bauman, G. L., & Bensimon, E. (2004, April 24). *Beyond diversity: Measuring success at a diverse campus.* Paper presented at the Council for the Study of Community Colleges Annual Meeting. Minneapolis, MN.

Weinstein, C. E., & Palmer, D. R. (2002). *Learning and study strategies inventory (LASSI): User's manual* (2nd ed.). Clearwater, FL: H & H Publishing.

Weinstein, C. E., Palmer, D. R., & Schulte, A. C. (2002). *Learning and study strategies inventory (LASSI)* (2nd ed.). Clearwater, FL: H & H Publishing.

7

EVALUATING THE EQUITY SCORECARD PROJECT

The Participants' Points of View

Edlyn Vallejo Peña and Donald E. Polkinghorne

I n previous chapters of this book, Estela Bensimon, Georgia Lorenz, and others wrote about the characterizing features that distinguish the Equity Scorecard Project (EqS) from other models of organizational change. Undergirding the EqS's unique approach to redressing inequities in educational outcomes is the idea that individuals can be the agents of change. When institutional members develop awareness and a deeper understanding of inequities in academic outcomes of students of color on their campuses, they are more likely to advocate for institutional changes designed to bring about equitable outcomes (Bensimon, Polkinghorne, Bauman, & Vallejo, 2004). Following this line of logic, developing awareness of inequities among faculty members and administrators becomes critical; it is a necessary step to laying the groundwork toward transforming institutions into organizations responsive to closing the achievement gap.

In our work with the fourteen EqS institutions in Phase I of the project, we specifically strove to develop individuals' awareness of inequities by engaging them in examination of and reflective dialogue about data on academic outcomes disaggregated by race and ethnicity. After investing two years of resources into raising participants' awareness of inequities, we (the Center for Urban Education [CUE] researchers) asked ourselves, "Did we accomplish our goal of increasing participants' awareness of inequitable outcomes? What were the challenges and opportunities in engaging in this kind

of work?" We desired to hear the stories of EqS participants who had benefited from learning about and discussing inequitable outcomes. In addition,
we wanted to understand the factors that hindered participants from engaging in the EqS process. As such, the whole story from the participants' points
of view were important to us—their struggles and triumphs, their challenges
in engaging in the process, and the opportunities to learn about how students fared on their campuses. Our curiosity resulted in an evaluation at the
end of Phase I of the project, and another at the end of Phase II. The
following pages detail the findings of both evaluative studies, providing an
"insider's perspective" on the EqS process.

Evaluation of Participants' Experiences in Phase I

The first evaluation was conducted at the end of the first two years of the
project, also known as *Phase I.* Though we ascertained from informal discussions with participants that many benefited from the EqS, we wanted to
take a closer, more systematic look at individuals' experiences. Particularly
intriguing were the experiences of team members who outwardly expressed
compelling enthusiasm toward or disagreement with the project. Participants
who openly communicated their perceptions about the project, whether positive or negative, had the potential to illuminate varying aspects of the EqS
experience. As a collective, they were able and willing to reveal more than
one perspective of how the experience of participating in the project
unfolded.

The focus of the study was on the range of experiences of selected EqS
participants, allowing us to capture differences in cases that spoke to the
challenges and opportunities in participating in the project. In conducting
this evaluative study we wanted to know how participants conceptualized
their involvement in the EqS.

Due to her extensive involvement in the project, Estela Mara Bensimon,
the principal investigator, developed familiarity with many of the sixty participants. Of these sixty, Dr. Bensimon selected ten participants whose comments most strongly expressed either positive or negative responses to the
EqS. Choosing ten individuals to participate in the study allowed us to gain
in-depth information from a small number of exemplars willing to provide
saturated descriptions of their involvement. In recruiting these individuals,
we were successful in interviewing eight. All ten were willing to be interviewed; however, because of time conflicts in scheduling interviews, eight

interviews were successfully arranged. The eight individuals represented faculty, midlevel administrators (e.g., institutional researchers), and senior-level administrators (e.g., deans)—five of which felt positively about the project and three who did not.

Donald E. Polkinghorne, a director of research of the EqS, conducted all interviews. Lasting from one to two hours each, the interviews opened with a statement about the purpose of the study. An excerpt from an interview transcript exemplifies the way in which Dr. Polkinghorne commenced his interviews:

> We're looking at what happened or didn't happen with the Equity Score-card [Project] in its first two years. We are looking more at what happened to the people that were involved in it rather than a program evaluation per se. For some people it was a significant event and for others it was more of a bother. Could you start by telling me about your experience of the project?

As interviews ensued, Dr. Polkinghorne inquired into the ways in which interviewees were recruited to participate in the project, the role they played on their respective teams, the nature of their relationships with members on the team, existing politics inside and outside the team, and other factors that were instructive of team dynamics. These contextual factors clued us into interviewees' perceptions and feelings toward the project, informing us of factors that affected their engagement or lack thereof. Fluid and unstructured, the direction of the interviews often depended on interviewees' responses and the flow of conversation. All participants were consistently asked to discuss (a) whether they learned or became more aware of inequities in educational outcomes of students of color, and (b) the extent to which they valued their participation in the EqS.

We found that all interviewees were open in their comments and easily relayed their experiences in the project. In order to maintain confidentiality, interviewees are not listed by name but by number, reflecting the order in which they were interviewed. Individuals' perceptions diverged into positive and negative themes, which are presented in this chapter. This dichotomous thematic structure was itself a reflection of the original choice to select the positive and negative participant outliers.

Positive Perceptions of Phase I

In this study, five of the eight interviewees felt optimistic and positive about the project. The participants who experienced new awareness of inequities in students' academic outcomes regarded the EqS as a process offering opportunities for personal learning and change—one that leads to institutional shifts in processes and practices. The following positive experiential themes were noted in individuals' narratives: (a) the examination of institutional data as an insightful process, (b) a greater understanding of context characterizing equity issues on their campus as a result of team dialogue, (c) participation in the EqS as increasing their awareness of ethnic inequities in academic outcomes on their campus, and (d) realization that the extent to which inequities existed deepened their commitment to communicate findings to campus leaders and to take personal action to improve the state of equity.

Utility of Examining Data

One of the most beneficial aspects of the EqS, according to interviewees, was the usefulness of the data teams examined. The EqS took place at a time in which accreditation and funding agencies placed special importance on the provision of data that demonstrated stated goals had been achieved. Consistent with this emphasis on a culture of evidence, the EqS aimed for its participants to recognize the importance of data-based knowledge in understanding the extent of inequity in the academic outcomes of students of color. Indeed, the project differed from other initiatives in which data monitoring did not occur. Interviewee 3 described the EqS approach as "different" because it is "data driven," admitting that "there have been a lot of things that aren't." Often institutional actors base their perceptions about students on anecdotal information. Instead, the EqS encouraged participants to utilize data in making informed decisions. Interviewee 1 expressed that looking at data "was a move from 'felt' understanding to data-based [understanding]; it brought greater clarity to what many people intuitively thought."

Not only did data confirm what some believed, it provided answers to questions individuals had never before considered. Interviewee 6 reflected,

> In a lot of ways it was an introduction to new ways of thinking; it's new ways of asking more questions but being trained to think about the next set of questions that you should be asking beyond, you know, the answers [in the data] that were initially presented.

In the same fashion, Interviewee 5 saw a relationship between asking new questions of the data and acquiring more refined answers that spoke to the root of the problem at his campus:

There were some questions that these numbers brought up. But [this] not only [prompted me] to think about those questions, but to realize that the numbers can start toward giving you answers to them. And in some cases watching the numbers get closer and closer to the causes—not just pointing out the problem but digging into the causes for the problem.

What participants found particularly useful about the data was that it was disaggregated by race and ethnicity. A new experience for some, participants reported that looking at disaggregated data allowed them to see disparities in outcomes across race and ethnicity clearly. "I looked at this data before, but this is far more detailed," said Interviewee 3. He admitted, "Some just have never been involved in looking at data in this way." The novelty of disaggregated data for participants was not simply attributed to the disaggregation itself but in the way the data were presented. That is, in addition to gathering data in disaggregated form, EqS teams created ways to display the data in meaningful ways, for example, by transforming the numeric data to colored charts and graphs. Interviewee 1 noted, "It had a tremendous impact. I don't know if it was seeing it so comprehensively for the first time or the use of the color printer to show those students who are below the average pass rate." The data made a similar impression on Interviewee 6: "I think there's so much power in the graphs, and you know, just to see it in writing, for example, that Asian Americans do not perform better here." The experiences and perceptions of these participants reveal that the EqS was successful in producing a commitment to the importance of data-based knowledge of the extent of inequities among ethnically diverse students.

Value of Dialoguing With Other EqS Participants

The format of the EqS called for members of the institutional teams to work together in analyzing the data. This joint productive activity had the potential to produce a shared knowledge of gaps in academic performance by ethnic group. Teams held "data parties" in which they culled through data brought to them by their institutional researchers. EqS team members had often not worked together before on a project, and some experienced these interactions around student equity as a constructive element of their participation in the project. Interviewee 7 viewed working on a team to improve equity as "really a positive team building kind of thing." Interviewee 6 elaborated on how team building ensued on his team:

[That there was] someone to talk to about these things, both on our own campus and also with the Scorecard team at CUE made a big difference—someone you can call to say, you know, "I have this thought and this question" and have someone to talk to about it.

Even when members previously knew each other before participating in the EqS, they had not related to each other in this way. "The EqS got us into discussions in certain ways we never thought about getting into," stated Interviewee 5, by socially constructing knowledge about students through team dialogue centered on data.

Increased Awareness of Inequity in Academic Outcomes

Although many participants began the EqS with the general idea that there were inequities in student outcomes by race, through their participation they became more aware of the extent to which this was true in their institutions. Suddenly the issues became clearer. Interviewee 5 had an idea of the disparities that existed before engaging in the work of the EqS; yet examining data in EqS meetings shed light on the severity of the performance gaps:

Well, I suppose some of the numbers that stuck out were when you look at measures of excellence in academic achievement—how White those groups were. I don't know that I was shocked by them. But they were probably more disturbing and worse than I expected.

Interviewee 1 shared a similar experience in examining the data:

What the Scorecard did was it validated what was intuitively and anecdotally thought. . . . The data was presented in such a way that it was overwhelming. I mean, I think everybody who saw the data said, "Wow, we have a serious problem."

Although the extent to which the inequities prevailed was made clearer for some, for others, examining the data served to refute assumptions entirely. Interviewee 6 expressed that he had ideas about "who is failing and succeeding and, you know, we debunked many of the myths through this deeper questioning of who our students really are." Inequitable educational outcomes were brought to the forefront for Interviewee 7 as a result of analyzing the data with his team members. Interviewee 7 said, "This is stuff I didn't know before [the EqS]." He continued, "Suddenly there were things that we hadn't looked at before that, you know, now I looked at them broken down by ethnicity." Not only was his awareness about performance gaps raised, he gained awareness about a different approach to collect and examine data to further inquire into the matter. Adopting the practice of disaggregating data by race was an important change, indicating that Interviewee 7 was willing to engage in equitable practices to continue to monitor the state of equity.

A departure from discussing changes in their own awareness, interviewees often discussed ways in which the awareness of fellow team members and colleagues on campus was raised. Interviewee 6 recalled that another EqS team member shared,

> [H]e learned to ask different questions of the data than [he] previously would have. It really changed the way he saw things because of the fact that he really didn't know these things. He didn't know that there were these inequities and disparities.

Similarly, the changes Interviewee 5 and his team members experienced prompted him to want to raise the awareness of others on campus: "You figure if it [the data] changed my attitude, I might be able to change somebody else's attitude." When interviewees and their EqS teams communicated the data to constituents on their campus, they noted a number of institutional actors became aware and interested in the data. For example, Interviewee 3 remembered, "People on this campus were very surprised [by the data]. . . . I think it raised the institution's awareness—my awareness, definitely." When Interviewee 4 shared the data with members on his campus, they became interested in institutionalizing the practice of examining data disaggregated by race and ethnicity. He exclaimed, "They're finally getting that we have to disaggregate our data!"

Empowerment to Communicate and Take Action

A significant benefit to having raised EqS participants' awareness included empowerment to take action toward redressing gaps in academic performance. As mentioned in the previous section, individuals' personal experiences in learning about inequities were enough motivation to spread the word to colleagues about how students of color were faring on their campuses. What else motivated participants to take action? In one way, participants expressed that having data-based knowledge gave them more credibility and authority on campus. Interviewee 3 said, "I think having the data

. . . gives more credibility to everything. It gives it more backing here for something to actually get done." In another way, Interviewee 3 saw the data as an effective tool to institute changes on campus. And when he presented the data to others on campus, they perceived it as a valuable instrument to advocate for change: "They love the fact that [disaggregating the data] is helpful for grants and things like that and to understanding what's happening with our students. Because if you don't understand that you can't plan the changes." Interviewee 7 also pointed out the utility of the Scorecard in communicating areas of inequity that deserve attention. He said, "The scorecard provides a mechanism, or a focus, or a way of communicating that [there are] problems." Interviewee 5 presented the data to his campus president at a time when the culture of the university placed value on equity.

> We finally got the President to move a couple of months ago by just simply presenting the numbers to him. And this comes off the heels of him proclaiming one of the signature characteristics of this place is Equity. . . . And it seemed to move him. . . . The numbers are absolutely crucial in that way.

EqS principal investigators intended to create opportunities for team members to communicate the data to colleagues and campus leaders. One means for accomplishing communication included teams preparing a report for their president that displayed their findings and proposed follow-up actions. Although it was expected of team members, some interviewees developed a personal commitment to share the data for institutional change. For Interviewee 5, it became

> a role that you take on. It might be an occasional conversation somewhere. It might be a meeting where I had some expertise that other people didn't. So sometimes in those committee meetings, I would find a reason to use the numbers to make an argument.

Interviewee 6 also prided himself on the fact that the data-based knowledge he developed resulted in a new kind of relationship with his campus president: "The president will often call on me or my colleague on the Scorecard Project to brief her prior to meeting [about] an outside agency or grant or about certain equity issues. I was prepping the president."

One of the most noteworthy findings in gauging participants' experiences pertained to the ways in which the data empowered them. Some reported that participation in the EqS revitalized their desire to bring about change. Interviewee 1 reported:

> We all, as a result of this, you know, kind of become a little bit more interested in wanting to become change agents. Not just merely people who facilitate the flow of work and the implementation of procedures and policies. We kind of take a conscious effort to bring about change.

Similar to Interviewee 1, Interviewee 6 expressed a deepened commitment to improve the state of equity. "We don't have the solutions, but many more of us are now invested and worrying about this issue, and that's the way it should be." He continued to reflect on how the data have made a difference in his personal and professional life: "Personally it has opened my eyes. This process has really given me new energy, a new life in my professional work. It made me excited again about my work and motivated me to pursue further studies for myself."

The four themes that emerged from participants who felt positively about the project are a reflection of the experiences intended by the EqS. Again, these themes constituted experiencing (a) the examination of institutional data as an insightful process, (b) a greater understanding of context characterizing equity issues on their campus as a result of team dialogue, (c) participation in the EqS as increasing their awareness of ethnic inequities in academic outcomes on their campus, and (d) realization that the extent to which inequities existed deepened their commitment to communicate findings to campus leaders and to take personal action to improve the state of equity. For these selected participants, the project's hopes were realized. Yet for the remaining interviewees, as illustrated in the following section, the EqS was more of a challenge than an opportunity to learn from the data to effect change.

Challenges and Problems With Phase I

In reading through the interview transcripts of those who felt negatively about the EqS, we noted a pronounced difference in tone and affect between these interviewees and those who viewed their participation in the project positively. The experiential themes of the negative texts had little overlap with those in the positive texts. Interviewee 8, for example, went as far as to say that her participation in the EqS "was actually an awful experience." The three themes that emerged from these particular interviews were (a) experiencing no change in awareness of inequity, (b) feeling as if there were too little time and too little rewards to engage in the EqS, and (c) perceiving the EqS as unsuitable for their campus contexts.

No Change in Awareness of Inequities

The three selected participants who reported that, in general, their experience in the EqS was negative said that they learned very little from their involvement. They reported already knowing there was inequity of outcomes at their institutions and that they did not need to have devoted so much time to the project to find this out. Of these three, Interviewees 2 and 8 were experienced in conducting research and data analysis. They felt that the kind of research the EqS required was redundant and did not offer any new insights. Interviewee 2 expressed that, for him, this kind of work was old hat; he did not "suddenly discover that something needs to be raised to a new level of priority." Interviewee 8 freely voiced similar concerns:

> It was frustrating to be spending a lot of time on this, which appeared to have no value at all. This was research we were doing here ten or twelve years ago . . . and we know very well what the issues are and we . . . have special programs for African Americans and Latinos. We felt we were way past the "look at the existing research, see where these discrepancies are, and make the President aware of them." We felt we were starting where your project was ending.

Too Much Time, Too Little Rewards

Because they felt the project was not producing new knowledge for them, Interviewees 2, 4, and 8 experienced it simply as a lot of imposed work. It was one more task added to their already too-busy workload and was not worth the time they put into it. "What initially was some enthusiasm became a great deal of effort," said Interviewee 2. He later continued,

> I would have a long time ago abandoned the project because right now we have no stake in this. The things that we will achieve from this which are meaningful are things that we could have done in another way without going through this laborious project with completing this [president's] report.

For Interviewee 4, it was not "worth all the time that was put into it on our part." Interviewee 4 was "too busy to be doing this" and felt that the Scorecard did not help her "to do my other job better; it was like an exercise."

Interviewee 8 also viewed the process of conducting the Scorecard as analogous to an exercise, rather than as a useful tool. She stated, "It was like a homework assignment: you don't know why the teacher gave it to you." Thus, Interviewee 8 perceived the project as time wasted: "The EqS seemed like an unnecessary, complicated time-consuming task to find out nothing."

Not only did the three interviewees mention that participation in the EqS demanded their time, they regarded this as time for which they were not receiving any reimbursement. All three cited lack of payment or reward as a challenge to becoming engaged in the process:

- "There's no reimbursement and there's no payoff for us in the sense of all the effort we've put in. . . . There needs [to be] some sort of financing." (Interviewee 2)
- "I think it would have been better had they given stipends." (Interviewee 4)
- "I was reluctant to get involved in something that looked like it might be a lot of work, . . . and there was certainly no money in it for us." (Interviewee 8)

In addition to perceiving the project as time-consuming with little or no rewards, Interviewee 2, an institutional researcher, felt that his expertise and experience in analyzing data were not acknowledged. In his interview, he recalled, "They never bothered to ask us what our credentials were, and it would be the same as me ignoring your extensive research background and assuming you had no idea about what was happening." Interviewee 2 became offended because he had "been doing this work for eighteen years and when individuals come in and begin to dictate the scope, course, and direction of your work . . . I find it very awkward and difficult to try to do." His position and opinion on the EqS were made clear when he stated, "Your approach is simply not mine; it was not something that I'd advocate to the campus."

Inappropriate Approach for Specific Campuses

A fundamental problem attributed to the project's lack of success for these individuals was that the EqS was not suited to their campuses' needs. Interviewee 2 expressed, "In fact, the problems we've got here are very different than imagined by the EqS." Interviewee 8 also felt that the project could not efficiently address the problems at her campus: "As we learned more about the [EqS] grant, it seemed poorly suited for this campus."

Both Interviewees 2 and 8 had been involved in previous failed efforts to bring about equity and had reservations about whether any new efforts would actually make a difference. Interviewee 8 shared,

> As soon as [campus administrators and faculty] are out of that [equity] program, they revert back to the norm again. So generally speaking we found that special programs have not made a sustainable difference. . . . So, we have no reason to believe that any of our interventions make a difference other than everybody feels good at the time.

Interviewee 2 mentioned that only more money, not the EqS, would make a difference. "By God," said Interviewee 2, "the only thing that will work is that influx of money so you can do more intensive interventions."

Evaluation of Participants' Experiences in Phase II

By the end of Phase II, we had worked with EqS participants over the course of four years. As the project culminated, we again yearned to know more about how the participants felt about their involvement in the EqS. For this evaluation, however, we wanted to know information that went beyond the opportunities and challenges of increasing the awareness of participants. After four years of intense efforts to engage partner institutions in the EqS, we desired to know the ways in which the project impacted campus practices and processes. Because the first evaluation took place in the middle of the four-year project, the information about challenges of the EqS benefited us as researchers and facilitators because we had two more years to make adjustments to the project. By the end of the project, however, our aim was to understand from highly engaged participants the ways in which individuals and institutions changed toward redressing unequal outcomes. After all, institutional change was a chief item on our agenda.

Because Dr. Polkinghorne had retired from the project by the end of Phase II, Estela Bensimon (principal investigator) hired an evaluation consulting firm[1] to conduct the interviews. We decided that in this evaluation, we wanted to recruit a larger pool of participants in order to attain a more comprehensive idea of the ways in which campuses were affected. Thus, the consulting firm successfully interviewed twenty-two participants. In this sample, campus leaders like college presidents and vice presidents were interviewed in addition to EqS team participants. The interviews in this evaluation lasted a much shorter time, usually fifteen to thirty minutes each, than those of the first study. The findings detailed in the following section are derived from the report written by the evaluation consulting firm. Because identifiers were not used in the report at all times, quotes shared in this evaluation's findings are not always accompanied by names or pseudonyms that identify individuals quoted. Again, the themes described in the following sections are separated into positive and negative responses.

Utility of Examining Data

As in the first evaluation, participants of the second evaluative study found the EqS to be an unparalleled project because of its focus on examining data. A college president who participated in the evaluation compared the EqS to other related projects in which he had been involved. He commented,

> It is the first equity related project that we have really done that has gone this deep. Most projects don't disaggregate the data and information . . . even by courses and within the same ethnic group. . . . It gives you a sense of what is happening.

Like this college president, many of the participants interviewed agreed that the EqS distinguished itself from other projects because of its orientation to institutional research. Other initiatives often used anecdotal information or did not disaggregate data by race or ethnicity.

Increased Awareness of Inequity in Educational Outcomes

Project participants shed light on the extent to which the EqS process raised their awareness of inequitable educational outcomes. The underlying disparities expressed in numbers brought EqS participants to "now pay way more attention to the educational outcomes." A dean of undergraduate studies at one partner institution eloquently described his experience:

> I think my level of consciousness is almost permanently at this raised state. It is not only about the numbers, but it is how those numbers look when we compare the different groups along key dimensions. I now raise this issue with others. In retrospect it seems so basic. Why haven't I done this before?

Like this dean, other interview participants mentioned how the data raised their awareness, allowing them to question institutional practices, as well as their own. This new kind of awareness led some to be critical about the "commitment my institution really has to Equity."

In addition to sparking critical questions about institutional practices, the EqS process offered individuals with answers that they previously were without. The use of examining data held instrumentality to promote learning and informed decision making. One interviewee stated,

> It lays the groundwork for organizational learning. Mostly it proves a pathway out of decision making on an anecdotal, myth-based basis and turns the organization toward planning and decision making on an evidentiary basis.

The learning that resulted from examining and reflecting on disaggregated data proved powerful. Another president said this kind of learning allowed institutional actors to make "more informed judgments," based on more accurate information. And, as one interviewee articulated, "Investing in that learning made the changes deeper: a complete change in attitude."

One associate dean in particular raved about the ways in which examining data affected him personally and professionally. He stated that as a result of the EqS,

> my thinking is completely different. It has gone through a radical paradigm shift—a revolution. Having the team look at the data and make meaning of it, that is completely different than anything I have ever been involved in. Totally different. It took my innocence. I can never view things in the same way. Now I always ask for data in terms of the classes, gateway classes. It has shifted the focus to administration, not the students.

In this statement, the associate dean highlighted an important principle of the project: examining data to become informed and take responsibility. His paradigm shift in how he viewed data and the problem of unequal outcomes allowed him to assume agency to request data and take responsibility for the disparities he discovered. Another statement evidenced this increased commitment to redressing unequal outcomes:

> It made me committed to doing my part to change organizations. I use the principle of disaggregating by ethnicity in my daily work now as a

result. I am not afraid of losing a job when I speak on behalf of social justice and equity.

Value of Interacting With CUE Facilitators

In this evaluation, interviewees discussed the ways in which CUE facilitators proved to be useful resources over the course of the project. Unlike in the first evaluation, participants spoke less about the value for fellow EqS participants than they did about their appreciation of CUE staff. An assistant dean of Ethnic and Intercultural Studies described the important roles that the facilitators assumed in the project. He explained,

> Even though it was their project, they were not directive in their style of working with us. They were clear about the outcomes and the process. They acted more as consultants working for us than individuals telling us what to do.

EqS participants appreciated the collaborative nature between facilitators and participants during the EqS team meetings. One president commented that this type of "collaboration was just extraordinary."

Facilitators also directed teams and other members on campuses to notice gaps in student achievement by pointing out pertinent data and completing the Scorecard. The facilitators were said to be responsible for "shaping the idea [and] at the same time able to articulate the [Scorecard] framework. They helped us into helping the team understand the framework." Understanding the framework was as valuable as comprehending the implications of the data themselves. In one case, a college president remarked about the moment he realized the significance of the project and the importance of the facilitator's role. Estela Bensimon had visited the campus for a retreat and shared the campus's data on student outcomes disaggregated by race and ethnicity. The president said,

> It was a bolt of lightning, a call to action, a slap in the face, a bucket of cold water—those metaphors all together. . . . It helped me move our conversation on campus . . . from how many students of color do we admit each year to what do we do with them when they are here.

This quote exemplifies one of many instances wherein a facilitator, in this case Bensimon, brought new information and ideas to the forefront for the president and other institutional actors.

Change in Institutional Culture and Practices

The most invaluable changes that the EqS process brought about pertained to shifts in campuses' institutional cultures and practices. Some partner institutions experienced a shift in the way decisions were made. One interviewee explained that the EqS

> helped the campus to move forward in acceptance around the whole notion of using data as a tool to make decisions. It helped people tell their own stories and take responsibility for change within their own units. Some units made extraordinary changes.

Similarly, another individual commented that "in all things with equity initiatives the Scorecard is always mentioned."

One specific outcome for a particular institution was the creation of a vision statement centered on equity. The assistant to the president on interculturalism said,

> It got us to do a whole lot of things. We had some Equity activities before the Scorecard. But what the Scorecard got us to do was develop a vision statement, goals. It got us to think about interculturalism.

For other campuses, the use of data became integral to conducting assessments on campus. One interviewee said that disaggregating data "will become part of the campus culture," while another said that it "is a continual practice [that] won't ever stop." Finally, the value of continuing to monitor data echoed in the following remark about the project:

> [The project] created an institutional expectation that these areas will be looked at, at least annually. And that is part of how we do business; it is not an add-on. It is part of a regular assessment of ourselves, to determine where we are, what successes we have achieved, and what challenges still remain. It is not about trying to be politically correct. It is about being an excellent organization.

Problems and Challenges With the EqS

Fewer negative comments emerged in the second evaluation of the project compared with the first evaluation. Six of the twenty-two interviewees expressed concerns about the EqS. Negative perceptions related to receiving little compensation, difficulty in understanding the theoretical principles of the project, and resistance from institutional members to change the campus culture. First, participants cited getting "a lot of work out of us for free." Participants contributed much energy and time without a stipend. One individual in particular noted, "It was the Scorecard that got the notoriety, not the work done by the individual campuses. . . . We felt disenfranchised."

Second, the way in which the facilitators communicated EqS principles to project participants was perceived as "very theoretical, which made it difficult." Some wanted "more applications or hands-on examples, things that were much more tangible." Another individual stated that understanding the organizational learning theory that underpinned the project "was a challenge sometimes because it is not my discipline."

Third, three of the twenty-two participants in the evaluation said that their colleges' resistance to change had prevented the EqS from affecting the campus. A president of one of the partner institutions admitted,

> It hasn't impacted the campus. We have a very evidence-resistant faculty. It has made me think differently about culture change here. In the accreditation world a big buzzword is creating a "culture of evidence." It has made it crystal clear that we need to work on that here. It hasn't had an impact because we don't have the structures for creating evidence-based conversations or the process of doing so and we don't have the tradition. The project has pointed out that we really have organizational change issues.

Although this president saw the potential the EqS might have for institutional change, campus constraints limited the project's capacity to be successfully implemented.

Advancing Our Understanding of How Participants Perceived the EqS

Fundamental to the EqS is the increase in awareness and sensitivity of its participants to the inequitable academic outcomes among different ethnic student groups who attended their institutions. The project sought to bring home the point that simply admitting a diverse student body was not sufficient. Namely, after admitting students of color, institutions are responsible for serving them in such a way that equitable academic outcomes are produced.

Project goals, however, are seldom achieved for each and every participant. Project success depends on a function of the interaction between the project activities and each participant. Its effect occurs within the individual project-participant dyad. Each participant brings his or her background, understandings, values, and needs to the dyad. In some cases, the project's offerings and the participant's background mesh to bring about a positive outcome, and in other cases, a negative one. And in still other cases, participants have mixed experiences.

As the two evaluative studies demonstrate, though the same EqS model was carried out in a similar fashion across participating institutions, the project did not produce the same effect for each participant. The experiences of the participants interviewed, even taking into account that the model underwent adaptations at each institution, varied for a number of reasons. Interviewing individuals from extreme ends of the continuum of experiences in the project, on the one hand, illuminated opportunities the EqS offered them—analyzing disaggregated data, interacting and dialoguing about the data as a team, raising awareness of inequities, and becoming empowered to address them. On the other hand, interviews revealed negative perceptions about the project. Unenthusiastic interviewees saw the project as a bothersome task from which they did not reap benefits, namely, new insight or reimbursement. Limited time and resources, according to certain individuals, restricted their engagement in the project.

In sum, the evaluations proved fruitful in two ways. First, though we take pride in those individuals who benefited from the EqS, we take seriously the feedback given to us by those who did not. The evaluations clue us into what we can improve upon, especially when we consider continuing this kind of critical work. Second, the findings derived from these evaluations give us hope that our work with institutions made a lasting effect. We now know that, for most participants, our work with the EqS teams was successful. Participants became more attuned to the magnitude of inequities that existed on their campuses. Confronted with data revealing incredible disparities, individuals became empowered to take on the responsibility of assisting their institutions to redress unequal outcomes. For some, examination of data disaggregated by race and ethnicity became a routine practice. For others, concrete outcomes, like developing a vision statement, were realized. These outcomes represent evidence that the EqS can change individuals and can change institutions.

Note

1. The consulting firm hired was PRISM Evaluation Consulting Services. Barbra Zuckerman and Hallie Preskill conducted the evaluation and submitted a final report on interview findings to the CUE.

Reference

Bensimon, E. M., Polkinghorne, D. E., Bauman, G., & Vallejo, E. (2004). Doing research that makes a difference. *The Journal of Higher Education, 75*(1), 104–126.

PART THREE

RESEARCHER PERSPECTIVE

What We've Learned About Organizational Learning to
Create Equity From the Equity Scorecard Process

8

AN ACTIVITY-BASED APPROACH TO PROMOTING EQUITY IN COMMUNITY COLLEGE SETTINGS

Considering Process and Outcomes

Robert Rueda

This chapter focuses on the problem of promoting equitable outcomes in higher education.[1] More specifically, the focus here is on community colleges, which are the initial step in the pathway to higher education for many non-White and poor students in the United States who fare less well in terms of educational outcomes than other groups. The chapter describes an approach that draws in part from sociocultural work in general, and activity theory specifically, to foster change in community college settings related to how these colleges view and address this problem. In addition to presenting how this theoretical approach was applied in a specific project, it considers the issues related to how such an approach reconceptualizes both the intended targets of the change efforts and where evidence of effects might be expected. Before describing the theoretical approach and specifics of the project, a brief review of educational outcomes in community college settings is provided in order to contextualize this work.

Community Colleges: A Brief Overview

Who attends community college? Although greater numbers of students are enrolling in college today than twenty years ago, the rates of college enrollment for African American and Latino students remain considerably lower than those of White and Asian students. In 1998–2000, the college participation rate of eighteen- to twenty-four-year-old White high school graduates was 46 percent, compared with 40 percent for African Americans and 34 percent for Latinos (Carnevale & Fry, 2000). There are also other interesting differences among subgroups. For example, first-generation students (those whose parents did not attend college and who are most often Latino or African American) have a lower rate of attainment than White students. Based on the National Education Longitudinal Study of 1988 (National Center for Education Statistics [NCES], 2005), 43 percent of the first-generation students who enrolled in postsecondary education between 1992 and 2000 "left without a degree" and 25 percent had attained an undergraduate degree by 2000. In contrast, 20 percent of the students whose parents had a bachelor's degree or higher "left without a degree" from a postsecondary institution, whereas almost 70 percent attained an undergraduate degree by 2000.

Community colleges have sometimes been seen as a stepping-stone for students who are unable, because of academic or financial reasons, to directly enroll in four-year colleges. Part of this is economics. It is clear that the cost of higher education is soaring, and thus would be expected to have a significant effect on the enrollment patterns of groups with higher levels of poverty. For the 2007–2008 academic year, annual prices for undergraduate tuition, room, and board were estimated to be $11,578 at public institutions and $29,915 at private institutions. Between 1997–1998 and 2007–2008, prices for undergraduate tuition, room, and board at public institutions rose 30 percent, and prices at private institutions rose 23 percent, after adjustment for inflation (NCES, 2008). Given the costs, it is not surprising that compared with students attending four-year colleges, community college students are more likely to be older, female, Black, or Hispanic, and from low-income families. Recent data suggest that the community college population is predominantly age twenty-four or older and is considered financially independent from parental support for financial aid purposes (Horn & Nevill, 2006). These data also indicate that almost two thirds (61 percent) of community college students are independent compared with 35 percent of students enrolled in public or private not-for-profit four-year institutions. These students also tend to differ from the younger traditional students who enroll in a four-year college right from high school. One third of community college students are married with children, and one fourth are single parents. With respect to poverty, when incomes are examined against established poverty thresholds, just over one fourth (26 percent) of community college students fall into the lowest income group (Horn & Nevill, 2006).

Achievement Patterns

Once they do get to college, African Americans and Latinos, as well as the lowest socioeconomic status students, are most likely to be found in remedial education. This stems in part from their lower levels of academic prepared-ness and in part to public policies that have relegated remedial education to community colleges (NCES, 2003; Swail, Cabrera, Lee, & Williams, 2005). Attewell, Lavin, Domina, and Levey (2006) show, even after controlling for high school academic performance, students in the public sector and in community colleges are more likely to be enrolled in remedial courses, as are Black students in comparison with their equivalently prepared White peers. These data and a variety of related indicators suggest that community college attendance and participation is stratified by students' racial-ethnic and socio-economic backgrounds. A recent analysis also suggests that racial and ethnic group differences are evident, especially among those in the more committed track (defined as college attendance intensity and intent to transfer to com-plete a degree). Compared with their representation among all community college students, White students were overrepresented and Hispanic students were underrepresented in the more committed applied associate degree track (Horn & Nevill, 2006).

Demographic Issues

In states such as California, demographic changes suggest that community colleges do and will continue to play a significant role in the educational pipeline (Cohen & Brawer, 2003). Currently, one quarter of current Califor-nians, 9.6 million children and adults, were born outside of the United States. This represents the highest proportion of foreign-born population in the state since 1890 and a fivefold increase in immigration since 1970 (Public Policy Institute of California, 2007). In California's public K–12 schools, over 40 percent of students (2.6 million) come from households where a language other than English is spoken (Rumberger, 2007). Significant num-bers of these students experience academic difficulty because of language differences, inadequate educational resources, and related factors (Callahan, 2005; Gándara, Rumberger, Maxwell-Jolly, & Callahan, 2003), and thus community colleges represent the only realistic track to higher education.

National data suggest the same conclusion, suggesting that students from non-White racial and ethnic groups, some of whom come from language minority backgrounds, rely on community colleges in particularly high numbers. Nationally, two thirds of Latino postsecondary students begin their higher education career in community colleges (Solorzano, Rivas, & Velez, 2005), and community colleges enroll over half of the total U.S. Latino college population (Saenz, 2002). In California, close to 75 percent of Latino first-time college students enroll in community college (Woodlief, Thomas, & Orozco, 2003), and almost half of California's community colleges have student bodies that are over 50 percent students of color.

A Perspective on Equity and Equitable Outcomes

In sum, the data just presented indicate that the community college system is an important link in the higher education chain, especially for non-White and poor students. The data also suggest that there are unequal outcomes for many of these students compared with their White counterparts. These and a multitude of related indicators suggest that there are significant issues related to group differences at the community college level. This is the context that led to the creation of the project described in this chapter, the Equity for All (EFA) project, housed at the Center for Urban Education (CUE) at the University of Southern California.

A major goal of this project was the promotion of equity-mindedness and equity-focused practices within the community setting. In this project, and in related action research (Bensimon, Polkinghorne, Bauman, & Vallejo, 2004; Dowd, 2005), *equity* was defined in terms of student "outcome equity" (Dowd, 2005) rather than surface indicators such as demographically representative enrollment. Disparities in student experiences and outcomes among racial-ethnic groups are viewed as prima facie evidence of inequities because such gaps in educational achievements are an unacceptable failure in a democratic society. In this sense, this work is "value laden," not value neutral (Bensimon, 2007).

When considering equity and inequitable outcomes, there are many student-related factors that can be pointed to as possible causes of the inequities noted previously, including students' inadequate prior education, students' and families' lack of resources, deficits in prior knowledge, poverty, language differences, and so on. In fact, there is a significant tendency in education to frame these factors as within-student deficits related to low motivation, intelligence, and so on (Valencia, 1998, 2010). However, these factors are not amenable to easy or quick fixes, especially as seen from the eyes of the individual educator. In the worst case, consideration of these factors sometimes leads educational practitioners to reduce expectations, provide low-quality instruction, or exhibit a sense of complacency, because this perspective focuses educational attainment as due solely to student-related factors. Although it is not useful to disregard these factors, the work to be described has tried to focus on things that individuals *can* affect through their day-to-day practice, in particular methods that can affect student outcomes *through changes in one's own practice* and by individuals' taking ownership of the problem.

Background and Goals of the Current Project

In previous work of the CUE (see, e.g. Bensimon, 2004, 2005, 2007; Bensimon et al., 2004; Bensimon, Rueda, Dowd, & Harris, 2007), we noted that the community colleges we observed were characterized by three critical features. First, achievement patterns for African American and Latino and Latina students mirrored those described earlier, and many of these students were mired in remedial education coursework that did not lead to transfer. Second, data related to student progress and outcomes was often collected by institutions, but it was not in a "user-friendly" form, did not disaggregate data by race or ethnicity, was rarely used to inform ways to improve student outcomes, and was rarely looked at or used outside of a very small number of administrators. Finally, equity was a sensitive and sometimes contentious issue, especially when the discussion focused on race and ethnicity. Thus, the project was designed to address these issues directly. The specific goals of the project were to assist participants and their institutions in (a) developing awareness of race- and ethnic-based inequalities in educational outcomes by being able to interpret and query the use of institutional data, (b) learning to interpret race-based disparities in academic outcomes through the lens of equity, and (c) viewing inequalities in outcomes as a problem of institutional accountability that calls for collective action. The long-term goal was to promote equity in educational outcomes for minority[2] students as an integral aspect of institutionalized processes in community college settings. A collaborative action research approach was adopted with the overall goal of fostering community college practitioner learning about racial inequities and fostering equity-minded[3] sense making of institutional data on equity indicators that normally is not provided to nor used by community college practitioners (see Figure 8.1 for a general conceptual framework). As the figure illustrates, each college is a unique sociocultural context. This context includes, among other factors not depicted, knowledge and attitudes about the key targets of the CUE's work: use of data, equity, attributions for student outcomes, and so on. The conceptual model assumes that changes in these areas can affect both individual practices and, over time, more widespread policies and practices.

Theoretical Framework

Neither a best practice nor a packaged intervention, EFA was seen as a *process*—built in part on social constructivist, sociocultural, and sociohistorical theories of organizational and individual learning and drawing on an action inquiry tradition. A fundamental goal was the construction of new knowledge and new practices for individuals as well as institutions related to fostering equitable outcomes for students of color. Specifically, EFA was designed

FIGURE 8.1
A conceptual model for change in the EFA project.

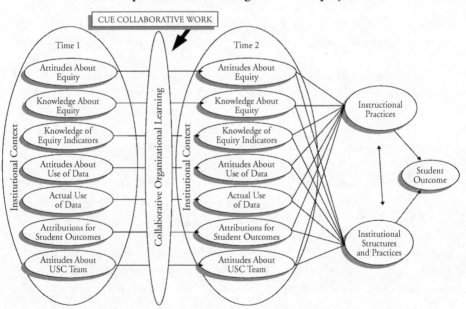

to produce practitioner learning about racial inequalities and foster equity-minded sensemaking for both individuals and the overall institution. In order to achieve these goals, we drew on complementary theories of individual and organizational learning and practice, as well as a suitable research methodology to investigate these efforts. The approach is based on what we loosely term a *situated organizational learning model* (Bensimon, 2005), one that rests in part on the principle that learning and change are socially constructed and facilitated by collective engagement in a joint productive activity. We describe these ideas in the following section.

Perspectives on Learning

Multiple theoretical perspectives on learning and change have informed this project. These perspectives are discussed in the following section.

Organizational Learning and Practice

Organizational learning is the study of how and under what conditions organizations can be said to learn (Kezar, 2005). This notion is based on a body of research and draws substantially from work in organizational psychology (Argyris & Schön, 1996). Kezar (2005) has noted some of the main concepts in this tradition that relate to learning: single- and double-loop learning, inquiry and advocacy, theories in use, overload, and information interpretation processes such as unlearning and organizational memory. *Single-loop learning* refers to using existing assumptions and values to deal with "errors of alignment with the environment" (Kezar, 2005, p. 10), whereas *double-loop learning* entails challenging assumptions and values and transformational change. *Inquiry* and *advocacy* are forms of dialogue that foster change in how individuals understand assumptions and values that block communication and learning. *Theories in use* are the mental models that guide action. *Overload* refers to when the information in a system exceeds the system's capacity to deal with it, as sometimes happens in highly bureaucratic systems. *Organizational memory* refers to the system's ability to maintain a connection among past, current, and future information and data such that important aspects are not lost or overlooked.

Some research in this area focuses on how the features of organizations such as structure, culture, and so on encourage or discourage learning. An example is how an unwillingness to look at information that challenges leaders' and practitioners' images of themselves as well as of their institution can be the biggest obstacle to institutional learning and change (Argyris, 1977; Argyris & Schön, 1996; Bensimon, 2005). More recent work that emanates from the domain of practitioners in the helping professions helps explain this common problem. Polkinghorne (2004) suggests that the everyday practices of professionals are guided by socially and culturally acquired knowledge that functions below the level of conscious awareness. This knowledge can lead to personal interpretations (about inequity and its causes and solutions, for example), leading to responses that can reduce or perpetuate inequitable educational outcomes. The personal theories that practitioners develop partly reflect their self-efficacy as agents of change, including the possible roles they might play creating or eliminating educational outcomes of students. This notion is related to cognitive psychologists' notion of automated knowledge, which has been shown to be a powerful influence on an individual's thought and behavior and yet is not subject to conscious monitoring (Bargh & Ferguson, 2000; Wheatley & Wegner, 2001).

A Sociocultural Perspective on Learning

A second theoretical perspective that has informed thinking about achieving the learning goals of the project is sociocultural theory, sometimes also known as *cultural-historical psychology*. Although Vygotsky is the name most often associated with this perspective (Vygotsky, 1987), many of the early ideas of Vygotsky have been developed by contemporary neo-Vygotskian scholars (Forman, Minick, & Stone, 1993; John-Steiner & Mahn, 1996; Kozulin, Gindis, Ageyev, & Miller, 2003; Lave & Wenger, 1991; Moll, 1990; Rogoff, 1991; Rogoff, Turkanis, & Bartlett, 2001; Tharp & Gallimore, 1988; Wenger, 1998; Wertsch, 1998; Wertsch, del Rio, & Alvarez, 1995), and more specifically in the related work in Cultural Historical Activity Theory model (CHAT) (Cole, 1996; Engeström, 1987).

Rather than being a single well-defined theory, sociocultural theory is really a family of theories with a set of related assumptions with differing emphases. The general common features of sociocultural approaches that we have drawn on in this work include the idea that (a) learning is social, (b) learning is facilitated by assisted performance that is responsive, (c) learning is mediated by cultural tools and artifacts, and (d) learning takes place in communities of practice and is indexed by changes in participation within these communities. In the following sections we explain these ideas more in detail and elaborate on how we have drawn on these theoretical notions in the implementation of the project.

Many approaches to learning assume that learning is an activity typically associated with students. It is likely that this is the reason that the study of learning among institutional actors such as faculty or administrators is not as developed as it could be in the scholarship on higher education (Bauman, 2005; Bensimon, 2005; Kezar, 2005). Whereas most approaches to learning regard it as an individual accomplishment (or failure) that takes place "between the ears," a basic assumption of our approach, based on a sociocultural perspective, is that learning is fundamentally a social process. From this theoretical perspective, learning is predicated on a collaborative relationship that allows the learner and "more competent others" to negotiate understanding, usually through discussion, sharing ideas, questioning, and other mediational means.

Learning Is Social

Sociocultural theorists point out that learning is facilitated or "scaffolded" by others in the social environment who are more accomplished, until over time one learns to do it for himself or herself. From this theoretical perspective, learning is predicated on the collaborative relationship that allows the learner and "more competent others" to negotiate understanding, usually through discussions, sharing ideas, questioning, and other mediational means. Vygotsky (1978, 1987) argued that learning occurs as individuals engage in culturally meaningful, productive activity with the assistance of these "more competent others" such as a peer or colleague. Thus, "more competent others" assist the performance of a learner.

It is this "assisted performance" that is the key to promoting learning. However, not all assistance is equally useful. Rather, the optimal level is somewhere above what the learner can already accomplish but not so advanced that it is beyond understanding. The learner must be engaged at a level that produces learning and induces development, that is, within the "zone of proximal development." This is defined as the range between the level of difficulty at which an individual can perform independently and the highest level at which she can perform with assistance. If the assistance is at a level that is either above or below a learner's current level of performance, learning will not be facilitated. However, when the assistance is within the learner's "zone," it is said to be *responsive* and is thought to produce learning. Specifically, learning takes place as novices participate in specific contexts with the assistance of those more experienced. Although novices may have an incomplete or inaccurate understanding of the overall goal initially, over time and with assistance they can become familiar with the values and identities embedded in the community of practice, so that they understand the broader purposes and have a clear sense of what they will eventually master and appropriate (Lave & Wenger, 1991).

This "assisted performance" (Tharp & Gallimore, 1988) approach to learning is consistent with an apprenticeship model in which social relationships are used as the foundation to help learners move through the zone of proximal development with the assistance of one or more "competent others" (Vygotsky, 1978, 1987). This more experienced "other" assists the novice in performing a task through various types of "assisted performance." Tharp and Gallimore (1988) have identified the seven most common forms of assisting performance, all with venerable histories in the social and behavioral sciences. These are questioning, feedback, instruction, modeling, task structuring, cognitive structuring, and contingency management.

Tharp and Gallimore (1988) point out that continuous assessment of the learner's performance and current level of understanding is essential to ensure that assistance or scaffolding is responsive. A useful illustration of these processes is found in the way that young children learn language. Initially they can do little more than make noises to communicate wants and needs. However, children will engage with more accomplished language users to accomplish everyday tasks. This can adjust the complexity of the language input to the child's current level of development. Eventually, children become accomplished language learners. The same processes can be used to describe learning how to drive, how to calculate statistics, or how to write a dissertation.

Learning Is Mediated

A key assumption of sociocultural perspectives is that learning is bound up in complex ways in larger cultural, contextual, historical, political, and ideological processes that affect learners' lives. Sociocultural theories place much importance on the role of mediation in learning processes, especially in regard to higher-order thinking. A strong focus of this perspective is how cultural practices and cultural resources mediate the development of thinking and learning. A major concern is to understand how culture, like other tools and artifacts, mediates thinking.

We often think of tools as physical objects. Yet cultural tools are things that we have inherited from those who have come before and they can be anything that helps accomplish everyday tasks in ways that were not possible

PROMOTING EQUITY IN COMMUNITY COLLEGE SETTINGS

without them. Think of how things like automobiles, computers, and the Internet have changed how we interact with the world, and how perhaps the most powerful of mediators, language and literacy, have changed what we do and how we do it. These artifacts and cultural practices are critical in mediating learning. From the earliest years of infancy to the last stages of one's professional career, people are socialized into particular cultural practices, including language and other artifacts that become tools for thinking and interacting with others. Simply put, all behavior involves mediation through the impact of cultural objects, symbols, and practices.

The basis of sociocultural theory is that learning is socially mediated and rooted in specific cultural-historical contexts (Cole & Engeström, 1993). The use of mediating tools is acquired through social and cultural experience. We know the world through symbolic mediation, such as when we perceive pieces of fruit as "apples" and "oranges," or when we categorize people into ethnic-, gender-, or even age-based categories. When we perceive objects and events, our understanding of them is not automatic but is based on constructed and shared meanings built up over time and in specific cultural contexts. Sociocultural researchers are uniquely concerned with the use of tools and mediators in specific contexts and in understanding and promoting learning. These tools and artifacts enable new meaning making, in essence helping to "re-mediate" one's understanding. Unlike the traditional notion of remediation, which focuses on the amelioration of specific deficits, the notion of *re-mediation* refers to changing the nature and type of mediation in order to promote the creation of new understandings and knowledge.

Communities of Practice

Consistent with the sociocultural view that learning is fundamentally social, knowledge is seen as being created through active participation in various social contexts, and strongly influenced by what is valued in those contexts. In sociocultural terms, these are known as learning communities or communities of practice, which Wenger (1998) defines as "a locus of engagement in action, interpersonal relations, shared knowledge, and negotiation of enterprises" (p. 85). Simply put, a community of practice is a social group developed over time through ongoing purposeful endeavor (Wenger, 1998). These communities of practice can be formal or informal "groups of people who have some common and continuing organization, values, understanding, history, and practices" (Rogoff, 2003, p. 80).

It is within these communities that learning takes place and individual identities (e.g., student, professor, parent, spouse), meaning, and social belonging are created. For example, people participate in the classroom community; a peer group; their family; and perhaps a variety of community or school groups, such as scouts, a soccer team, a profession, or a band. Any individual participates in multiple and overlapping communities of practice, with differing levels and types of participation in each (Wenger, 1998). These communities of practice help shape what Gallimore and Goldenberg (2001) describe as *cultural models*, or shared mental schema or normative understandings of how the world works, or ought to work, including what is valued and ideal, what settings should be enacted and avoided, who should participate, the rules of interaction, and the purpose of interactions. (It should be kept in mind that even though communities of practice may appear homogeneous and may widely share similar cultural models, these shared models can produce varying cultural practices among members, depending on features of specific social contexts.) These communities of practice are themselves shaped by cultural, historical, and institutional factors (Lave & Wenger, 1991; Wenger, 1998), part of the cultural inheritance of those who have come before.

One view of learning in this framework is that it is characterized by how a person participates in, contributes to, and is changed by specific communities of practice (Rogoff, 2003). Learning is always tied to a given community and always involves one's identity and membership with respect to that community. It needs to be kept in mind, however, that these are not static processes or fixed traits, but that they change dynamically over time. As one changes what one does (practices), how one views oneself and how others view that person change as well. The dynamic nature of this view of identity is captured by the notion of "trajectory." That is, the ongoing process and negotiation of identity may lie on a path leading to more central engagement with a community of practice or may lead (by choice or otherwise) to more peripheral engagement. As Wenger (1998) notes, "Membership in a community of practice translates into an identity as a form of competence" (p. 153). In a very real sense, learning can be seen in part in terms of the identity or identities one has formed with respect to a given community of practice and how those have changed over time.

Activity Settings

A key aspect of sociocultural approaches is that the focus or analytic unit needs to go beyond the individual learner. Thus, the key focus is the *activity setting*, not the learner in isolation. Activity settings can be seen as the "who, what, when, where, why, and how" of the routines that constitute everyday life—in essence, a more elaborated version of what we commonly call a social context.

The main components (Figure 8.2) are the subjects (participants), object (the goals participants are trying to achieve), and tools (the forms of mediation available in the setting, which can be symbolic like language or concepts, or more tangible like physical artifacts). In addition, activity settings include community, rules, and division of labor. The community refers to the specific community formed by those participating in the setting, but also the connections to the various extended communities with which they are associated. It should be noted that the community or communities with which the researcher identifies might be very different from the communities with which specific team members identify. But the existence of the project team meetings was designed to help shape the formation of a new community with jointly shared goals. The remaining elements of the activity setting also include the roles that participants play and the rules for what are appropriate and tolerated within the setting, and the division of labor consistent with those roles. We drew on the activity setting framework to situate the individual participants' learning and help connect that learning to the larger institutional context.

An Action Research Perspective

Our model belongs to that category of research known generally as action science or action inquiry, which is a "form of inquiry into practice" (Reason,

FIGURE 8.2
An activity setting framework.

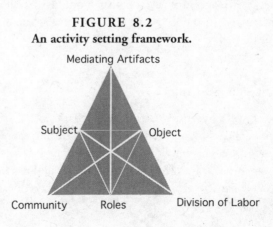

1994, p. 330). We call this model *practitioner as researcher* to emphasize that in it the roles of the researched and researcher are reversed to some extent. That is, practitioners take the role of researchers, and researchers assume the roles of facilitators and consultants. The practitioner-as-researcher model has elements of community (Smith, 1999), collaborative, and participatory action research (Bray, Lee, Smith, & Yorks, 2000; Stringer, 1996) in that the *purpose* of inquiry is to bring about *change* at individual, organizational, and societal levels.

The *methodology* consists of outsider researchers working as facilitators engaged with insider teams of practitioners in a process of collecting data and jointly *creating knowledge* about local problems as seen from a local perspective. Reason and Bradbury (2001) write that action research "is a participatory, democratic process concerned with developing practical knowing in the pursuit of worthwhile human purposes" and that its primary purpose "is to produce practical knowledge that is useful to people in the everyday function of their lives" (pp. 1–2). In the practitioner-as-researcher model, individuals conduct research about their own institutions, and by doing so they acquire knowledge that they can use to bring about change in these institutions. Because institutional insiders conduct the actual research, the role of the professional researcher shifts from research producer or expert to consultant and facilitator for the practitioner researchers. The practitioner-as-researcher model requires that the professional researcher be skilled in building and maintaining personal relationships as well as in research design. Above all, it is important for the insiders to assume ownership of their findings. The outcome is knowledge that heightens the members' awareness of what is occurring within their institutions and increases their motivation to effect change. Thus, the knowledge produced in this model is practical and effective in directing changes. In the following sections we describe how these principles were implemented.

The Equity for All Project

The project was a yearlong action-research project carried out with nine community colleges located across California during the period of May 2005 to June 2006. Previous publications have described the background and specifics of the project and have explored in detail the effect of the project on individual participants (Bensimon, 2004, 2007; Bensimon et al., 2004; Bensimon et al., 2007).

The Equity Scorecard Project, like its predecessor, the Diversity Score-card, is modeled on the business world's Balanced Scorecard Framework (Kaplan & Norton, 1998) and has been implemented in over thirty-five four- and two-year colleges in six states. In California and Wisconsin, the use of the Equity Scorecard process by groups of colleges was endorsed by state system leaders to meet state accountability requirements, and in Colorado it was implemented in collaboration with the Western Interstate Commission for Higher Education.

The primary method for increasing equitable and uniformly high student learning outcomes was by convening practitioners who were involved in an institution's formal learning systems or who were viewed as key actors in informal institutional networks. These meetings were also designed to facilitate the creation of a community of practice with the purpose of developing a culture of inquiry to promote minority student success. The teams were appointed by presidents based on specific project criteria (e.g., faculty members who teach "high-risk" introductory courses, academic leaders who sit on institution-wide committees and could serve as boundary spanners, racial and ethnic diversity).

The EFA process engages team members in a series of meetings that initially revolve around "vital signs" (indicators of student degree progression and student outcomes that include academic pathways, retention, transfer readiness, and excellence) but proceed to examination of "fine-grained measures" of the same types of indicators. An important difference between the vital signs and the fine-grained measures is the fact that the teams themselves select the latter indicators and request that they be provided for discussion to the team by the institutional research office. The selection of "fine-grained" indicators often involves narrowing the focus to student progression between particular course sequences, for example, from developmental to college-level coursework, or to particular groups of students, for example, African American males, who may have progressed through the curriculum at lower rates. The process of defining the indicators and specifically requesting the data is intended to promote problem framing, ownership of the assessment results, and general data literacy.

In addition, the project provides access to special tools and protocols and artifacts, including data sheets, vital signs protocols, interim reports templates, equity index formula, and examples of graphic displays to help make data easy to decipher. The project also introduced special language and concepts such as the differentiation between diversity and equity; deficit, diversity, and equity perspectives on institutional data; data versus inquiry approaches to data; and the notion of global versus local knowledge. Evidence teams met at least once a month for at least two hours. Before the project, there was no institutional "space" for this type of work, and thus it did not occur in any of the schools we worked with.

Characteristics of Teams

The president-appointed teams had the following characteristics: (a) two thirds of the members were female, (b) one third were White, (c) the number of African American (sixteen) and Latina and Latino (fourteen) members was about the same, and (d) faculty members (32 percent) composed the largest professional role represented in the teams. (See Tables 8.1, 8.2, and 8.3 for specific information on the team composition for all teams.) Over the twelve months the campus teams met on average once a month for at least two hours.

TABLE 8.1
Representation of Equity for All Evidence Team Members (All Schools) by Gender

Gender	n
Female	60 (67%)
Male	29 (33%)
Total	**89**

TABLE 8.2
Representation of Equity for All Evidence Team Members (All Schools) by Race and Ethnicity

Race, Ethnicity	n
African American	16 (18%)
Asian	5 (.06%)
Latino/a	14 (16%)
White	29 (33%)
Unknown	25 (28%)
Total	**89**

TABLE 8.3
Representation of Equity for All Evidence Team Members
(All Schools) by Campus Position

Campus Position	n
Classified Staff (Administrative Support)	1
Counselor	12
Dean, Academic Affairs	5
Dean, Student Services	3
Faculty Member	29
• (Math: $n=9$)	
• (English/Reading: $n=11$)	
• (ESL: $n=7$)	
Academic Department Chairperson	3
President/Superintendent	2
Research Analyst	4
Research and Planning Dean/Administrator	8
Student Services Coordinator	5
Student Services Director	5
Vice President, Academic Affairs	4
Vice President, Business Affairs	1
Vice President, Student Services	4
Other Administrator	3
Total	**89**

Project staff conducted two training sessions for team leaders and institutional researchers at the participating colleges in the methods, tools, and processes of the Equity Scorecard approach. Between June 2005 and July 2006, we facilitated ninety-one team meetings at the nine participating campuses in both northern and Southern California, an average of about ten meetings per team. Our role in the teams was to model "equity-minded" interpretations of the student outcome data, which we accomplished by asking questions, reinterpreting deficit-minded interpretations, providing feedback, and calling attention to data patterns.

A project researcher and at least one research assistant were present at each of the scheduled team meetings. Each of the team meetings over the yearlong period was transcribed for analysis. In addition, field notes from all contacts between project staff and team participants were kept. These contacts included records of formal meetings, informal meetings with individuals or subgroups of team members outside of the team meeting setting, phone calls, e-mails, and so on. In addition, all relevant documents that provided evidence of effect were kept for analysis. Finally, after the end of the formal project and the termination of formal team meetings, project staff continued to carefully document the participants' reports about their interactions with other people outside of the team meetings, their comments about institutional and organizational factors related to the project, and our own observations about institutional changes in activities or changes in practice or policy that took place and that could be directly attributed to the project, most often by the participants' or others' (e.g., administrators') reports.

Although nine community colleges participated in the overall project, we focus here on one college (in which the author served as the researcher) to achieve a more detailed understanding of how the theory and principles were implemented in practice, and how the institution was affected.

City Community College: Background of the College

City Community College is a large community college in the Southwest serving approximately 26,729 students annually. The college offers ninety-five associate of arts/science degree programs, eighty-one career certificate programs, and the opportunity to complete up to two years in any of fifty-eight baccalaureate programs for transfer to a four-year college or university. The college serves a diverse student population. Students identifying themselves as Asian, Pacific Islander, and Filipino made up about 17 percent of the head-count enrollment in the spring of 2007. White students represented about 26 percent of the student population, and Hispanics and Blacks represented about 36 percent and 13 percent, respectively.

In January 2005, City College was invited to participate as one of the partner institutions in EFA because its student body demonstrated ethnic diversity. The CUE purposefully invited colleges that were not struggling to diversify their student population so that the focus of the team would be on *student outcomes* rather than increasing diversity. The president accepted the invitation and appointed members to the EFA team because although City College had a long tradition of looking at data to track student performance it rarely monitored student outcomes by ethnicity. The president believed that the project's perspectives on educational outcomes and overall approach were a good match for the school's goals to increase the number of underrepresented students who migrate successfully through basic skills, earn a degree or certificate, and transfer.

Applying Theory to Practice: A Sociocultural and Activity-Based Approach to Change

At this point, it is useful to elaborate how we drew on the previously described frameworks in the EFA project. It should be recalled that the overall goal of the project was to affect individual and institutional attitudes and practices related to equitable outcomes for underrepresented students. Given this goal, we approached our work with the various institutions as an applied learning project. That is, the project tried to create communities of practice revolving around ensuring equitable outcomes in community college settings at each campus. Effecting change was seen as fundamentally an issue of professional development (Dowd, 2005) and learning, which is known to take place through collaborative social interaction over time (Bauman, 2005; Bensimon, 2004, 2005; Bensimon et al., 2004; Tharp, 1993; Tharp & Gallimore, 1988).

The team meetings were designed to create a special context or *activity setting* for collaborative inquiry, mediated by cultural tools and artifacts (the Equity Scorecard, for example, as well as the introduction of new concepts and discourse for thinking about equity) specifically constructed to make racial patterns of inequality visible. By forming communities of practice around equity, the goal was to create opportunity for participants to create new identities and new meaning or "sensemaking" around issues of equity, not in the abstract, but on their own campuses and in their own classrooms. This purpose was to ensure that locally developed solutions to issues of equity were "contextualized" and relevant to the specific setting.

Built into the team meetings was the principle that new knowledge is created—including new ways of examining and questioning data, new vocabularies, and new practices around diversity and equity. The team meetings served a "mediating" rather than a directive function in this respect. Rather than trying to change attitudes and practice directly, which emphasizes individual learning, the goal of the team meetings was to change the nature of the cultural practices that participants had at their disposal. In essence, we attempted to "re-mediate" thinking and practice around equity. In this context, then, *re-mediation* refers to changing the nature of mediation available to participants in the setting, rather than to the deficit-based connotation used to refer to compensatory programs and practices.

Within the activity settings known as *team meetings,* the EFA researchers provided strategic assisted performance to the teams. Rather than treating as deficient those participants who did not share a goal of equitable outcomes, we treated them as being at a certain level within a particular zone of proximal development. Wherever that starting point fell, the goal was to move forward. We were careful not to replicate the patterns of low expectations and inequitable treatment of team members similar to those we have often encountered in the ways that some institutions deal with underrepresented students (Valencia, 1998, 2010). Rather, the central task of the meeting facilitators was to provide scaffolding and assisted performance and to try to understand how to help learners move to the next level of understanding. Because learning was seen as social and mediated, we tried to reorganize key features of the social interaction and provide new cultural tools and artifacts and ways to use them (such as institutional data along with the strategies for becoming informed and critical consumers).

An Overview of Outcomes

It is useful to briefly summarize the major patterns that emerged related to participation in the team meetings for this and other colleges (Bauman, 2002; Bauman & Bensimon, 2002).

- Most team members believed data are essential, but few had the skills or confidence to examine them critically and ask relevant questions and use them as a tool for action. The Equity Scorecard process provided a context and setting to increase all evidence team members' (even those not quantitatively oriented) capacity to engage in data-based inquiry and make sense of student outcome inequities that are revealed by examining disaggregated data.
- Institutional researchers often saw their role as a technical activity rather than as helping others understand the data, ask questions of the data, or be proactive in looking at new data. The Equity Scorecard process assisted these institutional researchers to reconsider the formal roles to which they were socialized and to view themselves as "teachers" and "facilitators" of data-based inquiry. The roles and functions of institutional researchers are critical not only to evidence team members' learning, but also to the potential effect and overall success of the Equity Scorecard process.
- Leadership among teams was essential for effective action but was not necessarily found in one individual. Rather, it was most often

"distributed" among different members. The most effective team leaders were those who were able to facilitate learning and equity-mindedness by encouraging critical dialogue surrounding issues of race and ethnicity.

- Many patterns of student outcome inequities may remain hidden without systematic "unpacking" of the data that already exist. The Equity Scorecard process, including the vital signs perspectives and the disaggregation of all data helped bring otherwise concealed inequities to the surface, thereby allowing evidence team members to better recognize these patterns.

- The institutional context can influence the effect and outcomes of the Equity Scorecard process. A key aspect was the evidence teams. The characteristics of effective evidence teams included:
  - Team leaders who understood the goals and principles of the Equity Scorecard and who emphasized process and related learning rather than a final product
  - Support from the president and academic senate or related administrative bodies
  - A diverse team composition that included "boundary spanners," those who sat on multiple committees or had formal contact with multiple departments or divisions
  - Support from the institutional researcher regarding the notion that inquiry (rather than data) drives the Equity Scorecard process

Although these findings are useful, our sociocultural framework led us to consider a more theoretically driven perspective on outcomes. Tracking learning and change in a project such as this is both complex and dynamic, involving a myriad of factors. Student longitudinal outcome data over time, collected in an experimental or randomized control trial design, might be seen as the gold standard. Yet we would argue that there are additional ways that the effect of a complex change process might be conceptualized.

Conceptualizing Outcomes

Given the previously described project goals, activities, and processes, what are the best ways to think about effect? How do the theoretical frameworks underlying the project help guide the documentation of changes in individuals and the system? We have drawn extensively on sociocultural theory, in particular the notions of *community of practice, transformation of participation,* and *planes of development.*

Tracking Individual Learning

Earlier in the chapter, we described the notion of communities of practice. As we noted, these are social groups developed over time, and can be formal or informal, but share some degree of common values, understandings, history, and cultural practices. In this metaphor, one can think of concentric circles, where novice learners or participants are at the periphery, and more established participants or learners (experts, in cognitive terms) are more central. One way to track learning, then, is to examine the "trajectories of participation" (Rogoff, 2003) of one or more individuals as the nature and extent of their participation shifts over time. Learning is indexed through the nature and extent of participation, and how the participant(s) are changed as well as how they contribute to the community. These changes can be captured through the actions and discourse of an individual or group as they shift over time. How does the discourse reflect the norms and values of the community of practice? How do these change? How does the individual group contribute to or have an impact on the community?

Learning Beyond the Individual

In spite of the fact that learning is often seen as a characteristic of individuals, some sociocultural theorists (Rogoff, 1995, 2003) have elaborated on the view of learning and development as a dynamic process of transformation of participation, which occurs on three levels, or planes, of interaction. The first of these is the personal plane, which involves individual cognition, emotion, behavior, values, and beliefs. At this level, an important question to ask in terms of evidence for change is, "Do individuals feel, think, behave and talk differently than they did before (e.g., about the issue of equity)?" The second is the interpersonal or social plane, which includes factors that relate to how participants in a social context interact, including communication, role performances, dialogue, cooperation, conflict, assistance, and assessment. At this level, it is important to ask, "Is the nature of participants' interactions different from before?" Finally, the community or institutional plane involves shared history, discourse patterns or language, rules, values, beliefs, and identities. At this level, an important question to ask is, "How have the institution and the cultural practices and structures embedded within it changed?"

Whereas many learning theories focus primarily on the individual, sociocultural theory emphasizes that these three planes are inseparable, and a complete account of learning needs to consider all three. The important point is that the unit of interest is greater than the individual—rather, it is the individual in interaction with others in a specific social context or activity setting. Our framework pushes us to not only examine individual learning but to examine the "ripples in practice and structure" (Gallego, Rueda, & Moll, 2005) in the larger activity setting. What new communities of practice were created? How did these affect the larger institutional community? How were the cultural norms (roles and division of labor) within the institution changed? How did the organization integrate equity-minded principles and practices? In the following sections, brief examples of changes in each of the levels are provided.

Individual Change in the Personal Plane

At this level the focus is on whether participants have developed new skills, knowledge, or attitudes. In our analysis of the data, we found that team members displayed increased knowledge and more positive attitudes about indicators and equity. The following quote from a team member who is now engaged in follow-up work related to the project illustrates this point:

> Given the demographics of City College, there is no longer one American experience and there is no reason to force our students to read texts that do not speak to them. To invigorate the students' experience, as well as the instructor's, it is essential to try new texts written by authors whose experience is more like that of our students; as instructors we might be surprised at the ways in which these texts change the classroom experience and our students' dedication to learning more.

Interactional Change in the Interpersonal Plane

Qualitative analysis of meeting observation and field notes transcripts revealed that early in the project, members of the inquiry team were alarmed by the institutional data that showed significant gaps in transfer rates and degree attainment for underrepresented students. These findings were explored over the course of the project with the assistance of the data tools provided. This new knowledge created within the team meetings became the impetus for the team members to move their efforts beyond the confines of the team itself. In short, they partially redefined their roles as faculty and administrators, including the ways that they interacted among themselves and in the larger campus around issues of equity. For example, early on the student outcome data indicated that African American students were succeeding at a significantly lower rate in a key math course required for the associate's degree than the overall student population on the campus. A math faculty inquiry team member shared these results with other faculty in the math department. As a result, the math faculty formed a Math Evidence Team, modeled after the EFA project, to explore possible reasons for the underperformance of African American students in math through further data inquiry. Initially, the math faculty were particularly interested in examining how class size influenced student success in the course and conducted a series of statistical analyses to get more information. Based on this work during the project, the Math Evidence Team significantly expanded the scope of its inquiry activities. A follow-up study, for example, was conducted by the institutional researcher in collaboration with the new evidence team to assess student learning experiences in this math course through student survey data. Students were administered the survey and interviewed in the spring of 2007 and will be surveyed again next spring. Math faculty were also given a survey to examine their engagement in specific teaching practices thought to enhance learning. Finally, the Math Evidence Team made plans to conduct in-depth student interviews to learn more about student histories in learning math as well as their perceptions of the math classroom and of math instructors.

Change at the Institutional Level

The data that we collected allowed us to document overall changes in four key institutional areas: goal setting (e.g., strategic planning), self-assessment (e.g., student retention initiatives), academic decision-making (e.g., professional development) and administrative decision-making (e.g., resource allocation), and student support services (e.g., career counseling). Data analysis revealed that team members' involvement in the Equity Scorecard project appeared to have had a distinct "rippling" or "trickle down" effect on the larger campus community in these four domains. These included recognizable changes in cultural norms and institutional practices such as raising awareness of equity issues, creating intervention strategies, and assessing institutional practices.

The evidence team shared its work through meetings and formal presentations to key campus constituencies at various points throughout the project. For instance, some members presented key findings in a town hall meeting setting. Others made EFA the focus of a faculty retreat and professional development day activities. City College was particularly proactive in its dissemination strategy of the inquiry findings to other campus departments and divisions. The inquiry team's main goal was to facilitate a campuswide discussion regarding inequitable educational outcomes for underrepresented students of color. A key strategy utilized was a research e-newsletter, developed by the institutional researcher, which described the work of the project and student outcomes data disaggregated by race and ethnicity.

The newsletter was developed and distributed throughout the campus to inform faculty and administrators who were not on the evidence teams about the goings-on of the project. Since the creation of the newsletter, information regarding the work of the inquiry team and student findings have been regularly presented by inquiry team members to various campus constituencies, including the president's cabinet, academic senate, master plan committee, and student success committee.

Since the formal completion of the project, City College has also been particularly active in sharing the work of the project and raising awareness of equity issues to community college faculty and administrators throughout the state. This has been carried out by the institutional researcher and several other City College practitioners presenting their work with the project at approximately eight academic and professional higher education conferences throughout California (this figure is likely to be underestimated because we do not receive reports from City College about all of the presentations it has made). City College has also shared its experience with EFA directly with other community colleges outside of the state. For example, City College shared its work with a community college in Hawaii that was interested in learning more about how City College got involved with EFA and the overall process of the project.

City College also recently participated in an additional collaborative research project with the CUE's research team that was designed to follow up on a specific problem of the college related to transfer practices and policies. City College EFA data from 2006 had revealed that more than 20 percent of eligible students did not transfer, even though they were eligible. This meant that a significant number of students were "missing" from the group who did transfer. Consequently, City College decided to explore the benefits of various assessment strategies toward gaining a better understanding of why some transfer-ready students do not transfer and why some four-year-college-ready students transfer to less selective institutions rather than to the University of California system. Twenty-three volunteer faculty members and counselors participated in a five-month follow-up action research project that involved enrollment data analyses, interviews with "missing" transfer students who were eligible to transfer, and audits of institutional culture and resource use. A strategy was developed to identify and reach out to students who needed to complete only one additional course to become transfer eligible. In all, fifty students who were short one course of qualifying for transfer were identified. The committee then provided student information to counseling services, who in turn contacted the selected students to supply them with the necessary information and tools to help them become transfer ready. The committee also developed a proactive strategy aimed at increasing the numbers of students obtaining their associate degrees. The committee identified 1,600 students who were close to completing their general education degree requirements and sent students postcards and e-mails to encourage them to complete the necessary requirements in order to obtain their associate's degrees. It is safe to say that a definite effect of the project is that it is building a bridge between student services and faculty, areas that are typically disconnected. With these methods, they are trying to understand the role that college administrators, counselors, and faculty can play in increasing transfer.

There are several indicators that City College has moved toward the institutionalization of equity discourse. For example, "equity" became one of the goals in the college's master plan (required by the state system for all community colleges). In addition, City College has incorporated the work of the project with a previously separate student success initiative into professional development activities for faculty all around the campus and has used the project data for Title V and Title III grants. The college continues to monitor student outcomes in new ways (by race and ethnicity) that were not previously done.

Discussion

The overall design of the EFA project assumed that individual change is socially fostered and leads to institutional change. Thus, fostering individual equity-minded thinking and practices is seen as a stepping-stone toward changing institutional practices and culture and, ultimately, improved student outcomes. A problem with existing frameworks that address either one or both of these goals (changing individuals or changing institutions) is that they focus *exclusively* on either individual processes or institutional factors. The sociocultural framework we adopt here allows for a larger unit of analysis that includes both of these dimensions and thus helps bridge individual behavior and cultural practices to institutional ones. In essence, it situates individuals within specific communities of practice and incorporates not only individual goals and mediational means, but cultural norms and institutional goals as well.

An important change principle derived from this framework is that changes in any aspect of the activity setting can produce changes elsewhere in the system. Thus, by introducing new forms of cultural tools (e.g., new ways of talking about inequitable student outcomes, or data tools to track equity), it was possible to document changes in the larger system. We have noted that there are now new communities of practice (such as the Math Evidence Team) that have formed at the college, with new goals focused around equitable outcomes. The division of labor related to making sure equitable outcomes are produced has shifted so that previously uninvolved actors and academic units are sharing the responsibility. The traditional roles that have delineated efforts have begun to break down; in particular, divisions between faculty and key staff (e.g., in the area of transfer and counseling) are becoming less rigid. As the college begins to incorporate new cultural tools (equity-minded discourse, tools for unpacking and examining student outcome data), new activity settings are created such as a Transfer Academy that serve to promote student success over time. In essence, new knowledge and understandings about the issue are socially constructed and serve as a guide to future action.

Although it is possible to think about producing changes in behavior by trying to change the behavior directly, through didactic or similar means, such an approach focuses only on individuals and leaves several levels of learning unaccounted for. Consistent with the notion that learning is socially constructed, the project incorporated a perspective that focused on a unit of analysis larger than the individual actors. Thus, rather than adopting a didactic instructional approach, the project changed the nature of the mediation available to the team participants and created a special activity setting (team meetings) that allowed the creation of new, situated knowledge leading to a critical and proactive stance toward institutional change. The active ingredients that appear to be critical thus include (a) creating special activity settings that help form new communities of practice, (b) situated learning, and (c) data-driven inquiry. The framework adopted here, therefore, is useful not only in conceptualizing how to change individual and institutional cultural norms and practices, but in determining where to look for that change as well.

Conclusion

The economic reality of today's world is that there is a strong demand for highly skilled and educated workers who are both literate and able to think critically. Higher education is indispensable in helping meet this need. It is unthinkable on economic as well as moral grounds that major subgroups in society may not be able to contribute to the future development of the country because of issues related to access and inequitable outcomes at the level of postsecondary education. Given that a significant portion of under-represented community college students are less likely to complete their postsecondary education, it is likely that they will face limited career prospects and lower annual incomes compared with other groups. It is especially critical to counter the deficit-based thinking and practices that contribute to these outcomes via their assumption that students alone are responsible for their low academic achievement. The results of our work suggest that by creating a community of practice for practitioners centered on equity and institutional responsibility, new ways of conceptualizing and addressing issues of equity can be facilitated. In turn, this new knowledge can have a rippling effect that will influence the larger campus community and beyond. The project's findings underscore the importance of community college administrators, faculty, and personnel to view and address inequities of student outcomes on their campus through a lens of institutional responsibility.

Notes

1. This chapter builds on a chapter prepared for the 32nd Annual Association for the Study of Higher Education Conference, Louisville, Kentucky, November 2007, which included Amalia Marquez as a copresenter.

2. We use the term *minority* to refer to students from groups with a history of exclusion, discrimination, and disenfranchisement, primarily African Americans and Latinas and Latinos, the two groups that are central in the research project we draw on for this chapter. We recognize that the term is inaccurate in many urban settings where students of color are actually the majority; thus, we use this term primarily as a convenience.

3. Throughout the chapter we use *equity-minded* and *equity-mindedness* interchangeably.

References

Argyris, C. (1977). Double loop learning in organizations. *Harvard Business Review, 55*(5), 115–125.

Argyris, C., & Schön, D. A. (1996). *Organizational learning II: Theory, method, and practice.* New York, NY: Addison-Wesley.

Attewell, P., Lavin, D., Domina, T., & Levey, T. (2006). New evidence on college remediation. *The Journal of Higher Education, 77*(5), 887–924.

Bargh, J. A., & Ferguson, M. J. (2000). Beyond behaviorism: On the automaticity of higher mental processes. *Psychological Bulletin, 126*(6), 925–945.

Bauman, G. L. (2002). *Developing a culture of evidence: Using institutional data to identify inequitable educational outcomes.* Unpublished doctoral dissertation, University of Southern California, Los Angeles.

Bauman, G. L. (2005). Promoting organizational learning in higher education to achieve equity in educational outcomes. In A. Kezar (Ed.), *Organizational learning in higher education: New directions for higher education* (No. 131, pp. 23–35). San Francisco, CA: Jossey-Bass.

Bauman, G. L., & Bensimon, E. M. (2002, November). *The promotion of organizational learning through the use of routine data.* Paper presented at the Association for the Study of Higher Education conference, Sacramento, CA.

Bensimon, E. M. (2004, January/February). The diversity scorecard: A learning approach to institutional change. *Change,* 45–52.

Bensimon, E. M. (2005). Closing the achievement gap in higher education: An organizational learning perspective. In A. Kezar (Ed.), *Higher education as a learning organization: Promising concepts and approaches* (Vol. 131). San Francisco, CA: Jossey-Bass.

Bensimon, E. M. (2007). The underestimated significance of practitioner knowledge in the scholarship of student success. *The Review of Higher Education, 30*(4), 441–469.

Bensimon, E. M., Polkinghorne, D. E., Bauman, G. L., & Vallejo, E. (2004). Doing research that makes a difference. *The Journal of Higher Education, 75*(1), 104–126.

Bensimon, E., Rueda, R., Dowd, A. C., & Harris, F. (2007). Accountability, equity, and practitioner learning and change. *Metropolitan Universities, 18*(3), 28–45.

Bray, J. N., Lee, J., Smith, L. L., & Yorks, L. (2000). *Collaborative inquiry in practice: Action, reflection, and making meaning.* Thousand Oaks, CA: Sage.

Callahan, R. (2005). Tracking and high school English learners: Limiting opportunities to learn. *American Educational Research Journal, 42*(2), 305–328.

Carnevale, A. P., & Fry, R. A. (2000). *Crossing the great divide: Can we achieve equity when generation Y goes to college?* Princeton, NJ: Educational Testing Service. (ERIC Document Reproduction Service No. ED 443907)

Cohen, A. M., & Brawer, F. B. (2003). *The American community college.* San Francisco, CA: Jossey-Bass.

Cole, M. (1996). *Cultural psychology: A once and future discipline.* Cambridge, MA: Harvard University Press.

Cole, M., & Engeström, Y. (1993). A cultural–historical approach to distributed cognition. In G. Salomon (Ed.), *Distributed cognitions: Psychological and educational considerations* (pp. 1–46). New York, NY: Cambridge University Press.

Dowd, A. C. (2005). *Data don't drive: Building a practitioner-driven culture of inquiry to assess community college performance* (Research Report). Indianapolis, IN: Lumina Foundation for Education.

Engeström, Y. (1987). *Learning by expanding.* Helsinki, Finland: Orienta-Konsultit Oy.

Forman, A., Minick, N., & Stone, C. A. (Eds.). (1993). *Contexts for learning: Sociocultural dynamics in children's development.* New York, NY: Oxford University Press.

Gallego, M. A., Rueda, R., & Moll, L. C. (2005). Multilevel approaches to documenting change: Challenges in community-based educational research. *Teachers College Record, 107*(10), 2299–2325.

Gallimore, R., & Goldenberg, C. (2001). Analyzing cultural models and settings to connect minority achievement and school improvement research. *Educational Psychologist, 36*(1), 45–56.

Gándara, P., Rumberger, R., Maxwell-Jolly, J., & Callahan, R. (2003). English learners in California schools: Unequal resources, unequal outcomes. *Education Policy Analysis Archives* 11(36). Retrieved July 25, 2009, from http://epaa.asu.edu/epaa/v2011n2036/

Horn, L., & Nevill, S. (2006). *Profile of undergraduates in U.S. postsecondary education institutions: 2003–04: With a special analysis of community college students (NCES 2006-184).* Washington, DC: U.S. Department of Education.

John-Steiner, V., & Mahn, H. (1996). Sociocultural approaches to learning and development: A Vygotskian framework. *Educational Psychologist, 31*(3/4), 191–206.

Kaplan, R. S., & Norton, D. P. (1998). The balanced scorecard: Measures that drive performance. In H. B. Review (Ed.), *On measuring corporate performance* (pp. 123–145). Boston, MA: Harvard Business School Press.

Kezar, A. (2005). What campuses need to know about organizational learning and the learning organization. In A. Kezar (Ed.), *Organizational learning in higher education* (pp. 7–22). San Francisco, CA: Jossey-Bass.

Kozulin, A., Gindis, B., Ageyev, V. S., & Miller, S. M. (2003). *Vygotsky's educational theory in cultural context.* New York, NY: Cambridge University Press..

Lave, J., & Wenger, E. (1991). *Situated learning: Legitimate peripheral participation.* Cambridge, UK: Cambridge University Press.

Moll, L. (Ed.). (1990). *Vygotsky and education: Instructional implications and applications of sociohistorical psychology.* New York, NY: Cambridge University Press.

National Center for Education Statistics. (2003). *Postsecondary attainment, atten-dance, curriculum, and performance: Selected results from the NELS:88/2000.* Washington, DC: U.S. Department of Education.

National Center for Education Statistics. (2005). *First-generation students in postsecondary education: A look at their college transcripts (NCES 2005-171).* Washington, DC: U.S. Department of Education.

National Center for Education Statistics. (2008). *Digest of education statistics: 2008.* Retrieved from http://nces.ed.gov/programs/digest/d08/index.asp

Polkinghorne, D. E. (2004). *Practice and the human sciences: The case for a judgment-based practice of care.* Albany, NY: State University of New York Press.

Public Policy Institute of California. (2007). *Immigrants in California: Just the facts.* Retrieved from http://www.ppic.org/main/publication.asp?i=221

Reason, P. (1994). Three approaches to participative inquiry. In N. K. Denzin & Y. Lincoln (Eds.), *Handbook of qualitative research.* Thousand Oaks, CA: Sage.

Reason, P., & Bradbury, H. (2001). Introduction: Inquiry and participation in search of a world worthy of human aspiration. In P. Reason & H. Bradbury (Eds.), *Handbook of action research: Participative inquiry and practice* (pp. 1–14). Thousand Oaks, CA: Sage.

Rogoff, B. (1991). *Apprenticeship in thinking: Cognitive development in social context.* New York, NY: Oxford University Press.

Rogoff, B. (1995). Observing sociocultural activity on three planes: Participatory appropriation, guided participation, and apprenticeship. In J. V. Wertsch, P. del Rio, & A. Alvarez (Eds.), *Sociocultural studies of mind* (pp. 139–164). Cambridge, UK: Cambridge University Press.

Rogoff, B. (2003). *The cultural nature of human development.* New York, NY: Oxford University Press.

Rogoff, B., Turkanis, C. G., & Bartlett, L. (2001). *Children and adults in a school community.* New York, NY: Oxford University Press.

Rumberger, R. W. (2007). California's linguistic minority public school students, 2005. *EL Facts, 9.*

Saenz, V. (2002). *Hispanic students and community colleges: A critical point for intervention* [Electronic version]. ERIC Clearinghouse for Community Colleges, ED477908. Retrieved from www.eric.ed.gov/ERICWebPortal/recordDetail?accno=ED477908

Smith, L. T. (1999). *Decolonizing methodologies: Research and indigenous peoples.* New York, NY: Palgrave.

Solorzano, D., Rivas, M., & Velez, V. (2005). Community college as a pathway to Chicana/o doctorate production. *Latino Policy & Issues Brief No. 11,* UCLA Chicano Studies Research Center.

Stringer, E. T. (1996). *Action research: A handbook for practitioners.* Thousand Oaks, CA: Sage.

Swail, S., Carbera, A., Lee, C., & Williams, A. (2005). *Latino students and the education pipeline: Part III of a three-part series*. Stafford, VA: The Educational Policy Institute.

Tharp, R. G. (1993). Institutional and social context of educational practice and reform. In E. A. Forman, N. Minick, & C. A. Stone (Eds.), *Contexts for learning: Sociocultural dynamics in children's development*. New York, NY: Oxford University Press.

Tharp, R. G., & Gallimore, R. (1988). *Rousing minds to life: Teaching, learning, and school in social context*. New York, NY: Cambridge University Press.

Valencia, R. R. (1998). *The evolution of deficit thinking: Educational thought and practice*. Bristol, PA: Falmer Press.

Valencia, R. R. (2010). *Dismantling contemporary deficit thinking: Educational thought and practice*. New York, NY: Routledge.

Vygotsky, L. S. (1978). *Mind in society: The development of higher psychological processes*. (M. Cole, V. John-Steiner, S. Scribner, & E. Souberman, Eds.). Cambridge, MA: Harvard University Press.

Vygotsky, L. S. (1987). *L. S. Vygotsky, collected works Vol. I*. (R. Rieber & A. Carton, Eds.; N. Minick, Trans.). New York, NY: Plenum. (Original work published 1934)

Wenger, E. (1998). *Communities of practice: Learning, meaning, and identity*. New York, NY: Cambridge University Press.

Wertsch, J. V. (1998). *Mind as action*. New York, NY: Oxford University Press.

Wertsch, J. V., del Rio, P., & Alvarez, A. (Eds.). (1995). *Sociocultural studies of mind*. New York, NY: Cambridge University Press.

Wheatley, T., & Wegner, D. M. (2001). Automaticity of action, Psychology. In N. J. Smelser & P. B. Baltes (Eds.), *International encyclopedia of the social and behavioral sciences* (pp. 991–993). Oxford, UK: Elsevier Science Limited.

Woodlief, B., Thomas, C., & Orozco, G. (2003). *California's gold: Claiming the promise of diversity in our community colleges*. Oakland, CA: California Tomorrow.

9

INSTITUTIONAL RESEARCHERS AS TEACHERS AND EQUITY ADVOCATES

Facilitating Organizational Learning and Change

Alicia C. Dowd, Lindsey Malcom,
Jonathan Nakamoto, and Estela Mara Bensimon

"Langley, we have a problem." That was the headline of a *New York Times* article in the summer of 2006 lamenting the Central Intelligence Agency's (CIA's) loss of capacity for generating the strategic intelligence necessary for informed policy making (Weiner, 2006). Carl W. Ford, Jr., a former assistant secretary of state for intelligence and research, was quoted as saying, "Why spend $40 billion a year to store data on hard discs that analysts can't get to? We probably use 5 percent of the data we collect on a daily basis." The article pointed out that the CIA's inability to generate knowledge from mountains of data stemmed from "an inability to ask the right questions" and a tendency toward "instant analysis" in the information age.

Institutional Researchers as Teachers and Equity Advocates: Facilitating Organizational Learning and Change

Large segments of public higher education may soon face a similar problem. Although highly selective public- and private-sector institutions are adept at analyzing data for purposes of enrollment management and tuition pricing, open-access public colleges and universities have not been particularly successful in analyzing accountability data to increase student learning outcomes (Dougherty, 2002; Dowd & Tong, 2007; Erisman & Gao, 2006). This shortcoming is less due to a lack of available data than to a lack of capacity to use data for purposes of organizational learning and transformation (Bauman, 2005; Bensimon, 2004, 2005a, 2007; Kezar, 2005; Milam, 2005). In policy settings, there has been an emphasis on creating large federal and state databases for purposes of accountability and consumer choice (Ewell, Schild, & Paulson, 2003; U.S. Department of Education, 2006), which are expected to drive improvements in college quality and student learning outcomes.

There is a real risk, however, that the mountains of data available to colleges and universities will grow, but not the "craft of inquiry" (Alford, 1998) necessary to transform information into knowledge and knowledge into the basis for improved organizational performance (Bensimon, 2007; Dowd, 2005; Dowd & Tong, 2007; Polkinghorne, 2004). This problem is likely to be especially pressing for open-access colleges, which, in comparison to the highly selective institutions and private sector peers of equivalent size, have lower levels of resources (Titus, 2006), particularly the human resources necessary to interpret data in meaningful ways. In addition, their cause is not likely to be helped by the numerous "consumer friendly" ranking and rating systems that have proliferated in the age of instant news and analysis.

In this chapter, we present a case study of the role of institutional researchers at nine community colleges engaged in the Equity Scorecard process, an institutional assessment project designed to bring about organizational learning to reduce racial and ethnic gaps in student outcomes. Inequities in student outcomes are a pressing issue for higher education. Despite a host of outreach, access, and remedial programs for "at-risk" students, attainment gaps have essentially stayed the same over the past several decades (Advisory Committee on Student Financial Assistance, 2001, 2002; Bensimon, 2007; Tierney & Hagedorn, 2002). To address the underrepresentation of low-income and minority students in higher education, many postsecondary institutional leaders are increasingly recognizing the need to engage in ongoing data analysis to measure progress in terms of reducing gaps in college access and graduation rates. But how will examining institutional data lead to actual progress in reducing educational inequities?

Certainly, publicly reporting data about minority and low-income student enrollment and outcomes can keep the pressure on for change. However, data alone are not sufficient to create equity. Instead, as is argued earlier in this volume, the Equity Scorecard process, which is a structured process that facilitates learning and change among practitioners, is an effective way to improve equity in higher education. We agree that data are an important, even critical, aspect of what is needed to accomplish that goal. But it is also important to ask: How specifically can data be used to bring about improvements in equity? We have previously argued that what is needed is a culture of inquiry in which practitioners engage in assessment practices to frame problems of institutional effectiveness in terms of equity (Bensimon, Rueda, Dowd, & Harris, 2007; Dowd, 2005; Dowd & Tong, 2007). A culture of inquiry is distinguished from a culture of evidence by placing practitioners, not data, at the center of change efforts.

In this chapter, we draw on our experiences from the Equity Scorecard project to illustrate the challenges—and potential—of using data as a tool to reduce inequities in higher education. We show that the institutional researchers played a key role in the Equity Scorecard process; they were called on to act not only as "knowledge workers and infomediaries" (Milam, 2005, p. 61), but also as teachers and equity advocates. In doing so, we demonstrate how institutional researchers more broadly can adopt the role of a teacher in helping colleagues first to make sense of data and then to use data-based knowledge to improve institutional effectiveness and student outcome equity. We describe what we learned through this project about the role of the institutional researcher in organizational learning, knowledge production, and institutional change.

In the scholarly and policy literature, the institutional researcher role has primarily been conceptualized and structured administratively in terms of the knowledge and technical skills required; institutional context; organizational functions, constraints, and needs; and strategies for improved effectiveness (Delaney, 1997; Hackman, 1983; Knight, Moore, & Coperthwaite, 1997; Peterson, 1999; Terenzini, 1999; Volkwein, 1999). A more limited number of studies have considered institutional research as a teaching role (Bagshaw, 1999) or as an "infomediary" with an important role in knowledge production (Milam, 2005). A few authors have specifically addressed, as we do, the particular power of institutional researchers to advocate social equality and reform (Darder, 1994; St. John, McKinney, & Tuttle, 2006; Terrass & Pomrenke, 1981). Therefore, our purpose in this chapter is to provide a rich portrait of institutional researchers in the roles of teacher and equity advocate. We locate the institutional researchers in our study in a social context by demonstrating how the inquiry team members, and the design of the project itself, facilitated this conceptualization of the institutional research function.

Data and Methods of the Study

We used a variety of complementary research methods based in the empirical traditions of case study (Stake, 1995), evaluation (Patton, 1990), and action research (Bensimon, Polkinghorne, Bauman, & Vallejo, 2004). There were nine teams, one at each of nine colleges participating in the project. Each college team typically had eight to ten participants, all of whom were employed at the college as an institutional researcher, an administrator, a counselor, or a faculty member. One team participated without an institutional researcher after the person in that role resigned, but two teams involved two institutional researchers, so our study focuses on ten individuals. Of these, eight were White, one was African American, and one was Asian American; six were male and four female.

One or two members of our research team of eight people attended each monthly meeting of the college teams and recorded written or audiotaped field notes. Our data collection took place primarily at the meetings of the inquiry teams. The data were recorded and managed using the qualitative data analysis software ATLAS.ti. We wrote researcher memos, categorical coding, and biweekly debriefings in research team meetings to analyze our data on an ongoing basis. The role of the institutional researcher in facilitating the discussion of the team, assisting members' understanding of the data, and responding to requests for additional data displays was of particular interest as we coded our data based on the conceptual framework, expectations, and goals of the project. We developed categories of correspondence and propositional assertions about the attitudes, beliefs, and behaviors of institutional researchers with different levels of agreement or disagreement with our project goals (Stake, 1995). We then sought confirming and disconfirming evidence for these categories and assertions and refined our interpretations based on what we found. These categorical analyses were combined with narrative analysis to create "coherent developmental accounts" (Polkinghorne, 2004, p. 15) of institutional researchers on the inquiry teams.

The project can be characterized as a design intervention, which "entail[s] both 'engineering' particular forms of learning and systematically studying those forms of learning within the context defined by the means of supporting them" (Bannan-Ritland, 2003; Cobb, Confrey, diSessa,

Lehrer, & Schauble, 2003; Design-Based Research Collective, 2003). In addition to our role as researchers, we were facilitators of the inquiry teams and were active participants in team meetings in a number of different ways. For example, we would ask questions intended to ensure that everyone on the team had the chance to understand what had been presented (even if they were too shy to ask for clarification). We offered interpretations of the data that we believed would aid the team in reconceptualizing the problem of student outcomes from the perspective of student deficits to one of institutional responsibility. And, as shown in our analyses, we suggested approaches to conducting the data analyses (to the institutional researchers) and facilitating team meetings (to the team leaders).

Using pseudonyms throughout, we present our results using thick descriptions based on our field notes to enable readers to generate naturalist generalizations (Stake, 1995). We would like institutional researchers to be able to see themselves in the settings we describe and to consider what it would mean to recast their work in the role of teacher and equity advocate. We would also like to enable college leaders to see what is required if they would like to generate "strategic intelligence" about the state of equity at their colleges.

The Institutional Researcher as Teacher

Too Difficult to Understand

It is far more difficult for practitioner audiences to take meaning from institutional data than might be expected by advocates of data-driven decision making. Take, for example, the case of Michael and the inquiry team members at Plateau Community College. Michael typically presented data by reading the numbers off the charts he produced. In general, he seemed comfortable responding to his teammates' questions regarding the data and answered readily. However, by the fourth team meeting, it became apparent that Michael had not been accurately gauging his teammates' understanding of the data. During that meeting, Katharine, a vice president at Plateau Community College, noted that the data could be misinterpreted without Michael there to explain it. A discussion ensued in which Michael attempted to clarify the misunderstanding, but Michael did not indicate during the exchange that he would alter the chart to avoid similar confusion in the future.

Not surprisingly, then, in the seventh meeting when a draft of the report to the college president had been completed, Katharine again raised an objection about the chart, saying, "Just the way it's presented right now is too difficult to understand and get your arms around it." A perplexed Michael countered by saying that he had been showing the team that chart since the start of the project. Katharine responded that "this is the first time we've actually sat down" to look closely at the chart. Later in that meeting, another teammate who was also confused stated, "But to understand [the report] is where we're having the trouble. Michael's data is presented as he understands it. We're just saying from someone who's not a statistician [it is difficult to understand]."

This case illustrates that institutional researchers cannot assume that their colleagues understand the data they present. Once his colleagues told him they did not understand the chart, despite it having been presented to them repeatedly, Michael spent a significant amount of time altering the report. During the eighth meeting, he made a point of asking the other members of the team if they were happy with the presentation of the data, showing a shift from simply presenting information to communicating with his peers.

Becoming Comfortable With Error

Misinterpretations of the data were common among our inquiry team members. In particular, we observed a great deal of confusion between interpretations of proportional shares, or the percentage of different racial-ethnic groups in a particular class or cohort (i.e., a group's slice of the pie), and participation rates, or the percentage of a particular racial or ethnic group present in a class or cohort (e.g., a graduation rate). At Fielding Community College, the willingness of the team leader, Joyce, to act as a "test case" and to offer her interpretation of the data, mistakes and all, illustrated the challenges of working in groups to inform problem framing with data.

At the team's third meeting, Joyce offered a "test case" interpretation of a graph, explicitly saying, "Okay, I'm the test case," for how well other audiences on campus would be able to understand data presented in the team's report. In fact, she misinterpreted the data, which showed the enrollment shares of each racial and ethnic group in a particular basic skills mathematics course, as an enrollment rate. Kim, the institutional researcher, then explained the proper interpretation. This exchange led another team member, Janet, to say, "That's why these columns need to be more descriptive." Janet added, "You would need a little more narrative in terms of how you interpret that in order to either apply it or understand." After Joyce's misstep in data interpretation, James, a faculty member at Fielding, also offered his interpretation of the data, which was also incorrect. Kim explained again the correct interpretation, with Janet echoing her and stating, "Once again for user friendliness, and please don't be offended," the graphs needed to be more clearly labeled.

These exchanges between Michael and Kim and their colleagues indicate to us that the reluctance of the inquiry teams to offer interpretations of the data was in part due to difficulty understanding the data displays. Joyce's confusion between enrollment shares and rates was very common among the inquiry team members in our project. It seemed that the level of information sufficient for an institutional researcher to feel comfortable with a data display was typically much more minimal than what less-experienced data users would require. When team members were willing to state their mistaken data interpretations aloud, it was helpful in that it gave the institutional researcher the opportunity to see that their initial explanations had not been effective.

Researchers who were attentive to signals of confusion or lack of understanding from their colleagues were able to adjust their presentation practices. This often came late in the project, which highlighted for us that we and others interested in using data as a key ingredient in organizational change efforts would need to be more active in the future in helping institutional researchers to see the differences between their understanding of data and that of their colleagues.

Two of the nine institutional researchers in our project were quite resistant to the idea that the data displays needed to be simplified and elaborated to serve as effective communication tools and three others expended only minimal effort to improve data displays. The tables and graphs brought to meetings seemed to overwhelm their teams, which would then spend a good part of the meetings asking for clarification of the data definitions and the sample, or, even worse, sitting passively while the institutional researcher presented the data. These five institutional researchers seemed to prefer to retain their role as data authority rather than shift into a role as a communicator or teacher.

The Reluctant Teacher

To some extent, our project created an expectation that institutional researchers would facilitate learning among inquiry team members. As a result, the majority of them were pulled, if somewhat reluctantly, into a more instructional role. (The exceptions are provided by three institutional researchers who readily accepted the role of teacher.) For example, Brian, the institutional researcher at Plateau Community College, initially viewed his role primarily as a provider of data. In one instance, when the research associate (RA) meeting with the Plateau team asked Brian to "walk the team through the data," he responded, "It's pretty clear. I've done a very thorough job of answering all these questions, and there are lots and lots of data, but in every data set African Americans are the low achievers in any outcome." The latter part of Brian's statement also reveals his personal objections to the way in which the project framed disparities in student outcomes as a matter of institutional responsibility. He emphasized instead differences in student preparation, cultural values, and goals as explanations of differences in student success.

Despite his objections to the project goals, toward the end of the project Brian began to reframe his role from one of "data provider" to "data instructor and interpreter." We believe this is due to the fact that the president appointed the members of the inquiry team and because Brian faced specific requests for help from the facilitator and other team members. In the ninth and final team meeting, Brian spent a good part of the time explaining the data to the team. He guided the team, page by page, through the tables, explaining key variables and drawing the team's attention to trends he noticed in the data. He sympathetically noted, "I know it's a lot of numbers to look at," which showed an initial awareness of the experience of the team members in encountering so much data.

Later in that meeting, Brian also called the team's attention to findings in the data that raised equity issues for the team to consider:

> The next page is probably more interesting to you because these are the excellence measures we just discussed, but they also show that equity index. The top two tables are the measure of selective institutions we were just discussing. And you'll see that African Americans are underrepresented in their transfer to selective institutions.

When a team member asked, "Say that again. . . . About whether . . . is this based on where they transferred to?" Brian confirmed that the team member was correct and also elaborated helpfully:

> Let's look at African Americans. One hundred thirty-two African Americans transferred to a four-year institution. Of those, twenty-seven went to selective institutions. For rate or percent, 20.5 percent. That Equity Index is below 0.5. Hispanics are also below equity in that measure.

As we see from the team member's follow-up comment, Brian's instruction enabled the team member to synthesize this information with statistics presented previously: "These results are very similar to what we saw [in] transfer in general, the difference between transfer intent and transfer ready."

Brian acted as more of an instructor by explaining the data, providing an alternative explanation for the sake of clarity, and then answering a team member's question regarding his explanation. After it was clear that the team member who asked the question now understood, given her statement noted previously, Brian confirmed her interpretation by saying, "Exactly." This is significant to us because interactions of this type were rare in the previous eight meetings. These findings suggest that the interactive structures of the project had an influence on Brian's practice. Although Brian continued to interpret educational inequities as a result of student characteristics and deficits, he acknowledged that the ways in which he had presented the data in the early meetings "overwhelmed the team." Over time, he also agreed to use the data template provided by the project because it was "easy, . . . intuitive, . . . [and] comfortable" for the inquiry team members to use.

The Institutional Researcher as Equity Advocate

So I'm Bringing It Up Again

Although it was clear to us that the institutional researchers in our project needed to move beyond presentation to communication, even when data were presented well and clearly labeled, our inquiry teams were reluctant to engage in discussions of equity based on college data. Here we relate how Kim, an institutional researcher at Fielding Community College, acted as an equity advocate by pressing the discussion of racial and ethnic disparities revealed in the college data. In the first three of Fielding Community College's team meetings, it was very clear to our research team that the data that had been presented to the team revealed that African American and Latina and Latino students were not doing as well at the college as their White and Asian peers. Although it was true the charts and graphs could have been labeled more clearly, these shortcomings did not obscure some glaring inequities. At the end of the second meeting, the CUE RA collaborating with the Fielding College team clearly stated a point that the team members had avoided in their discussion of the data:

> If you look across the board at first glance, even at grade point average for all the groups, there seems like there are some inequities . . . some gaps

there in terms of Asian students and White students. Their GPAs are consistently better across the board than most of the other student groups. Regardless of what chart you are looking at, if you do an eyeball comparison of grade point average, the Asian students, the Filipino, and the White students typically outperform other student groups as measured by GPA, regardless of what semester you are looking at.

The inequities that jumped off the page at our RA had not been discussed by the team, which seemed to become mired for the most part in clarifying data definitions. However, the team was able to interpret the data well enough to answer "a question to satisfy . . . anecdotal reasoning that circulates around the campus" as to the effects of late enrollment on drop-out behaviors. The team members looked closely at drop-out rates for students who had enrolled in different weeks at the beginning of the term and were able to conclude that those anecdotes were wrong: There was no clear association between the week of enrollment and a student's departure from class. We noticed that where the team members were willing to look closely at the data, they were able to make sense of it.

In contrast, the team shied away from discussion of the racial and ethnic gaps in the grade point average (GPA) data. At Fielding College's third meeting, Kim had reformatted tables into graphs and had even included the "interpretive" information requested by a team member at the previous meeting. She also pushed again, gently, to call the team's attention to the GPA gaps, pointing out the relatively low GPAs of African Americans in relation to other groups. However, as there was a great deal of data to get through, most of the meeting was spent with Kim presenting and the inquiry team listening. The team members asked a few questions for clarification, but for the most part were passive. There was very little discussion of the inequities illustrated by the data.

They were the same data presented in the previous meeting, but now in graphs rather than tables. Still the team did not seem to be moved by what they were seeing, despite the troubling implications of the data concerning the inequitable experiences of African American students at the college. The format of the data was clearly not the only factor keeping the team from discussing equity issues. Therefore, between the third and fourth meetings, Kim and the project's RA decided that Kim would not only present the graphs but also ask the team questions about what had been presented, in order to place the team members in a more active learning role. At the fourth team meeting, Kim reminded the members that they had already seen the data she was presenting in previous meetings. She projected the graph with the GPA data and said,

> We thought that we would bring this back up, the GPA indicators, because there wasn't much discussion about it at our last meeting. So I'm bringing it up again [laughter]. It seems to me that the average GPA . . . this part represents matriculating students' GPA [pointing to graph]. . . . The average GPA for female students is 2.91 and every group is at par or above that with the exception of African Americans. African American females are at 2.69, so there's a huge disparity there between African Americans and the other group with GPA. . . . So I just wanted to bring that up.

Kim's somewhat tentative approach is reflected in the group's laughter after she first said, "So I'm bringing it up again." Despite this, she continued trying out her new role of teacher and equity advocate, perhaps not expertly—we note she repeated the same expression ("So I just wanted to bring that up") that had not brought a response initially—but persistently. When the team did not respond, Kim tried again to stimulate discussion, saying, "If there are any ideas as to why this is occurring from this one group, why there is this disparity? . . . Anyone have . . . are there any ideas?" Still, she received no response. The team leader, Joyce, and the RA each took a turn. Joyce noted, "We didn't really talk about that discrepancy in our last discussion, at our last meeting, [but] there is a huge discrepancy in terms of GPA." The RA referred to the "deliverable" of the project, the team's report to the president, and asked the team to consider what to say about the disparities in GPA: "What would you like to say about [these results] in the report?"

After several more minutes of discussion about data definitions, Kim attempted again to elicit discussion. She asked, still somewhat "tentatively," as our field notes record it, "Any questions or comments?" Again, she received no response. James, a faculty member and administrator, responded not with an interpretation, but with a request for clarification regarding "where these numbers are coming from." The reluctance of the team to discuss the inequities revealed by the GPA data is significant to us. This was the third time the team had looked at these data, but the team members continued to question what the indicators measured.

They were hesitant to reach any interpretations or statement of a problem that they would feel comfortable including in a report to their campus and the college president. As noted previously, to some extent it reveals

202 CONFRONTING EQUITY ISSUES ON CAMPUS

difficulty understanding the data, but we believe it also illustrates the significant discomfort groups encounter in discussing racial and ethnic disparities in college students' experiences and outcomes. The team members may have perceived that they were presented with two unhappy options: to draw attention to poor institutional performance in helping African Americans achieve (the purposes of our project) or to draw attention to the poor performance of African Americans at the college. Instead they seemed to prefer to draw attention to imperfections in the data displays. The team moved on to look at new data without reaching any interpretation about the GPA gaps. It is quite possible that our team did not want to allow the data to feed into negative portrayals of African Americans as "low achievers," to use Brian's words, knowing that such deficit perspectives are commonly held.

An "Aha" Moment

Moving on from the GPA data, Kim presented her team with side-by-side pie charts showing the racial and ethnic distribution of students who completed basic skills courses at the college and the racial and ethnic distribution of students who were successful at the next level course, which is the first course in the curricular sequence that carries credits eligible for transfer to a four-year college. As she had at other points during this fourth team meeting, to no avail, Joyce put the equity agenda on the table:

> So the huge disparity for transferable math, I'm going to say this and you tell me if I'm wrong, is—I won't go to [speak now about] the over represented, only to the under—would be African American students, Hispanic/Latino students, and that's it. Those are the two groups where we would have some issues going on.

After some discussion, James described his understanding of the chart and asked for clarification about the sample represented. Based on requests from the team at the second meeting, the sample had been restricted to students who completed prior-level, "basic skills" courses at the college. This step was taken to show only the college's "own" students. Students who completed their basic skills courses at another college or enrolled in the transfer courses as a first-time student at the college were excluded. Looking at these side-by-side pie charts, James was powerfully struck by the data. He saw the changing share of African Americans and the very large proportion, 60 percent, who were not successful in the transfer-level class. James stated:

> Really what this shows is that there are really two groups that are . . . something is . . . something is or isn't happening that is not acceptable.

Somehow or other, [even] when African American students pass a basic skills math class, a tremendous number of them do not pass the next course. And the same is true for Hispanic/Latino. . . . When we look at the percentage of students who do not pass the next sequenced course in math, 60 percent are African American, 20 percent are Hispanic/Latino, and every other ethnic group on campus is below 10 percent. . . .[1] What's important is to figure out why. Right?

Because the first pie chart showed that the enrollment shares of African Americans and Latinas and Latinos were significantly lower than their shares of the group of students who were unsuccessful in the transfer-level course, the magnitude with which these two groups were overrepresented among unsuccessful students became very clear to him.

Joyce picked up on James's statement by indicating that these were results the group should bring to the campus, by including them in their report. Toward the close of the meeting, when Joyce asked the teams which indicators they should include in the report, James reiterated, "I'm visual, there's something about the pie chart that is pretty dramatic. . . . So in terms of making it powerful and dramatic and easily recognizable for the statement of the problem, that's a problem." Later he added, "We can just say to the campus, 'Look what we found!' We don't have to know all of the other stuff [report all the other findings] but look what we found."

This statement is significant to us because it demonstrates James's ownership of the data and his willingness to highlight equity issues as a problem. The data finally spoke to him. The long road it took to reach this point in James's understanding underscores the challenges of generating new practitioner knowledge through data analysis. It also suggests that just putting numbers in front of people is not sufficient in itself to generate new knowledge or a willingness to argue for institutional change to address inequities revealed by institutional data. Kim's and Joyce's persistence in placing equity issues on the table was also important to create a setting in which James was pushed to look at the data until he had a chance to digest them.

It is clear that Kim was willing to step into uncharted territory professionally to attempt to bring attention to the disparities she saw. Her actions helped us to see the challenges an institutional researcher would face in taking on the role of teacher and equity advocate. Although a skilled data analyst, presenter, and interpreter, Kim did not have experience as a teacher. Other members of the team were faculty members who were experienced teachers, and most had many more years of experience at the college than

Kim did. Several team members were well versed in the intricacies of certain aspects of the data, particularly concerning the enrollments within particular courses or programs in their department.

Multivariate Thinking

The charts that produced James's "aha moment" told the story of a group of students who were unequivocally the college's *own* students, successfully completing one course and moving on to the next. At that next level, racial and ethnic disparities in success rates emerged. James was willing to own the problem, it seems to us, because explanations about lack of student prepared-ness had been ruled out, or at least significantly diminished. All the students had passed the college's own course to prepare them for the transfer-level course. Because the purpose of the prior-level course was to prepare them, if they were not prepared, it was the college's problem, as we see in James's response where he stated "that's a problem." The team members decided to restrict the sample to their own students so they would not be unfairly blamed for the ineffectiveness of other community colleges or of the high schools. When the poor success rates of African American and Latina and Latino students were revealed in the data, limited to the college's own sam-ple, external explanations for the lack of success were ruled out (or at least diminished to the point where the balance of responsibility shifted).

The side-by-side pie-chart analysis dispelled, in James's mind at least, what we call "multivariate thinking," the tendency to look for explanations of disparities in student outcomes rather than to recognize the problematic nature of those disparities. Multivariate thinking can be at odds with what Bensimon (2005a, 2005b, 2007) has called "equity-mindedness." Equity-mindedness is a cognitive frame of reference for understanding disparities in student outcomes that views those problems as a matter of institutional responsibility. The equity-minded frame of reference is contrasted with "deficit thinking," which is a tendency to assume that student success gaps can be explained by characteristics ascribed to African American and Latina and Latino (and other traditionally underrepresented) students, such as low aspirations, poor academic preparation, and family values opposed to higher education.

Multivariate thinking, which we recognize as valuable in identifying the magnitude of effects of various factors on variation in student outcomes, was also associated with deficit thinking among our team members, particularly those with statistical and mathematical training. The tendency toward multi-variate thinking at times precluded the recognition of equity issues. We noted previously that Brian tended to explain differences in student out-comes based on student characteristics and stated that he was opposed to the conceptualization of equity adopted by the project. In the following state-ment, Brian used multivariate thinking to explain disparities in student out-comes. The data showed that Asian American students were succeeding at higher rates than Latinos and Latinas and African Americans, a pattern Brian attributes to "cultural values":

> What I think it informs me is that there might be some cultural differences in the goals of students. And that just on this data alone, clearly not enough to make that kind of assumption, but it's possible that some stu-dents have different goals based on their culture. For example, we might assume that Latino and African American students come here, perhaps, to improve their academic skills but not get a degree. Whereas there is a cultural bias in Asians to get a degree. Is that the kind of thinking that you get from this? For example, four out of ten Asians are behaving as if they want to get a degree and transfer where only one out of four African Ameri-cans are.

Although differences in student preparation, aspirations, and goals do exist, they are not predetermined by immutable cultural characteristics as Brian seemed to assume here. Multivariate thinking, applied consciously and unconsciously, was often used to attempt to cut down attention to equity at our team meetings. As a result, Brian's participation in our project was often uneasy. He objected to the use of simple descriptive statistics, pointing out that none were "statistically significant." He argued against disaggregating data or viewing educational inequities through the lens of race and ethnicity, supporting instead the use of socioeconomic indicators, which he argued held greater explanatory power. Finally, his political beliefs and professional authority seemed to be challenged by the project's methods and goals, and the analysis strategies he proposed would have sanitized the discourse of educational inequities by eliminating race and ethnicity from the discussion.

The team's RA therefore underscored the importance of identifying racial-based gaps. At the beginning of the project, Brian actively countered the project's goals by providing indicators of student outcomes in a format that made comparisons only "within group" instead of across groups, as structured by the project data analysis template. In Brian's presentation, the data for each racial and ethnic group were presented on their own pages, essentially thwarting the goal of helping the team gain a better understanding of racial and ethnic disparities in student outcomes. The RA asked, "I was wondering, is there a way of looking at [the indicators] all together, like for each of the variables, rather than on separate sheets?" Brian responded:

> We were concerned if we were making accurate comparisons between groups because we know that groups are dissimilar in their SES [socioeconomic status], academic preparation, high school, etc. So these are first described as a within group comparison and I understand the natural desire for people to take one variable and go across.

The facilitator responded to Brian that the point of disaggregating data by race and ethnicity was to make disparities between groups easier to see and asked that he present data to the team using the data template provided by the project. His discomfort with that approach stemmed from his disagreement with the project's conceptualization of equity and from his statistical sense that comparisons of differences in student outcomes by racial and ethnic group were inappropriate if statistical controls were not included for socioeconomic status, academic preparation, and other factors. He objected to the statistically simpler, but in his view politically charged, goal of demonstrating the magnitude of racial and ethnic disparities in outcomes.

However, due to the concerns of some team members that Brian's approach would preclude the analysis of disparities in outcomes of different racial and ethnic groups, the team did not adopt the "within-group" analysis strategy. Ultimately, as we noted previously, Brian did express some appreciation of the "simple" and "intuitive" benefits of using simple descriptive statistics to demonstrate differences in student success. We attributed this to the fact that he was faced with a request for help from his team members who needed assistance to understand the tables and graphs he brought to the team meetings.

Inquiry Teams as Incubators of Strategic Intelligence About Equity

Keeping Equity Issues on the Table

Brian's decision to follow the approach of the project did not reflect a change in his thinking concerning the project's conceptualization of equity. For example, he raised the political specter of "quotas," stemming from the project's use of proportional representation as the benchmark for equity. Though noting his discomfort, he eventually indicated, "I'm fine with doing it any way you like. If it informs policy and it's useful," essentially agreeing to participate in the project despite his disapproval.

These developments were significant to us because they suggest that when leaders commit a college to equity as a goal, they can take a first step toward creating a culture of inquiry concerning racial and ethnic inequities in student outcomes. Brian continued to hold his beliefs, but by bringing data to the team in his professional role as institutional researcher, he enabled a broader discussion of those data and the introduction of different perspectives on outcome inequities. His personal agreement was not necessary for him to play a professional role in allowing counter-narratives to begin to emerge.

This counter-narrative was largely provided by us as facilitators of action research at Brian's college (see chapter 10). However, we note that even at the early meetings when Brian was bringing the within-group data to the team, his team members made attempts to keep the issue of equity on the table. For example, at the third meeting Brian brought what he described as "stacks of data" organized to show within-group differences. Instead of guiding the team members through these tables, he waited for them to examine the data on their own.

Other team members therefore stepped in and discussed how they went about examining the data to make across-group comparisons. The team leader described taking apart the large, stapled packet of tables and placing them in an order that made sense to him. Another team member described how she selected one variable and went through the data sheets to see what gaps existed among the racial and ethnic student groups. By convening the inquiry team, we created a setting for data-based inquiry, despite the fact the team members initially had little support from their institutional researcher.

Coconstructed Understanding of Equity

By the tenth meeting of the Fielding College inquiry team, in order to get team members more involved in the data interpretation, Joyce, Kim, and the RA had decided to ask several members of the team to play the role of "reporter" for various segments of the data. The reporter's role was to facilitate the discussion of their data segment and write the text for that section of the report. In the tenth meeting, where the team was focused on data concerning students' preparedness for transfer to four-year colleges, James was the designated reporter. At the beginning of the meeting, Joyce turned the role of facilitator over to him, saying, "So at this point, I tend to become a participatory researcher, because James is now going to lead his area on transfer, along with Kim, presenting the transfer data."

Kim got the meeting started by presenting the data, walking the team through the first couple of graphs. She spoke at length, giving a fair amount of attention to defining the samples and comparison groups. Over the length of the project, she consistently integrated improvements to the data displays, based on what she had learned from previous reactions from the team, as well as new teaching strategies. At this meeting she informed the team that after explaining the first few slides she would ask for the team members' active participation by having them explain the data presented. After she described the first slides, several team members, including James, in his role as reporter, asked numerous questions about the data and how they were defined. After this discussion, Kim turned to a new slide and asked if some-one would like to "take a shot at reading this one?" At first no one answered, so she said she would do it, but before she did Jose interjected

> Jose: I'm not sure. What are you asking?
> Joyce: To read the slide.
> Jose: To read it?
> Joyce: So we can all . . .
> Jose: Oh, I don't mind reading. . . . Oh, what does it mean?
> RA: What it means. What is the information present [in] this . . .
> Joyce: Can we look at it for a second, before we . . . ?
> RA: Yeah, definitely.
> Mariana: So what you're saying is 17 percent of matriculating population
>   is Asian and that 21 percent of them have completed half . . . 11 and a
>   half units of transferable work?
> Kim: OK, you're close.

Kim then went on to clarify a finer point about the data. What is significant to us about this exchange is the change in the nature of the interactions from the early team meetings, in which Kim presented slide after slide of data and team members primarily asked questions to clarify data definitions. Here Kim asks them to read the slide and the group slows down to take a minute to look at what is displayed. Two people respond positively to the invitation to read the slide, with one ultimately doing so.

In and of itself, this may seem like a fairly unremarkable incident. How-ever, in the context of our data, in which we have observed nine inquiry teams involved in data discussion over an average of ten meetings per team (i.e., over ninety two-hour meetings), we highlight this as significant. Due to the highly specified nature of student progression data and definitions, practitioners are hesitant to offer interpretations of such data outside explanations given to them by the data authority, typically the institutional researcher.

James was also very active in interpreting the data and we note how he developed in his capacity to discuss data. In earlier meetings, he typically qualified his questions and comments with statements such as, "Maybe because it's not my strong suit dealing with statistics and numbers," and "I get lost when I look at data. The interpretation does not leap off the page." In the following excerpt, which is part of a longer passage in which he interpreted the data under review by the team, he still turns to Kim for support (saying "help me out here, boss") but forges ahead much more confidently than he had previously:

> So it seems to me, just off the top of my head, that a student who's taking . . . and help me out here, boss . . . transfer units, but not English or math, is less likely to transfer than the student who has the units, but has one of the math or English because what they do is they avoid the math and English and if they've jumped into that pool, then it's much more likely that they're going to get the unit criteria than if they just have . . . they circle around getting the units, but they avoid the two tough gateway subjects.

This meeting is also significant to us because James moved beyond data interpretation to strategic thinking about the use of the data in communicating with the campus. We also are struck by the way in which the interpretation of the data was coconstructed by the team at this meeting in ways that enabled James to interject a strategic, "big-picture" focus on how to communicate the results to the campus and Kim and Joyce to interject an equity-minded perspective on the importance of reporting transfer rates to selective universities.

At this tenth meeting, the team members were discussing the transfer data and whether they should set a threshold of 5 percent before they treated a disparity in participation among racial-ethnic groups as a gap. James said he did not think they should adopt such a strategy, because "you start to have a whole bunch of difficulty about where [to] draw the line between parity and [a group being] underrepresented." He argued that it would be more useful to focus on the group where the "discrepancy is the broadest." James also talked about the data in terms of the story it can tell. As the following excerpt shows, he related what he was seeing in the numbers to his experience as a faculty member and how he goes about counseling students:

> What I'm thinking about is all this data is a reflection of what real life is and what happens in real life is you sit with a student who's been going here for a long time and then they say, "Oh, am I close to an [Associate's degree] or whatever?" And you say, "You're close to transferring." So we don't introduce the subject of transferring to a UC or transferring to [a selective university]. . . . [W]e just introduce the subject of transfer, "Have you ever thought about transferring?" And many of our students haven't even thought about that, and so that's the important part . . . to expand their scope or their vision or their dream into transfer.

James was not seeing the importance of counseling African American and Latina and Latino students to transfer to selective universities. His view was based on his experiences in talking with his students. At this point, Kim and Joyce contributed to the discussion. They were uncomfortable letting the issue of disparities in access to selective institutions be left out of the report. As shown in the following excerpt, Kim echoed a suggestion posed initially by Joyce that they at least put the data about transfer to selective institutions into an appendix of the report, where it would be available for everyone to see. Kim pointed out:

> Latinos and African Americans are not really transferring to [selective universities]. They're disproportionately transferring to [less selective universities]. . . . So there are disparities. Asians are transferring more to [selectives] and not transferring to [less selectives] and the same for White kids. . . . So I think that there is some distinction, but we don't have to go on this level of detail and depth probably not at this point is what I'm hearing from everyone, but to state that we're seeing ultimately it ends up there are disparities amongst our students.

Kim, while stating that she would agree with Joyce's proposed compromise, actually managed to shift the discussion by calling the team's attention to the data. When the RA pointed out that they still needed some data for another section of their report, focused on indicators of excellence in student outcomes, James, Joyce, and Kim agreed that the data about disparities in transfer to selective institutions should be included in that section.

We find it striking in these data that the "strategic intelligence" of the group was coconstructed among the team members, with James inserting the initial emotional component of the equity issue by talking about their role in expanding the "scope or vision" of their students, Kim calling their attention to the disparities shown by the data, and Joyce playing a negotiating role by proposing a friendly amendment (placing the data in an appendix) to James's stated strategy for reporting the data.

By placing James in the role of reporter, the project helped support the development of such strategic intelligence, a focus on the big picture. Because James was not an institutional researcher, not immersed in the data the way Kim was, he treated the results more readily as a communication tool. He cut away detail in a way that Kim was not inclined to do in his interest in telling a story. Kim's role in bringing him to this level of confidence in discussing the data was clearly evident to us. Month after month, she brought the data to the team meetings, presented it, and proceeded to successively place more and more of the task of interpretation in the hands of her inquiry team members. In this way, she became a coconstructor of knowledge that could contribute in significant ways to organizational learning.

Implications

Data are viewed in many accountability systems as the primary drivers of institutional accountability and change (see, e.g., U.S. Department of Education, 2006). Yet data, like other types of resources, are not "self-acting" to bring about improvements in practice (Cohen, Raudenbush, & Ball, 2003). Individuals must interpret and act on them (Alford, 1998). Therefore, specific and effective approaches to using data to promote organizational and individual learning must be developed to address the longstanding and inequitable gaps in student achievement. The institutional researcher will be a central figure in attempts to integrate data into decision-making and improved practice. The findings of this study, therefore, have implications for conceptualizing and structuring the institutional researcher role to include a teaching and organizational change function. This implies that the skills of individuals employed in institutional research offices must be inclusive of those with knowledge of pedagogy and adult learning.

In presenting our findings, we focused in particular on the case of Kim, a researcher at Fielding Community College. Kim's case was featured for three reasons. First, Kim readily accepted the role of teacher and equity advocate. Because she was inexperienced in those roles, she welcomed and acted on suggestions from us as facilitators. Therefore, we were able to observe how the different teaching strategies Kim adopted played out in the inquiry team setting.

Second, the Fielding College team included a faculty member, James, who often talked about how he liked to learn and what he understood, or didn't, when looking at the data. Therefore, it is possible to see changes in James's participation and an evolution in his data-based knowledge during the yearlong span of the project. We observe two critical incidents that occurred through interaction between Kim and James, at points when Kim adopted new teaching strategies. Finally, Kim consistently received assistance from Joyce, the team leader. With Kim and Joyce, as well as the team's RA, consistently raising equity issues throughout the project, we are able to see the team's responses to these issues. In addition, the collaboration between Kim and Joyce helps us to demonstrate the social construction of beliefs about equity.

Toward the end of the project, Kim's adoption of an active learning strategy put James in the role of team "reporter," in charge of facilitating discussion, and subsequent reporting, of the college's transfer data. Although initially self-deprecating in regard to his data analysis capabilities, by the tenth meeting, we see James leading the data discussion and advocating particular strategies for presenting the findings to the broader community. At this point, as we highlighted, he was engaged not only in data analysis and knowledge creation, but in the development of strategic intelligence as well.

Kim played a role in this transformation by carefully preparing the data in graphic form with accompanying text and by taking time to explain data definitions and terms. She also willingly handed over the role of data interpreter and authority to James, while remaining at the ready to assist him when he ran into difficulty understanding the data. This in many ways is the definition of a good teacher, someone who uses different strategies to find out what the "pupils" know or do not know to guide their learning and move them on the path to self-guided learning. Therefore, the Fielding College case provides a model for understanding how to structure the interactions of institutional researchers and campus committees formally or informally convened as "inquiry teams" in order to produce strategic intelligence about the steps needed to reduce inequities in student outcomes at a college.

Notes

1. The magnitude of these numbers is accurate, but they have been adjusted slightly so they do not match the data of any one of the participating colleges.

References

Advisory Committee on Student Financial Assistance. (2001, February). *Access denied: Restoring the nation's commitment to equal educational opportunity.* Washington, DC: Author.

Advisory Committee on Student Financial Assistance. *Empty promises: The myth of college access in America.* Washington, DC: Author.

Alford, R. R. (1998). *The craft of inquiry.* New York, NY: Oxford University Press.

Bagshaw, M. (1999, winter). Teaching institutional research to the learning-inhibited institution. *New Directions for Institutional Research, 104,* 73–82.

Bannan-Ritland, B. (2003). The role of design in research: The Integrative Learning Design framework. *Educational Researcher, 32*(1), 21–24.

Bauman, G. L. (2005). Promoting organizational learning in higher education to achieve equity in educational outcomes. In A. Kezar (Ed.), *Organizational learning in higher education* (Vol. 131). San Francisco, CA: Jossey-Bass.

Bensimon, E. M. (2004, January/February). The diversity scorecard: A learning approach to institutional change. *Change,* 45–52.

Bensimon, E. M. (2005a). Closing the achievement gap in higher education: An organizational learning perspective. In A. Kezar (Ed.), *Organizational learning in higher education* (Vol. 131). San Francisco, CA: Jossey-Bass.

Bensimon, E. M. (2005b). *Equality as a fact, equality as a result: A matter of institutional accountability* (Commissioned Paper). Washington, DC: American Council on Education.

Bensimon, E. M. (2007). The underestimated significance of practitioner knowledge in the scholarship of student success. *The Review of Higher Education, 30*(4), 441–469.

Bensimon, E. M., Polkinghorne, D. E., Bauman, G., & Vallejo, E. (2004). Doing research that makes a difference. *The Journal of Higher Education, 75*(1), 104–126.

Bensimon, E. M., Rueda, R., Dowd, A. C., & Harris, F. (2007). Accountability, equity, and practitioner learning and change. *Metropolitan, 18*(3), 28–45.

Cobb, P., Confrey, J., diSessa, A., Lehrer, R., & Schauble, L. (2003). Design experiments in educational research. *Educational Researcher, 32*(1), 9–13.

Cohen, D. K., Raudenbush, S. W., & Ball, D. L. (2003). Resources, instruction, and research. *Educational Evaluation and Policy Analysis, 25*(2), 119–142.

Darder, A. (1994, Spring). Institutional research as a tool for cultural democracy. *New Directions for Institutional Research, 81,* 21–34.

Delaney, A. M. (1997). The role of institutional research in higher education: Enabling researchers to meet new challenges. *Research in Higher Education, 38*(1), 1–16.

Design-Based Research Collective. (2003). Design-based research: An emerging paradigm for educational inquiry. *Educational Researcher, 32*(1), 5–8.

Dougherty, K. J. (2002, April 1–5). *Performance accountability and community colleges: Forms, impacts, and problems.* Paper presented at the American Educational Research Association, New Orleans, LA.

Dowd, A. C. (2005). *Data don't drive: Building a practitioner-driven culture of inquiry to assess community college performance* (Research Report). Indianapolis, IN: Lumina Foundation for Education.

Dowd, A. C., & Tong, V. P. (2007). Accountability, assessment, and the scholarship of "best practice." In J. C. Smart (Ed.), *Handbook of higher education* (Vol. 22, pp. 57–119). New York, NY: Springer.

Erisman, W., & Gao, L. (2006). *Making accountability work: Community colleges and statewide higher education accountability systems.* Washington, DC: Institute for Higher Education Policy.

Ewell, P. T., Schild, P. R., & Paulson, K. (2003). *Following the mobile student: Can we develop the capacity for a comprehensive database to assess student progression?* Lumina Foundation for Education Research Report: National Center for Higher Education Management Systems.

Hackman, J. D. (1983). Seven maxims for institutional research: Applying cognitive theory and research. *Research in Higher Education, 18*(2), 195–208.

Kezar, A. (Ed.). (2005). *Organizational learning in higher education* (Vol. 131). San Francisco, CA: Jossey-Bass.

Knight, W. E., Moore, M. E., & Coperthwaite, C. A. (1997). Institutional research: Knowledge, skills, and perceptions of effectiveness. *Research in Higher Education, 38*(4), 419–433.

Milam, J. (2005). Organizational learning through knowledge workers and infomediaries. In A. Kezar (Ed.), *Organizational learning in higher education* (Vol. 131). San Francisco, CA: Jossey-Bass.

Patton, M. Q. (1990). *Qualitative evaluation and research methods.* Newbury Park, CA: Sage.

Peterson, M. W. (1999, Winter). The role of institutional research: From improvement to redesign. *New Directions in Institutional Research, 104,* 83–103.

Polkinghorne, D. E. (2004). *Practice and the human sciences: The case for a judgment-based practice of care.* Albany, NY: State University of New York Press.

Stake, R. E. (1995). *The art of case study research.* Thousand Oaks, CA: Sage.

St. John, E. P., McKinney, J. S., & Tuttle, T. (2006, Summer). Using action inquiry to address critical challenges. *New Directions for Institutional Research, 130,* 63–76.

Terenzini, P. T. (1999, Winter). On the nature of institutional research and the knowledge and skills it requires. *New Directions for Institutional Research, 104,* 21–29.

Terrass, S., & Pomrenke, V. (1981). The institutional researcher as change agent. *New Directions for Institutional Research, 1981*(32), 73–85.

Tierney, W. G., & Hagedorn, L. S. (Eds.). (2002). *Increasing access to college: Extending possibilities for all students.* Albany, NY: State University of New York Press.

Titus, M. A. (2006). Understanding college degree completion of students with low socioeconomic status: The influence of the institutional financial context. *Research in Higher Education, 47*(4), 371–398.

U.S. Department of Education. (2006). *A test of leadership: Charting the future of U.S. higher education.* Washington, DC: Authors

Volkwein, J. F. (1999, Winter). The four faces of institutional research. *New Directions for Institutional Research, 104*, 9–19.

Weiner, T. (2006, May 14). Langley, we have a problem. *New York Times*, p. 4.1.

IO

THE MEDIATIONAL MEANS OF ENACTING EQUITY-MINDEDNESS AMONG COMMUNITY COLLEGE PRACTITIONERS

Estela Mara Bensimon and Frank Harris III

One of the most critical challenges facing institutions of higher education in the twenty-first century is overcoming their limited capacity to produce equitable educational outcomes for African American and Latina and Latino students. We believe that a significant, but often overlooked, aspect of the problem is the inadequacy of practitioners' knowledge and practices that decrease their effectiveness with particular students. Our observations of college practitioners in a variety of action-oriented inquiry activities designed by researchers at the Center for Urban Education (CUE) demonstrate an urgent need for developing funds of knowledge that are grounded in local understandings of racial inequalities in educational outcomes and the belief that their elimination is an institutional responsibility (Bensimon, 2007).

The Mediational Means of Enacting Equity-Mindedness Among Community College Practitioners

According to Polkinghorne (2004), practitioners are not "locked into their socially transmitted backgrounds" and they can change or expand their practical knowledge by engaging in reflective inquiry. The data for this chapter come from *Equity for All: Institutional Responsibility for Student Success* (EFA), a project that was designed as a yearlong intervention (Cobb, Confrey, diSessa, Lehrer, & Schauble, 2003) to engage practitioners in an extended reflective inquiry activity and facilitate their development of equity-minded practical knowledge that they draw on when making judgments about students (Polkinghorne, 2004). Essentially, we created a structure and process to engage practitioners in situated learning activities that focused on making racial inequalities in educational outcomes visible and openly discussed.

Previous publications have described the background and specifics of EFA (and its predecessor, the Diversity Scorecard) and have described in detail the theory of action, research methods, and effect on campus teams and individual participants (Bensimon, 2004, 2007; Bensimon, Polkinghorne, Bauman, & Vallejo, 2004; Bensimon, Rueda, Dowd, & Harris, 2007; Harris & Bensimon, 2007). EFA has three goals for the practitioners who are engaged in the project: (a) to develop awareness of race-based inequalities in educational outcomes; (b) to learn to interpret race-based inequalities in educational outcomes through the lens of equity; and (c) to view inequalities in outcomes as a problem of individual and collective responsibility that calls for new knowledge, practices, and policies.

In this chapter we focus on two EFA community colleges to illustrate the mediational means (Scollon, 2001; Tharp & Gallimore, 1988) through which we facilitate the three goals of the project.

Theoretical Perspectives on Practitioner Learning and Change

A fundamental aspect of EFA is that the improvement of postsecondary educational outcomes for African American and Latina and Latino students depends on practitioners becoming equity-minded, a concept discussed in more detail in the organizational learning and the critical race discourse analysis sections of this theoretical framework. The practitioner-oriented activities of the project as well as the research methods to document the process and outcomes are multidisciplinary and reflect the diverse theoretical and methodological backgrounds of the lead researchers. The dominant theoretical and analytical themes undergirding the project are practice theory, as recently elaborated by Donald Polkinghorne (2004) in relation to the caring professions; sociocultural theory, as elaborated by neo-Vygotskian scholars (Forman, Minick, & Stone, 1993; Lave & Wenger, 1991; Moll, 1990; Rogoff, 1991; Rogoff, Turkanis, & Bartlett, 2001; Tharp & Gallimore, 1988;

Wenger, 1998; Wertsch, 1998), principles of organizational learning (Argyris, 1991; Argyris & Schön, 1996), and critical theories of race and discourse analysis (Pollock, 2001; West, 1993).

Practice Theory

According to Polkinghorne (2004), the everyday practices of professionals are guided by socially and culturally acquired knowledge that functions below the level of consciousness. The premise of the EFA project is that institutional practitioners have been socialized to expect autonomous and self-regulating students who take responsibility for their own learning. Consequently, the lower rates of success that are experienced by African American and Latina and Latino students, regardless of institutional selectivity, are far more likely to be attributed to students' individual characteristics or experiences than to educational practices or institutional culture. Attributing inequalities to students' academic preparation, motivation, help-seeking behaviors, or engagement casts them as predictable and unsolvable. Consequently, EFA was designed as an inquiry activity to make racial disparities in routine educational outcomes visible to practitioners and help them learn to interpret disparities as unnatural racial inequalities whose existence and elimination require practitioners and institutional leaders to assume collective responsibility. Thus, the aim is to create a structure and processes that enable practitioners to recognize the need for new knowledge and practices.

Sociocultural Theory

To facilitate the development of equity-minded practical knowledge we drew on the sociocultural idea that (a) learning is social, (b) learning is facilitated by assisted performance that is responsive, (c) learning is mediated by cultural tools and artifacts, and (d) learning takes place in communities of practice and is indexed by changes in participation within these communities. The primary means of implementing these principles is to convene practitioners who are involved in an institution's formal learning systems or who are viewed as key actors in informal institutional networks. These practitioners form a community of practice that is referred to as an "evidence" or "inquiry" team. Learning in the evidence teams is mediated by a "data tool" that facilitates the examination of disaggregated data on educational outcomes and helps participants discover the nature and extent of racial and ethnic student outcome inequities. Practitioners' analysis, interpretation, and explanation of the racial inequalities are expressed in the naturally occurring talk (Perakyla, 2005) that goes on among the team members as they sift through data tables. Although we cannot presume to deduce the practices of instructors, counselors, or administrators from their sensemaking conversations, what is said as well as not said about racial inequalities indexes how success (and lack of it) in educational outcomes is produced (Pollock, 2001).

Although most approaches to learning regard it as an individual accomplishment (or failure) that takes place "between the ears," a basic assumption of sociocultural perspectives is that learning is fundamentally a social process. From this theoretical perspective, learning is predicated on a collaborative relationship that allows the learner and "more competent others" to negotiate understanding, usually through discussion, sharing ideas, questioning, and other mediational means. Vygotsky (1978, 1987) contended that learning occurs as individuals engage in culturally meaningful, productive activity with the assistance of these "more competent others," who may be a teacher, peer, sibling, parent, or colleague.

Sociocultural theories place great emphasis on the importance of mediation in learning processes, especially in regard to higher-order thinking. A strong focus of this perspective is how cultural practices and cultural resources mediate the development of thinking and learning. A major concern is to understand how culture, like other tools and artifacts, mediates thinking. Practitioners have been socialized into particular cultural practices, including language and other artifacts that become tools for thinking and interacting with others (Bensimon, 2007). We know the world through symbolic mediation, such as when we categorize people into ethnic, gender, or socioeconomic categories. However, in other instances our understanding is not automatic but is based on constructed and shared meanings built up over time and in specific cultural contexts. An example of this is how we analyze data on student outcomes. As indicated previously, practitioners in higher education have attributed meanings to race-based inequalities that make them appear natural. Accordingly, in EFA the intervention consists of understanding and promoting equity-minded learning by introducing tools, artifacts, and cultural practices that reveal established meanings and facilitate the making of new ones.

Sociocultural theorists contend that learning is a socially constructed phenomenon that is created collectively through individuals' interaction and participation in a variety of social contexts—or learning communities (Wenger, 1998). Learning communities are created and maintained by way of participants' collective action and interaction toward a "purposeful endeavor" (Wenger, 1998). Thus, within a given learning community, some knowledge, or ways of knowing, will be valued and prioritized above others.

These communities of practice help shape what Gallimore and Goldenberg (2001) describe as cultural models, or shared mental schema or normative understandings of how the world works, or ought to work, including what is valued and ideal, what settings should be enacted or avoided, who should participate, the rules of interaction, and the purpose of interactions.

Organizational Learning

Sociocultural theories suggest that individuals learn and change as a consequence of collaborative engagement in a productive activity. Organizational theories of learning suggest that there are different types of learning and that not all learning results in transformative change. In fact, they suggest that most learning within organizations consists of single-loop learning, whereas change—whether at the individual or institutional level—requires double-loop learning (Argyris & Schön, 1996). Single-loop learning can be understood as operational learning that results in the revision of existing practices or the development of new ones (Kim, 1993). In contrast, double-loop learning is more akin to conceptual learning, which results in the creation of new frameworks and ways of looking at familiar problems (Kim, 1993). The difference between single-loop and double-loop learning is that the former encourages individuals to view a problem functionally and search for structural or programmatic solutions, whereas in the latter learning entails the ability to reflect on a problem from within, in relation to one's own values, beliefs, and practices (Coburn, 2003). The major distinction is that the single-loop learner locates the problem externally and seeks to change others. Conversely, the double-loop learner is more apt to focus attention on the root causes of a problem and self-changes that need to be made in attitudes, values, beliefs, and practices to bring about enduring results (Bauman, 2002). Looking inward is the capacity to reflect on how practices (also beliefs and expectations) at the individual and institutional levels produce racial inequalities.

In particular, according to Argyris (1991), individuals "must learn how the very way they go about defining and solving problems can be a source of the problems in its own right" (p. 2). Argyris maintains that highly skilled professionals are very good at single-loop but bad at double-loop learning. The explanation he gives for this counterintuitive claim is,

> Because many professionals are almost always successful at what they do, they rarely experience failure. And because they have rarely failed, they

have never learned how to learn from failure. So whenever their single-loop learning strategies go wrong, they become defensive, screen out criticism, and put the "blame" on anyone and everyone but themselves. In short, their ability to learn shuts down precisely at the moment they need it most. (p. 4)

The development of equity-mindedness is a double-loop learning problem because it requires the willingness of practitioners and institutional leaders (a) to disaggregate data on student outcomes by race and ethnicity as a routine and necessary practice to self-assess progress toward equity in educational outcomes, (b) to identify equity in educational outcomes as an essential indicator of institutional performance and quality, and (c) to assume responsibility for the elimination of unequal results.

Double-loop learning (Argyris 1991, 1994; Argyris & Schön, 1996) that reflects equity-mindedness is likely to be evidenced in:

1. Changing the interpretation of racial disparities in educational outcomes, from simply detecting the problem to questioning the values and beliefs that shape the way in which the problem is being articulated
2. Willing to reveal inequalities in outcomes rather than hide them (e.g., making information public)
3. Becoming aware of how racial and cultural assumptions, stereotypes, and biases are embedded in one's everyday actions
4. Discussing openly the emotional or value-laden aspects of race and racism

Critical Race and Discourse Analysis

In the context of the EFA project, achieving equity means achieving equal educational outcomes for college students from racial and ethnic groups that have a history of enslavement, colonization, or oppression in or by the United States, relative to groups that have not experienced such conditions. "Equity-mindedness" is a multidimensional theoretical construct derived from concepts of fairness, social justice, and human agency articulated in several disciplines, including critical race theory, feminist theory, and critical discourse analysis.[1] In essence, equity-minded individuals are more aware of the sociohistorical context of exclusionary practices and racism in higher education and the effect of power asymmetries on opportunities and outcomes for African Americans and Latinas and Latinos. Individuals who are

222 CONFRONTING EQUITY ISSUES ON CAMPUS

equity-minded attribute unequal outcomes to institution-based dysfunctions. Whereas deficit-minded (Valencia, 1998) individuals construe unequal outcomes as originating from student characteristics, equity-minded individuals reflect on the roles they and their colleagues play and the responsibility they share for helping students succeed.

Equity for All: Background of the Project

EFA involved nine community colleges in southern, northern, and central California. The participating colleges were selected because they met one or more of the following criteria:

- The percentage of enrolled Latino and Latina students was 25 percent or greater.
- The enrollment of African American students exceeded the California Community College systemwide average of 7 percent.
- The enrollment of Native American students exceeded the systemwide average of 1 percent.
- The total enrollment of non-Caucasian students was 50 percent or greater.

Upon agreement to participate in the EFA project, the presidents of the nine colleges were asked to create a campus "evidence team" (sometimes also referred to as an "inquiry team") that included an institutional researcher and an individual designated as team leader. We expected the team leaders, in addition to having the interpersonal skills to facilitate collegial conversations and encourage the questioning of taken-for-granted knowledge, would have easy access to their presidents and keep them informed and engaged throughout the project.

To assist the presidents in the formation of their teams, we gave them basic guidelines. One guideline was to include influential faculty members, particularly from the English and mathematics departments. These faculty members should be "boundary-spanners," such as administrative leaders, who served on important campuswide committees such as retention, strategic planning, and so on, and are well situated to "spread" what they learned about equity in educational outcomes to other groups. We also recommended that the team include individuals with different opinions about issues such as affirmative action, the practice of disaggregating data by race, and the concept of equity in educational outcomes.

The nine teams had eighty-nine members, most of whom were women (67 percent). White ($n = 29$) and Unknown ($n = 25$) were the largest racial and ethnic groups, followed by African American ($n = 16$), Latina and Latino ($n = 14$), and Asian American ($n = 5$). Faculty members consisted of the largest group ($n = 29$), which is unusual for projects of this kind;[2] the second largest group ($n = 12$) were counselors. The teams included nine vice presidents and deans of academic affairs, and twelve institutional researchers. The other members were in student services or other administrative positions.

The EFA project lasted from June 2005 to July 2006. During this period there were 91 two-hour team meetings that took place across the nine teams. At the conclusion of the project each team completed an institutional report on its findings and presented it to various groups, including trustees, presidents' senior staff, academic senates, and English and mathematics departments, and in specially organized retreats and professional development activities.

The colleges and team members were not compensated for their participation, and the time they dedicated to the project was voluntary. The major benefit to the colleges was access to new inquiry methods and tools that enabled them to transform existing data into new and useful knowledge. We theorized that not compensating the EFA team members or colleges, as is typically done in similar projects, increased the likelihood that the work would continue after the project came to an end.

To accomplish the three goals of the project—awareness of racial inequalities, equity-minded interpretations, and the assumption of institutional responsibility for their solution—we created an activity setting that involved teams of practitioners in the analysis and interpretation of routine student outcome data disaggregated by race and ethnicity. The culmination of the activity was the completion of an Equity Scorecard that consists of four perspectives: academic pathways, retention and persistence, transfer readiness, and excellence. The teams, with guided assistance from a CUE researcher, selected numerical indicators and goals for each of the four perspectives. For example, "the percentage of first-time students, by racial and ethnic categories, who transfer to the UC [University of California] within three years," was an indicator of excellence selected by several of the participating colleges. Similarly, "increasing transfer to the UC among African Americans within three years by a specified percentage" could be an excellence goal.[3]

The construction of the Equity Scorecard consisted of a series of mediated actions (Scollon, 2001), for example, completing the vital signs data tables, collaborative sensemaking, asking for more data to answer new questions, creating indicators to populate the Equity Scorecard framework, writing and editing reports, making campus presentations on the project, participating in the teams' monthly meetings, participating in training sessions, and so on.

Sociocultural researchers are uniquely concerned with the use of tools and mediators in specific contexts and in understanding and promoting learning. These tools and artifacts enable new meaning making, in essence helping to "re-mediate" one's understanding. Unlike the traditional notion of remediation, which focuses on the amelioration of specific deficits, the notion of *re-mediation* refers to changing the nature and type of mediation in order to promote the creation of new understandings and knowledge, for example, equity-minded interpretations of data (Rueda & Marquez, 2007).

In this chapter, we describe the mediational means we introduced into the project to facilitate equity-minded analysis, interpretation, and explanation of race group–specific unequal outcomes. We illustrate the mediational means by providing excerpts from conversations among team members within two of the EFA campuses. Three questions frame our discussion of mediational means:

1. What were the mediational means of facilitating equity-mindedness among practitioners?
2. How were the mediational means of equity-mindedness enacted and by whom?
3. In what ways did participants respond to the mediational means of equity-mindedness?

Cultural and Social Mediational Means of Facilitating Equity-Mindedness

In the context of EFA, the "mediational means" are the social and cultural processes (and other members of the teams) through which EFA brings about new learning about race-based disparities in outcomes at the participating colleges. The mediational means include artifacts like the Scorecard; the team meetings; and the questions, comments, and feedback that are exchanged within the team meetings. As such, mediation is what produces the learning, but it is not learning in and of itself. Sociocultural theorists contend that all action and learning are mediated by language, by interaction with others, and by one's own thoughts and feelings. In essence, EFA served to "re-mediate" learning that had already taken place by assisting practitioners in developing new ways to think about racial inequities in student outcomes at their institutions. Five mediational means were enacted in the EFA project to facilitate equity-mindedness among team members: (a) equity-minded discourse, (b) guided analysis of data on educational outcomes, (c) criteria for the composition of the campus teams, (d) artifacts and tools, and (e) activity settings. In the sections that follow, we elaborate further on each of these mediational means and demonstrate them with qualitative data from the EFA team meetings.

Equity-Minded Discourse

Deficit and diversity talk are ways of discussing racial and ethnic minorities in higher education. For example, it is not uncommon for practitioners and researchers to interpret the consistency of unequal success among some racial and ethnic groups in the language of deficit. The discourse of deficit can be compassionate (e.g., "These students have many personal responsibilities that take precedence over school") or judgmental (e.g., "These students don't take advantage of all the resources the college provides"). It is also not unusual for practitioners to construe racial and ethnic minorities in the language of diversity: "We [the college] are like the U.N."

The discourses of deficit and diversity are more often than not used in well-intended ways; nevertheless, they can be disadvantageous to the academic achievement of underrepresented students. In the discourse of deficit, inequality is represented as a condition produced by outside circumstances, making it practically unpreventable. In the discourse of diversity, the social justice language of the Civil Rights Act (e.g., achieving "equality as a fact and equality as a result"[4]) shifted in the 1980s to the relational language of interracial communication and understanding; and, more recently, in response to the legal attacks on affirmative action, there has been a shift to the language of assessment (e.g., measuring the cognitive benefits that are derived by students who attend racially diverse colleges).

In contrast to the narratives of student deficit and diversity, EFA introduces practitioners to a discourse of equity. The characteristics of equity-minded discourse that the project promotes are as follows:

- Being color-conscious (as opposed to color-blind) in an affirmative sense. To be color-conscious means noticing and questioning patterns of educational outcomes that reveal unexplainable differences for minority students and viewing inequalities in the context of a history of exclusion, discrimination, and educational apartheid.

- Being aware that beliefs, expectations, and practices can result in negative racialization. Examples of racialization include attributing unequal outcomes to students' cultural predispositions and basing academic practices on assumptions about the capacity or ambitions of minority students.
- Being willing to assume responsibility for the elimination of inequality. Rather than viewing inequalities as predictable and natural, allowing for the possibility that they might be created or exacerbated by taken-for-granted practices and policies, inadequate knowledge, a lack of cultural know-how, or the absence of institutional support.

Guided Analysis of Data on Educational Outcomes

Researchers[5] from the CUE were assigned to campus teams and their role was to purposefully enact the discourse of equity by means of critical questioning and probing, modeling critical analysis of data, reinterpreting attributions of individual and cultural deficits, instructing, reframing, explaining, challenging, and providing feedback.[6] Specifically, three means of equity-minded discourse were enacted: (a) *Critical probing* entails questioning or calling attention to hidden patterns of inequality, (b) *racial reframing* entails a critical race response to counter interpretations that evade or fail to notice racial inequalities in educational outcomes, and (c) *institutional accountability reframing* entails a critical response to data that reinforce the role of institutions (in general) and institutional agents (in particular) in redressing race-based inequities and disparities in student outcomes. These means were employed when race-based inequalities made evident by student outcome data failed to catch team members' attention or engage them in sensemaking; when team members attributed unequal outcomes to students' characteristics, predispositions, and cultural values; when unequal outcomes were framed as culturally justifiable; or when team members' sensemaking redirected the analysis away from racial inequalities. Researchers also used these strategies to assist and reinforce equity-mindedness among members of the team.

Criteria for the Composition of Campus Teams

Equity-mindedness is both an individual and a distributed characteristic of a group of people. At the micro level the aim of the project is to facilitate the development of equity-mindedness as a shared schema among the members of the evidence team. At the macro level our goal is for the members of the team to foster equity-mindedness at the institutional level. Consistent with principles of organizational learning, individuals learn on behalf of their organizations (Huber, 1991) and share their learning with other organizational members in committees, meetings, reports, participation in institutional governance, and through changes in their own practices.

To increase the likelihood of teams having members who embodied the qualities of equity-mindedness, we provided the campus presidents with guidelines on whom to include in their evidence teams. In addition to specifying racial diversity, we recommended the inclusion of individuals with different opinions about issues such as affirmative action, the practice of disaggregating data by race, and the concept of equity in educational outcomes. Our expectation was that each team would have at least one member who would "naturally" display equity-mindedness in the analysis, interpretation, and explanation of the data and thus assist in the enactment of EFA's specialized discourse.

Artifacts and Tools

The project provides various special artifacts and cultural tools including vital signs protocols, the Equity Scorecard framework, report templates, new constructs, equity index quantitative formula, resource notebooks, and examples of graphic displays to help make data easy to decipher. Each of these tools and artifacts serves to facilitate the analysis, display, and reporting of race group–specific data. Artifacts and cultural tools, which can be physical, conceptual, or ideational, help us see things differently than before.

Activity Setting

A key aspect of sociocultural approaches is that the focus or analytic unit needs to go beyond the individual learner. Thus, the key focus is the activity setting, not the learner in isolation. Activity settings can be seen in the "who, what, when, where, why, and how" of the routines that constituted the creation of the Equity Scorecard. The activity settings of the nine participating colleges evolved differently based on their composition, the interpersonal and organizational skills of team leaders, the attitude of institutional researchers toward the data requirements of the project and their skills in making data (see Dowd, Malcom, Nakamoto, & Bensimon, 2007) accessible

228 CONFRONTING EQUITY ISSUES ON CAMPUS

in nontechnical ways, and the relationships among the members. Power differences, whose voices were heard, and the relationship between the team and the CUE researchers also influenced the activity setting.

EFA created a special type of activity setting that is constituted to create new types of knowledge and thinking about equity, particularly in relation to the educational outcomes of African Americans and Latinas and Latinos. Activity settings specifically designed to promote organizational learning are scarce or nonexistent in most academic organizations (Dill, 1999; Garvin, 1993).

The activity setting encompassed the evidence teams, their actions, and the mediational means to facilitate learning and change. Our observation and subsequent analysis of the activity settings at two EFA colleges serve as the focus of this chapter.

The Veeder Community College and Gillroy Community College Equity for All Activity Settings

In this chapter, the focus is on the enactment of cultural and social mediational means of equity-mindedness in the activity settings of two community colleges to which we refer by the pseudonyms Veeder (VCC) and Gillroy (GCC). To protect the identity of the colleges and maintain the confidentiality of the team members, we provide general, but informative, descriptions of VCC and GCC.

VCC and GCC, located in California, are urban community colleges that enroll approximately 25,000 full-time-equivalent students. Both campuses serve racially and ethnically diverse student populations. Collectively, African American, Asian and Pacific Islander, Latino and Latina, and Native American students compose more than 75 percent of the campuses' total student enrollments. The colleges are engaged in a range of initiatives and offer support programs and services that aim to facilitate students' achievement of successful outcomes. Yet in spite of these interventions, racial and ethnic disparities on basic indicators of student success exist on both campuses. For instance, a critical mass of students of color is concentrated in nondegree-credit basic skills programs, few of whom ever matriculate to college-level coursework. In addition, African American, Latina and Latino, and Native American students earn degrees and certificates at significantly lower rates in comparison with their White and Asian and Pacific Islander peers. These disparities persist among transfer indicators as well. GCC and

VCC are considered among the top feeder colleges to California's four-year institutions. For example, in a recent year, VCC and GCC collectively transferred to the UC more than five hundred Asian Pacific Islanders and almost two hundred White students; however, they transferred fewer than one hundred Latinas and Latinos, and fewer than twenty African Americans.

Collectively, a total of twenty practitioners served on the VCC and GCC EFA teams. Eight were full-time faculty members, five were program directors, three were senior administrators (e.g., dean or vice president), two were counselors, and two were other administrators. Both teams were ethnically diverse and balanced on the basis of gender (nine men and eleven women). We now turn to a description of the methods we used to identify and examine the mediational means in the VCC and GCC activity settings.

Research Methods

Data Collection

The data on which this chapter is based are composed of ethnographic field notes and transcribed audiorecordings that were collected and maintained during the VCC and GCC EFA evidence team meetings. During the course of the project, the VCC team held eight team meetings at which a CUE facilitator was present and field notes were collected. The GCC team held seven meetings. Verbatim statements that were made by team members in discussing the data were captured in the field notes, as were their nonverbal expressions and physical activities of the meetings. Prior to the first team meeting, all team members were informed of our purposes in collecting field notes and asked for their informed consent to observe and document team meetings at which they were present.

Data Analysis

Our analysis of the data was informed by the case study qualitative methodological tradition (Stake, 1995). The formal analysis of the data occurred in two phases. During the first phase, we carefully read the raw field notes and analyzed them by applying major code concepts and categories that were derived from the project's conceptual framework. Our purpose in phase one of the analysis was to evaluate the project's effectiveness in achieving the learning and instrumental goals that were described previously in this chapter. In doing so, we applied three sets of codes: (a) those that captured team members' beliefs, attitudes, and reactions to the data and patterns of race-based inequities in student outcomes; (b) those that captured observations of the institution's context, culture, practices, and policies that seemed to have meaningful impact on equity and mediated the range of options available to address the inequities; and (c) those that captured team dynamics, interactions, and the strategies team members relied upon to fulfill both formal and informal team roles.

During the second phase, we assumed a more narrow and focused approach to our analysis of the data. Here we sought greater depth in understanding the mediated means that were applied *within* the activity settings and how the means facilitated equity-minded sensemaking about observed outcome inequities among team members. We examined the coded field notes and meeting transcripts from the VCC and GCC teams and coded instances in which the five mediational means (described previously) of enacting equity discourse were evident. In addition, we noted the (a) team members who consistently employed the mediational means during team meetings, (b) other team members' responses and reactions to the mediational means, and (c) shifts in the team's discourse and sensemaking about student outcome inequities that can be attributed to the mediational means. We used the ATLAS.ti qualitative data analysis software program to code, organize, and maintain the data.

In conducting our analyses, we relied upon both "direct interpretation" and "categorical aggregation" (Stake, 1995). In using direct interpretation, a discrete instance serves as the unit of analysis. For example, we often observed philosophical disagreements or contentious exchanges between two or more team members that occurred during the meetings. Elaborated discussions among the team in which important decisions were made also captured our attention. In these instances, we made sense of the data by "pulling it apart and putting it together again more meaningfully" (Stake, p. 75). Again, we paid close attention to the actors involved, responses and reactions from other team members, and the noticeable effects these interactions had on team dynamics. Categorical aggregation involves the "emergence of meaning from the repetition of phenomena" (Stake, p. 76). By using categorical aggregation, we arrived at meaning by identifying and analyzing themes and patterns that consistently emerged over the course of the eight VCC meetings and the seven GCC meetings.

Trustworthiness

We established trustworthiness by way of two strategies that are proposed by Patton (2002). First, in our review of the field notes we sought "alternative themes, divergent patterns, and rival explanations" that challenged our interpretations of the data. For example, we periodically came across statements in which team members attributed outcome disparities to student characteristics. Rather than immediately coding these statements as reflections of "deficit thinking," we considered other reasonable interpretations.

Second, we used triangulation to establish trustworthiness. Patton (2002) suggests "comparing and cross-checking the consistency of information" (p. 467) derived from one source with other sources. The meeting field notes were our primary source of data. However, we also relied on our observations of team members during the course of the project as well as the aforementioned artifacts to triangulate our findings. When we arrived at inconsistencies, we sought to understand the contextual factors that may have accounted for these differences. Our coresearchers who served as facilitators to the VCC and GCC teams were also key sources of insight in making sense of inconsistencies. We regularly presented our interpretations of the data during bimonthly EFA research meetings. During the meetings, our coresearchers questioned, challenged, and supported our interpretations of the data. In the next section we describe the five mediational means as used in the activity settings at VCC and GCC.

The Enactment of Mediational Means Within Two Activity Settings

To illustrate each of the mediational means of equity-mindedness, we will present situations in which team members are interpreting data that depict a racial and ethnic group experiencing a specific unequal educational outcome. Inequality in the EFA project was based on proportionality as well as on comparison with other groups. The only measures that were used were numbers and percentages. Although the focus of this chapter is not on the quantitative data findings, we provide a brief description of the data examined by both teams to make it easier to envision the activity setting.

Some EFA teams decided to use snapshot data, whereas others focused their attention on a single cohort of first-time students who enrolled in a particular year (e.g., 1999) or multiple cohorts who enrolled over three to four years (e.g., 1999–2001, 1997–2000). Other teams concentrated their attention on students who had completed a specified number of credits or college-level courses. The VCC team analyzed the educational outcomes for a single-year cohort of first-time students disaggregated into eight categories:

African American, Asian/Asian American, Filipino/Pacific Islander, His-panic/Latino, Native American, Other, European Caucasian, and Declined to State.

The VCC team, like most other teams in the project, examined data on (a) educational goals, (b) enrollment and success rate in developmental and college-level English and mathematics, (c) transfer rates to a four-year college within three years, (d) transfer rates for selective and less selective four-year colleges, (e) degree and certificate completion within three years, (f) semester-to-semester persistence, and (g) enrollment in advanced-level courses in science and mathematics.

The percentage for African Americans in the VCC study cohort saying that "transfer to a four-year college" was their educational goal in the admissions application was higher than for all the other groups. However, the data on successful transfer to four-year colleges within three years of starting at VCC showed African Americans as well as Latinas and Latinos as experiencing the greatest inequality in transfer rates to all colleges, regardless of selectivity. No African Americans and just one person of Latin descent transferred to the state's selective public institution. In comparison, Asian Americans represented 75 percent of all the transfers to the selective institution.

Over the twelve months of the project, the VCC team engaged in many interpretive conversations about the transfer inequality being experienced by African Americans and Latinas and Latinos. These conversations allowed for our observation of the project's mediational means within the activity setting.

We present four conversation excerpts; each is selected to foreground one of the five mediational means. However, within each of the four excerpts other mediational means are being used besides the one that is foregrounded. For example, the mediational means highlighted in the first VCC excerpt is "artifacts and cultural tools"; however, it also shows the CUE facilitator using "guided analysis" to bring out implicit meanings in the interpretations being offered to explain the racial and ethnic differences in transfer rates.

Artifacts and Cultural Tools

This excerpt shows Veeder's Team Member 1 (VTM1) at the first meeting of the team noticing ("jumps out") race group–specific ("disproportionately Asian") differences in transfer outcomes and sharing this knowledge with the other members of the team. The noticing by VTM1 of large racial and ethnic disparities in transfer patterns to the most prestigious public university is facilitated by EFA's data practices: disaggregating data by race and ethnicity and reporting the results in numbers and percentages for each group in a manner that makes comparisons across groups easy to grasp; and determining whether outcomes are at, below, or above equity based on population proportionality rather than using Whites or Asian Americans as the norm. In the excerpt VTM1's learning is facilitated by the format in which the data are presented, which makes patterns of inequality clear. Additionally, he makes sense of the data by means of "proportionality," one of EFA's cultural tools to facilitate the noticing of unequal outcomes and their magnitude. By focusing on proportionality, VTM1 compares whether transfer outcomes for each group are proportional to their percentage in the student population and is able to describe the evidence of inequality very specifically. Proportionality helps him to determine that the transfer outcomes for Whites are proportionally equitable, and that Asians compose the largest group of transfers numerically and the percentage of transfers is proportionally larger than their overall population (i.e., they are well above equity). In contrast, VTM1 points out that Hispanics, who compose 13 percent of the population, represent only 8 percent of the transfers and the same holds true for African Americans.

In the following text, we provide the conversation excerpt that starts out with VTM1's proportional analysis and is followed by comments from other members of the team. The excerpt brings out the various ways in which team members make sense of the new knowledge revealed by the data. Following the excerpt, we will provide additional discussion of what mediational means are in use.

> VTM1: One thing jumps out at me. Transfers to Research University are disproportionately Asian. White transfers reflect the student population [they are proportionally equal]. Asian number is higher than overall student group. Hispanics are about 13 percent of the population but only 8 percent transfer and the same holds for African Americans.
>
> VTM2: Black students may go to Historically Black Universities and so their transfer rates may actually be higher. Can we get private school transfer [data]?
>
> VTM3: I have asked my students and they say that if they major in liberal arts they will not be able to transfer to Research University. . . . Many of my students are going into science and engineering or mathematics or even business. I always ask students what their major is and very few Asian students say, "My major is liberal arts."
>
> VTM1: I think that's a function of the students you are seeing. They are the cream of the crop.

>   VTM4: It's a good question, but based on my experience with students a
>   lot of decisions about majors are based on economics. Also, since Prop
>   209 African American and Latino students were not applying to
>   Research University and I think only now they are just recovering
>   from that.
>   VTM3: I can see that you need the income to go to Research University
>   as opposed to State College.
>   CUE Facilitator: I'm not sure I understood VTM3's point about students
>   being in the right major to transfer.

Although EFA's cultural practices around data analysis facilitated VTM1's
learning about transfer inequality for Latinas and Latinos and African Americans, his fellow team members respond with explanations about the causes
for the inequality. Although it is unintended, the explanations make the
racial transfer patterns brought to their attention by VTM1 appear circum-
stantial rather than an indication of inequality in opportunity.

Team Member 2 (VTM2) offers the possibility that African Americans
are going to historically Black colleges and universities. Team Member 3
(VTM3) thinks that Asian Americans, by selecting majors outside liberal
arts, increase their chances of transferring to the selective university.
Although unsaid, VTM3's line of reasoning implies that African Americans
are more likely to choose liberal arts majors and, as a consequence, have a
reduced chance of transferring to the selective university. Even though
VTM4 recognizes the inequalities evidenced in the transfer data, she attributes them to external circumstances that are beyond the influence of VCC.

In saying, "I'm not sure I understood VTM3's point about students
being in the right major to transfer," the CUE facilitator employs mediational means of "guided analysis" (critical probing) to call attention to the
improbability that inequalities in transfer patterns are created by Asians
choosing the "right" majors and African Americans and Latinas and Latinos
choosing the "wrong" majors. However, the CUE facilitator's use of critical
probing did not elicit responses that exemplify equity-minded learning
within the moment of this conversation.

Guided Analysis

At the second meeting of VCC's team, the conversation on racially distinctive patterns of transfer resumes with a discussion of whether the disparity
between Asian and African American transfer rates might be a reflection of
unequal sample sizes, rather than unequal opportunities. We offer this excerpt

to demonstrate how the concept of proportionality is used as a mediational tool in the Equity Scorecard process:

> VTM3: [B]ut the issue here is that the enrollment of African Americans is very low and that makes it hard to actually see things clearly. If the success rate is proportional to those in other groups, then there doesn't seem to be any problem at all, right?
>
> VTM4: [B]ut we can say that even though the number is small, proportionally the success rate is out of whack. I think that's kind of the way we've been going at this [referring to the project's focus on proportionality as a measure of equity] is to say even though there's a small group of African Americans, they're like 4 percent of the population as compared to Asian students that are like what, 38 percent of the population. . . . I don't have it right in front of me . . . but the Asian students . . . about 50 percent of those students transfer to Research University. . . . [T]hat's a little high. . . .
>
> VTM3: What I'm saying is actually it may not be that different. If you have one hundred African-American male students and only four of them transfer and if you have ten thousand say Caucasians and four hundred transfer, that's the same proportion.
>
> VTM4: Exactly, exactly. But do we really have that issue?
>
> VTM3: My concern is the population. It's 37 percent Asian, only 3 percent African American. . . . That's the issue: small sample size.
>
> CUE Facilitator: But what about Hispanics, for example? Where you have a larger sample size, but once again, a relatively low percentage.

This excerpt shows VTM3 insisting that the small number of African Americans in the study population makes it appear as if their transfer rates are much lower than the rate for Asian students. VTM4 draws on EFA's principle of proportionality to persuade VTM3 that African Americans are truly experiencing considerably lower rates of transfer success. VTM3 continues insisting that the issue is not inequality but small sample size. At the point that VTM3 asserts the correctness of his analysis, "That's the issue, sample size," the CUE Facilitator enters into the conversation to assist VTM4 and persuade VTM3 that sample size is not the issue. To maintain the focus on the inequality shown by the data on transfer without arguing about sample size, she draws attention to a similar pattern of transfer inequality among Hispanics, who compose a much larger group.

However, the discussion on unequal transfer patterns comes to a stop when VTM5, who up to that point had not said anything, suggests that it may be more accurate to look at "transfer-ready" students. VTM5 paints a scenario in which students are ready to transfer but, for reasons unknown, do not do so. What is important, however, from VTM5's perspective is that "we've done our job, if the student is transfer ready or transfer prepared." The possibility that transfer disparities are not a substantiation of racial inequality resonates with the other team members. VTM4, who previously had been focusing on the proportional inequalities, offers that students may have decided to "take a break from college" but it could also be lack of "money"; and VTM3 thinks that many students want the degree or certificate as well as transfer but "they decide not to [transfer] for some reason, for a private reason."

The possibility that the transfer rates for African Americans and Hispanics were much lower as a consequence of "transfer-ready" students not transferring was an appealing positive spin on data that might otherwise cast the institution in a negative light. But data demonstrating large disparities across race groups in the successful completion of basic skills math offered a more plausible explanation for unequal transfer rates. The CUE facilitator called attention to the 23 percent gap between White and Black students and, in an attempt to recontextualize equity as an institutional responsibility, she said to the team members:

> One of the questions you could ask yourselves would be, "What would it take to bring all groups up to a success rate of 65 percent?" "And how long would it take?" "What kind of conversations would we need to have in order to meet that goal?"

Despite the CUE facilitator's attempt to shift the discourse away from student characteristics to a consideration of institutional practices, the team members' interpretations and questions brought the problem back to the students: Might there be gender differences? Might it have to do with day versus evening students? Might there be a need for more interventions?

Equity-Minded Discourse and Guided Analysis

Over the course of the seven GCC team meetings, an issue that received considerable attention was the reliability of students' self-declared goal as a baseline indicator of student success. Some members of the team compared the high percentage of underrepresented students whose self-declared educational goal was to transfer to a four-year college to the very low percentage who actually transferred as a sign of inequality. Other team members interpreted the data as demonstrating the unreliability of self-declared goals. They felt that students made uninformed choices when selecting from among the long menu of options on the admission application. It was felt by some that a very large number of students at the college "had no idea what they wanted to do" and chose goals based on their perceived popularity and social desirability.

The following excerpt captures the discussion prompted by a team member's suggestion that self-declared goals are not reliable and, instead of accepting them at face value, from a research perspective it would be more accurate to infer students' goals from their course-taking patterns. The excerpt begins with GTM1 reacting to another team member saying that students' self-declared goals are not a reliable indicator and should not be used as a basis for assessing outcomes. The excerpt focuses on the mediational means enacted by GTM1 and the CUE facilitator, both of whom reframe the problem as one of institutional responsibility, rather than the truthfulness of students' goals.

> GTM1: I could be wrong. I don't have the research [refers to himself as not being a researcher] but I don't think it's fair to say it's not accurate. Why am I able to say that this is not an accurate goal for them when this is actually what they have indicated that is their desire? The reality, however, is that they are not attaining that, why are they not attaining that? That's what I would want to know. . . .
>
> GTM2: That's got to be one of the first questions. . . .
>
> GTM1: If I know that Latinos make up 41 percent of the population, and their numbers reflect pretty consistently the goal of transfer, but they only transfer at a 2 percent rate, again it's not that it's not an accurate goal that they describe for themselves, it's just that they're not attaining it. So how can we impact that?
>
> GTM3: I think that's a very good point. . . .
>
> GTM4: That's a very good point and we should not get away from seeing what the student goals are, . . . there are African Americans who have the transfer goal and yet there is something that's blocking. . . .
>
> GTM3: I think from an administrative point of view . . . they found that students were just picking the first choice. So, from that, people were assuming that educational goals weren't a true picture of what they wanted. But that's a good point, that's a good question. Is there a true and untrue picture of what they want [regardless] of what they achieve?
>
> GTM2: I would think that would have to be one of the first questions for us to consider.

CUE Facilitator: If I were sitting in your shoes I mean the big thing I
would be worried about is: What is the role of the institution? I think
it's important to just lay on the table that the purpose of the project
is not to blame institutions or compare institutions but if it turns out
that 41 percent say they want to transfer and only 2 percent are, then
whatever the reasons are, you know, what can the institution do to fix
it, I think that's really important, without saying we're doing a horri-
ble job.

GTM3: And I think we have a great question in the student's ed goal, and
if it is something that they want to do or if it's something that they
picked out of the air, and if it is truly something that they want to do,
why are they not achieving it? And from that, what can faculty and
administrators do to help?

In most community colleges there is an enormous gap between students'
self-reported aspirations and actual outcomes, which can make the institution appear badly in the eyes of trustees and policymakers concerned with
issues of efficiency and accountability. Understandably there is a reluctance
to compare transfer outcomes to transfer aspirations as most institutions will
not look very effective. In contrast, when outcomes are based on course-
taking patterns, the rate of transfer success will be significantly higher
because the thousands of students who are channeled into basic skills
courses, a great many of whom are likely to have indicated transfer to a four-
year college as their educational goal, would not be counted.

GTM1 introduces into the conversation the inherent unfairness of viewing students' goals as inauthentic because they do not attain these goals. It is
more important to consider why students are not attaining their goals and
what can be done about it than to search for ways to inflate success. GTM1
models equity-mindedness by using words that connote values (e.g., *fair*),
questioning the rightfulness of invalidating students' goals, and by placing
the responsibility for students' goals at the institutional level.

Similarly, the CUE facilitator, sensing that some team members may be
more worried with what the data say about the institution than with the
implications for students, reminds them of the purpose of the project, which
is not to blame institutions but to find ways of being more responsive to the
inequalities experienced by some students. Regardless of how the data are
presented, the reality is that if 41 percent of Latinas and Latinos say they
want to transfer and only 2 percent actually do, the institution has a responsibility to fix it.

Equity-minded modeling by GTM1 and the CUE facilitator helped
GTM3 and GTM4 concur on the need to take students' goals into account

and consider what might be "blocking" African American students. In contrast, GTM4, while agreeing that GTM1 has a good point, continues to view students' goals in terms of "true" and "untrue" and is interested in finding out whether goals represent "something they [students] want to do" or "something they picked out of the air."

The GCC team analyzed multiple cohorts of "first-time freshmen" who entered the college in the fall semesters in four consecutive years. The cohorts were disaggregated into the following racial and ethnic categories: African American, Asian, International, Caucasian, Hispanic, Mexican American, Pacific Islander, and Southeast Asian.

The interpretive event we focus on took place on the fourth meeting of the team. The team was reviewing a draft of its report to the president on the academic pathways perspective of the Equity Scorecard. The report consisted of tables and graphic displays with data on a cohort of students, disaggregated into racial and ethnic categories, who had completed a specified number of units and whose course-taking patterns identified them as students who were on a pathway to transfer. The data show that African Americans, followed by Latinas and Latinos, have the lowest percentage of students in the pathway to transfer and International and Asian students have the highest. The event starts with a team member trying to make sense of why there are such large differences in course-taking patterns among racial and ethnic groups.

> GTM1: What I think it informs me is that there might be some cultural differences in the goals of students. And that just on this data alone, clearly not enough to make that kind of assumption, but it's possible that some students have different goals based on their culture. For example, we might assume that Latino and African American students come here, perhaps, to improve their academic skills but not get a degree. Whereas there is a cultural bias in Asians to get a degree. Is that the kind of thinking that you get from this? For example, four out of ten Asians are behaving as if they want to get a degree and transfer where only one out of four African Americans are.
>
> GTM2: That's what I think about it.
>
> GTM3: I don't see it that way.
>
> CUE Facilitator: Why is that?
>
> GTM1: Yeah, I'd like to hear another opinion.
>
> GTM3: I would suggest . . . let's look at Latinos. Culturally, they would probably value a degree as much as the Asian students but there are other roadblocks hindering them, academic preparation being the first

one. They are not in [college-level English or math] so they can't be transfer intent, right? Because that's part of the definition.

GTM1: They have to attempt [college-level English and math to be considered an aspiring transfer student].

GTM3: They have to attempt it. And many of them, a high proportion, a disproportionate number of them, Latino and African American, are placing into [basic skills English and math]. I mean, that's across the board . . . and they aren't passing those classes either. Culture can be one aspect, but that wouldn't be my first thought. My first thought is academic preparation, limited knowledge of higher education, those kinds of . . . navigating the system [issues].

GTM1 attributes unequal participation in the transfer pathway to cultural predispositions that result in different educational goals. He speculates that Asians might be "culturally biased" to transfer and earn a baccalaureate, whereas African Americans and Latinas and Latinos might be more "culturally biased" toward improving their basic skills rather than earning a degree. Minority students behave as basic skills students and Asian students behave as degree-seeking students. The data demonstrate different behavioral and choice patterns for different groups.

Although one of the team members agrees that transfer pathway outcomes may be culturally determined, GTM3 disagrees and the CUE facilitator encourages him to elaborate. GTM3 explains that Latinas and Latinos may be as culturally predisposed to value a degree as Asians, but they face many obstacles. The reason why they do not behave as if they want a degree is because in being placed in noncredit college courses they are precluded from the transfer pathway, even if their aspiration is to transfer. GTM3 reframes the problem as academic preparation and lack of college knowledge, which prevent the majority of these students from behaving like degree-seeking students. GTM1 seemed open to hearing a different interpretation but there is no indication in the transcript as to whether he agreed with GTM3 or changed his mind in any way.

Discussion

To illustrate the mediational means of enacting equity-mindedness, we analyzed team talk on two topics that adversely affected African Americans and Latinas and Latinos: unequal transfer outcomes and the phenomenon of very high transfer aspirations and very low transfer outcomes. Both topics recur, in one manner or another, in the fifteen meetings held by the Veeder and Gilroy teams; they were also very much in evidence in the discussions that took place in the teams of the other seven campuses.

On both teams, the data elicited deracialized interpretations that justi-fied, normalized, or circumvented unequal outcomes among African Ameri-cans and Latinas and Latinos. From an organizational learning perspective (Argyris, 1991), de-racializing inequality represents single-loop learning. In the context of this study, single-loop learning resulted in participants defin-ing the problem in a manner that diminished the possibility of a conscious and careful examination of how race is implicated, for example, in data practices (e.g., not counting students' self-declared goals), beliefs (e.g., the notion that culture determines outcomes), and academic culture (e.g., avoid-ing value-laden conversations).

Within the two teams there was at least one member who, along with the CUE facilitators, employed the cultural and social tools of EFA to medi-ate awareness of unequal opportunity in the educational patterns of African Americans and Latinas and Latinos and to develop a sense of responsibility for change. From a sociocultural perspective, action is successfully mediated when our understandings correspond. Although the conversations demon-strated the various ways in which mediational means were used by CUE facilitators and team members to counteract deficit and de-racialized analy-ses, the conversations do not provide evidence of having elicited the desired responses. For example, both CUE facilitators introduced the notion of insti-tutional responsibility (e.g., "What would it take to bring all groups up to a success rate of 65 percent?" "If it turns out that 41 percent say they want to transfer and only 2 percent do . . . what can the institution do?"), but there was no evidence that the questions generated equity-minded responses.

There are several reasons we can offer to explain the apparent lack of response to the mediation of equity-mindedness. One response is that equity-mindedness was well defined at the level of data practices and arti-facts, but the discourse practices were underdeveloped. The reporting of data broken down by race and ethnicity, the focus on racial equity, the methods of calculating equity, and the various data and report templates were fully developed. The data practices were effective in facilitating the noticing of inequalities comprehensively. Moreover, the project was effective in demon-strating how routine data that are highly accessible can create new knowledge when they are organized and reported with a specific learning goal in mind (see chapter 9). One way to view this is in terms of scaffolding. That is, learning is dynamic and takes place over time, especially when previously overlearned or "automated" learning is present. New learning takes place in small steps over time. We can see the "buds" of new learning being created, but it is likely that the time frame of the project was too short. In other words, the "zone of proximal development" (ZPD) of the team participants was very wide, and it is unrealistic to think that it would change in a short period.

In the very beginnings of this work, the project relied primarily on the theory and literature of organizational learning (e.g., theorists such as Argyris and Schön). Organizational learning was very helpful in guiding the design of team structures and data practices to facilitate collaborative sensemaking, and in developing our understanding of equity as a double-loop learning problem. However, the literature on organizational learning does not address the means of facilitating learning, particularly the means of facilitating double-loop learning. Similarly, critical race theories, while helping us delineate the qualities of equity-mindedness, did not provide the means of facilitating it.

It was not until we turned to sociocultural theories of learning that we began to define the project's data practices, data tools, structures, and critical discourse as mediational means purposefully designed to enact equity-mindedness. The turn toward sociocultural theory came after the project was implemented and although we, as facilitators of the evidence teams, were well-grounded in the values, practices, and discourse of equity-mindedness and were clear that our role within the teams was to facilitate its enactment, we did not specify the actual discourse practices, when and how to use them, or how to assess their effect. Simply put, we were conscious of modeling the discourse of equity-mindedness, but we did so more intuitively than strategically.

The conversational excerpts demonstrate that the CUE facilitators modeled equity-mindedness through a variety of mediational means, for example, by asking questions, reinforcing the principle of institutional responsibility, redirecting team members' attention to unnoticed inequalities, and providing support to team members who viewed the data through the lens of equity. Our enactment of equity-mindedness was not sufficiently attentive to "scaffolding" equity-mindedness. Sociocultural theorists (Lave & Wenger, 1991; Tharp & Gallimore, 1988; Vygotsky, 1978, 1987) point out that the learner must be engaged at a level that produces learning and induces development, that is, within the ZPD. This is defined as the range between the level of difficulty at which an individual can perform independently and the highest level at which she or he can perform with assistance. If the assistance is at a level that is either above or below a learner's current level of performance, learning will not be facilitated. However, when the assistance is within the learner's zone, it is said to be "responsive" and is thought to produce learning.

It is possible that the mediational means by which we enacted equity-mindedness were not responsive to the ZPD of the participants. For example, the project has an orientation session for the teams and training sessions for team leaders and institutional researchers, but the focus of these is on the activities, products, and data practices of the project and how to facilitate them. These sessions do not address the concept, meaning, and practices of equity-mindedness directly. Nor do they introduce team leaders and institutional researchers to the means of assisting team members in developing awareness of inequities, how to view data through the lens of equity, and how practitioners collectively can assume responsibility for producing equitable outcomes.

Without a more structured approach,[7] the equity discourse we enact in team meetings may be too nuanced to bring about equity-mindedness in others. Moreover, to be equity-minded requires that inequality be viewed as an indication of ineffective practice or lack of knowledge. The admission of ineffective practice or lack of knowledge may be particularly difficult in institutional contexts that actively discourage the examination of failure and where the leadership cultivates an institutional image of quality, innovation, and high performance. Both institutions had developed a reputation as high transfer institutions and team members from time to time reacted defensively to the data.

Notes

1. We are grateful to Alicia C. Dowd for her insightful contributions to the definition of equity-mindedness.

2. EFA was very successful in involving faculty members and gaining their support. The project is appealing to faculty members because it engages them in new research activities that are relevant to their classroom experiences.

3. The technical aspects of the Equity Scorecard are discussed in Harris and Bensimon (2007) and are available online at www.usc.edu/cue.

4. Address given by Lyndon B. Johnson at the 1964 Howard University commencement as cited in Bensimon, 2005, p. 1.

5. E. M. Bensimon, A. C. Dowd, F. Harris, III, and R. Rueda were the lead researchers.

6. At the outset of the project we did not specify the strategies of enacting a discourse of equity. The researchers and assistants met almost weekly during the

duration of the project to discuss the implementation of the project, report on the teams' activities, and review field notes through the theoretical perspectives that informed the project. The discourse strategies we were enacting became clear in the review of meeting transcripts and the naming of these strategies was inspired by Tharp and Gallimore's (1988) description of means of assisting performance in a teaching and learning situation.

7. As a consequence of the findings reported in this chapter the training model has undergone major changes and more directive methods are being used to teach team members the meaning of "equity-mindedness" conceptually and practically. Additionally, team members can now access a Web-based module on equity.

References

Argyris, C. (1991). Teaching smart people how to learn. *Reflections, 4*(2), 4–15.

Argyris, C. (1994). Good communication that blocks learning. In C. Argyris (Ed.), *On organizational learning.* Boston, MA: Harvard Business Review Press.

Argyris, C., & Schön, D. A. (1996). *Organizational learning II: Theory, method, and practice.* New York, NY: Addison-Wesley.

Bauman, G. L. (2002). *Developing a culture of evidence: Using institutional data to identify inequitable educational outcomes.* Unpublished doctoral dissertation, University of Southern California.

Bensimon, E. M. (2004, January/February). The diversity scorecard: A learning approach to institutional change. *Change,* 45–52.

Bensimon, E. M. (2005). *Equality as a fact, equality as a result: A matter of institutional accountability* (Commissioned Paper). Washington, DC: American Council on Education.

Bensimon, E. M. (2007). The underestimated significance of practitioner knowledge in the scholarship of student success. *The Review of Higher Education, 30*(4), 441–469.

Bensimon, E. M., Polkinghorne, D. E., Bauman, G. L., & Vallejo, E. (2004). Doing research that makes a difference. *The Journal of Higher Education, 75*(1), 104–126.

Bensimon, E., Rueda, R., Dowd, A. C., & Harris, F, III. (2007). Accountability, equity, and practitioner learning and change. *Metropolitan Universities, 18*(3), 28–45.

Cobb, P., Confrey, J., diSessa, A., Lehrer, R., & Schauble, L. (2003). Design experiments in educational research. *Educational Researcher, 32*(1), 9–13.

Coburn, C. E. (2003). Rethinking scale: Moving beyond numbers to deep and lasting change. *Educational Researcher, 32*(6), 3–12.

Dill, D. D. (1999). Academic accountability and university adaptation: The architecture of an academic learning organization. *Higher Education, 38,* 127–154.

Dowd, A. C., Malcom, L., Nakamoto, J., & Bensimon, E. M. (2007). *Institutional researchers as teachers and equity advocates: Facilitating organizational learning and change*. Paper presented at the annual meeting of the Association for the Study of Higher Education, Louisville, KY.

Forman, E. A., Minick, N., & Stone, C. A. (Eds.). (1993). *Contexts for learning: Sociocultural dynamics in children's development.* New York, NY: Oxford University Press.

Gallimore, R., & Goldenberg, C. (2001). Analyzing cultural models and settings to connect minority achievement and school improvement research. *Educational Psychologist, 36*(1), 45–56.

Garvin, D. A. (1993, July/August). Building a learning organization. *Harvard Business Review*, 78–90.

Harris, F., III, & Bensimon, E. M. (2007). The Equity Scorecard: A collaborative approach to assess and respond to racial/ethnic disparities in student outcomes. In S. R. Harper & L. D. Patton (Eds.), *Responding to the realities of race on campus: New directions for student services, 120* (pp. 77–84). San Francisco, CA: Jossey-Bass.

Huber, G. P. (1991). Organizational learning: The contributing processes and the literatures. *Organization Science, 2*(1), 88–115.

Kim, D. (1993). The link between individual and organizational learning. *Sloan Management Review, 35*(1), 37–50.

Lave, J., & Wenger, E. (1991). *Situated learning: Legitimate peripheral participation.* Cambridge, UK: Cambridge University Press.

Moll, L. C. (Ed.). (1990). *Vygotsky and education: Instructional implications and applications of sociocultural psychology.* New York, NY: Cambridge University Press.

Patton, M. Q. (2002). *Qualitative research & evaluation methods* (3rd ed.). Thousand Oaks, CA: Sage.

Perakyla, A. (2005). Analyzing talk and text. In N. Denzin & Y. S. Lincoln (Eds.), *The Sage handbook of qualitative research* (3rd ed., pp. 869–886). Thousand Oaks, CA: Sage.

Polkinghorne, D. E. (2004). *Practice and the human sciences: The case for a judgment-based practice of care.* Albany: State University of New York Press.

Pollock, M. (2001). How the question we ask most about race in education is the very question we most suppress. *Educational Researcher, 30*(9), 2–12.

Rogoff, B. (1991). *Apprenticeship in thinking: Cognitive in social context.* New York, NY: Oxford University Press.

Rogoff, B., Turkanis, C. G., & Bartlett, L. (2001). *Children and adults in a school community.* New York, NY: Oxford University Press.

Rueda, R., & Marquez, A. (2007). *Reconceptualizing institutional impact from a sociocultural lens: A case study view from a successful partner in a university-based equity project.* Paper presented at the annual meeting of the Association for the Study of Higher Education, Louisville, KY.

Scollon, R. (2001). *Mediated discourse: The nexus of practice.* New York, NY: Routledge.

Stake, R. E. (1995). *The art of case study research*. Thousand Oaks, CA: Sage.

Tharp, R. G., & Gallimore, R. (1988). *Rousing minds to life: Teaching, learning, and schooling in social context*. New York, NY: Cambridge University Press.

Valencia, R. R. (1998). *The evolution of deficit thinking: Educational thought and practice*. Bristol, PA: Falmer Press.

Vygotsky, L. S. (1978). *Mind in society: The development of higher psychological processes*. (M. Cole, V. John-Steiner, S. Scribner, & E. Souberman, Eds.). Cambridge, MA: Harvard University Press.

Vygotsky, L. S. (1987). *L. S. Vygotsky, collected works Vol. I* (R. Rieber & A. Carton, Eds.; N. Minick, Trans.). New York, NY: Plenum. (Original work published 1934)

Wenger, E. (1998). *Communities of practice: Learning, meaning, and identity*. New York, NY: Cambridge University Press.

Wertsch, J. V. (1998). *Mind as action*. New York, NY: Oxford University Press.

West, C. (1993). *Race matters*. Boston, MA: Beacon Press.

II

CHRONICLING THE
CHANGE PROCESS

Edlyn Vallejo Peña, Frank Harris III, and Estela Mara Bensimon

I n the education community, discourse that centers on improving academic performance of students of color typically focuses on changing the students—their behaviors, attitudes, and academic skills (Bensimon, 2005). Although students and their outcomes remain our primary focus, the Center for Urban Education's (CUE's) approach to the closing of the achievement gap is grounded in the perspective that postsecondary institutions and the faculty and administrators within them should be the target of change. In particular, we view the problem of inequitable educational outcomes as an organizational learning problem. When organizations learn and apply new knowledge to their practices, they are more likely to meet the needs of students who have historically been underserved and placed at the margins.

From the summers of 2005 to 2006, we engaged nine California community colleges in a practitioner-as-researcher process that involved examining, understanding, and redressing inequitable educational outcomes that existed on their respective campuses. Each of the nine partner institutions formed teams of faculty and administrators to conduct this work. The teams convened on a monthly basis to examine institutional data on student outcomes disaggregated by race and ethnicity. Together, team members collaboratively looked at these data, discussed the gaps in outcomes among student groups, considered the gaps' implications on students and the institution, and reflected on various ways to close the gaps.

Through this joint productive activity, the Equity Scorecard process created a space that brought issues of race and ethnicity and academic performance to the forefront. In this chapter we describe how examining, discussing, and reflecting on disaggregated data on student outcomes resulted in individual and organizational learning. In the sections of this chapter that follow, we first detail the theory of action that underpinned our work in the Equity Scorecard process. We then provide evidence of the ways in which faculty and administrators assuming the role of practitioner-researchers resulted in changes in beliefs, attitudes, and perceptions about inequity in student outcomes. Thereafter, we discuss how the approaches to create conditions for organizational learning led to changes in institutional practices at participating community colleges.

Theory of Action

Disparities in educational outcomes continue to affect critical masses of students of color enrolled at community colleges. Meanwhile, controversy brews over the most appropriate ways to hold community colleges accountable for educating their students (Dowd, 2005). While legislators and postsecondary associations debate possibilities to hold institutions accountable, community colleges continue to do business as usual. As a number of faculty members and administrators have witnessed, change in community colleges is slow, just as it is in higher education in general.

Resistance to postsecondary institutional change has sparked a disquieting consternation among educators (Tharp, 1993). Faculty members', administrators', and scholars' concerns stem from the dichotomous behavior of postsecondary institutions. On the one hand, postsecondary institutions promote and create learning (although inequitably); on the other hand, they have thus far achieved little success in applying new knowledge to improve their own activities (Garvin, 1993). Consequently, even though colleges create spaces for students to learn, the institutions themselves do not engage in organizational learning.

Organizational Learning

We believe organizational learning is a missing link to changing institutional practices toward the goal of improving the academic outcomes of historically underserved student groups. Organizational learning entails acquiring new ideas that lead to institutional improvements (Garvin, 1993). Although acquiring new knowledge is a necessary prerequisite, applying that knowledge constitutes the critical element in organizational learning. Once knowledge is applied, practices, behaviors, and actions change or shift. Although a number of scholars have documented evidence of organizational learning, a dearth of literature exists that depicts ways in which organizational learning actually happens (Bauman, 2005). The process and characteristics necessary for organizational learning have not been made transparent to educators who wish to develop conditions to promote this kind of learning.

Our objective in this chapter is to demonstrate how the Equity Scorecard process created opportunities for organizational learning to occur at nine community colleges in California. We offer evidence of postsecondary organizational learning and the ways in which it is fostered by the project. We specifically aspired to promote learning to achieve equity in educational outcomes for historically underserved groups.

The premise underlying our approach in the Equity Scorecard process is that organizational learning in community colleges can be fostered given several conditions. First, participating faculty members and administrators assume the role of practitioner-researchers. Practitioner-researchers "conduct research about their own institutions, and by doing so they acquire knowledge that they can use to bring about change in these institutions" (Bensimon, Polkinghorne, Bauman, & Vallejo, 2004, p. 108). Second, through joint productive activity, practitioner-researchers collaboratively inquire into achievement gaps by examining student outcomes data disaggregated by race and ethnicity. Data examination, discussion, and reflection are facilitated by individuals on teams who engage in various means of assisted performance (Tharp, 1993). That is, key individuals on the team assist the learning of other team members, or practitioner-researchers.

These theory-based elements of the Equity Scorecard process allow individuals to become more equity-minded. Equity-mindedness encompasses not only understanding inequities, but also understanding that the elimination of inequities becomes a shared responsibility among faculty, administrators, and institutions. On most campuses, inequitable outcomes are solely attributed to students' academic, cultural, and social deficits. From this perspective, interventions are often created to remediate such deficits. Equity-minded individuals, conversely, "are more prone to notice and question patterns of educational outcomes" and "are far more likely to understand that the beliefs, expectations, and actions of individuals [e.g., faculty and administrators] influence whether minority group students are construed as being capable or incapable" (Bensimon, 2005, p. 102). The focus of equity-minded individuals, then, centers on changing institutions and their actors rather than changing students.

Practitioner as Researcher

The practitioner-as-researcher model was developed and shaped by our desire at CUE for practitioners (a) to learn about the current status of educational outcomes that exist on their respective campuses, and (b) to use the newly acquired knowledge to influence their practices to achieve equity in students' educational outcomes (Bensimon et al., 2004). The Equity Scorecard process served as the vehicle for developing practitioner-researchers. Typically, faculty and administrators have hunches or ideas about how students fare at their respective institutions. Yet such ideas are based on personal experiences and are rarely substantiated by data. In the Equity Scorecard process, faculty and administrators conduct collaborative inquiry that centers on data about academic outcomes disaggregated by race and ethnicity. By analyzing disaggregated data, team members learn about the state of equity in student outcomes at their respective institutions.

Learning about glaring inequities in academic outcomes can prompt team members to question patterns of inequities. Team members move from blaming inequitable outcomes on students and their characteristics to questioning their institution's role in perpetuating achievement gaps. Faculty and administrators ask questions such as, "What kinds of services or attention are the students not getting along the way to achieve transfer?" "What can the math department do differently to enable students of color to move from basic skills to college-level math?" "What do we, as faculty members, need to change when we teach English?" These questions reflect an equity-minded perspective. Team members become critical about the ways in which institutions produce and perpetuate inequitable educational outcomes. They desire to know what processes, structures, and practices impede students from attaining the associate of arts degree, certificates, and the ability to transfer to a four-year postsecondary institution.

Once learning and questioning occur among individuals, organizational learning is possible. After becoming aware of the status of inequities on their college campuses, faculty members and administrators are more likely to feel empowered to take action. They apply their new knowledge to their own practices and advocate for institutional changes on a wider scale.

Assisted Performance

Although assuming the role of practitioner-researcher is important, becoming equity-minded and engaging in organizational learning is more likely to occur in conversation with others. Thus, the collaborative and social nature of the Equity Scorecard process constitutes a key element to fostering individual and institutional changes. Selected team members play a crucial role in facilitating and guiding team dialogue. CUE researchers, elected team leaders, and institutional researchers often assume this responsibility by engaging in seven means of assisted performance and guided learning, as described by Tharp (1993). The seven functions, which have been adapted by researchers at CUE, are (a) *modeling* behavior, such as questioning data and discussing institutional responsibilities to redress inequities; (b) offering *feedback* on examining, interpreting, and discussing data on student outcomes and action steps to improve student success; (c) providing *contingency management* by reinforcing or discouraging interpretation of data, student outcomes, and solutions; (d) *instructing* by offering clarity, giving information, and making decisions; (e) *questioning* to prompt a mental operation that team members would not normally produce alone; (f) *cognitive structuring,* which involves providing explanations that lead to equity-minded perceptions; and (g) *structuring tasks* into components, such as examining vital signs and identifying indicators (as explained in more detail later in this chapter). For more information on the social learning process that is facilitated by assisted performance, see the appendix on page 269.

Over the course of the project, "the assisters," as Tharp calls them, carried out these seven means to assist team members' learning and understanding of the problem of unequal outcomes. Researchers from CUE worked closely with team members—especially team leaders and institutional researchers—to build their capacity to employ these behaviors and strategies. Developing these individuals' capacity to assist others' learning on the team uniquely positioned them to cultivate equity-mindedness among team members. Learning to assist others' performance becomes a tool that can be applied to other professional situations (e.g., committee work, institutional planning, and curriculum design) and influence institutional decision-making about student outcomes. In this way, the effect of the Equity Scorecard process is scaled up beyond the team to other institutional contexts.

The *Equity Scorecard Process: Institutional Responsibility for Student Success* Project

Key to the effectiveness of the Equity Scorecard process were the structure and processes that provided the foundation to cultivate learning and equity-mindedness. The project structure and processes entailed (a) examining what we call *vital signs* data, (b) raising questions about the data, (c) requesting new data to answer questions prompted by the vital signs, (d) identifying and benchmarking student success indicators, and (e) reporting to the campus. To orient the teams to these activities, we held a two-day workshop in May 2005 at the University of Southern California. The workshop served to introduce team leaders, institutional researchers, and all other team members to the activities, as described in the following sections.

Examining Vital Signs Data

At the beginning of the project, institutional researchers on each team filled out and disseminated a vital signs worksheet to the team. These worksheets organized data on student outcomes into four perspectives on inequities in educational outcomes: academic pathways, retention and persistence, transfer readiness, and excellence. For each perspective, team members examined basic- or global-level measures to pinpoint potential areas of unequal outcomes (Bensimon, Hao, & Bustillos, 2006).

Raising Questions About the Data

After each team examined the vital signs worksheets, team members collaboratively identified troubling gaps and agreed on what additional data were needed to understand the source of the gaps. For example, after analyzing vital signs data on transfer rates disaggregated by race and ethnicity, some teams decided to look into the specific courses that became gatekeepers to transferring. Thus, teams examined students' progression, or lack thereof, from basic skills courses to transfer-level courses. By doing so, they identified specific courses that appeared to block students' progression along the transfer pathway.

Requesting New Data to Answer Questions

After identifying gaps that team members desired to further examine, the institutional researcher brought the data needed by the team members to define more precisely the conditions contributing to the gaps revealed in the vital signs. CUE researchers worked with the institutional researchers and team leaders to ensure that the data were presented in a manner that would generate insightful discussion and facilitate the learning of team members. Making sense of the data entailed discussions among the team members about the meaning of the findings. Through these discussions the teams identified what student groups, the administration, and faculty needed to become aware of in order to take action.

Identifying and Benchmarking Student Success Indicators

After having examined and discussed the data, team members identified indicators of student success to include in the Equity Scorecard. An indicator illustrates measures of equity or inequity of educational outcomes among ethnic and racial groups of students. These indicators were selected to designate a measure that would be monitored by the institution on a systematic and ongoing basis. For each indicator in the Equity Scorecard, teams documented the baseline, which represents the numeric value identifying the current status of the measure; the improvement target, which represents interim objectives or benchmarks; and the equity goal, which represents the point at which equity would be achieved for the particular measure (see Figure 11.1).

Reporting to the Campus

The final step in the Equity Scorecard process entails reporting the team's findings to the campus. Each team wrote a report to the president, which was widely disseminated throughout the campus. Reports described pertinent findings and selected indicators for each perspective, a completed Equity Scorecard, and recommendations for future action steps to redress inequities in educational outcomes. Equity Scorecard process teams strategically disseminated reports to relevant constituencies, some of which included campus academic senates, academic departments (e.g., English, math, English as a second language), strategic planning committees, and boards of trustees.

The following sections detail how the Equity Scorecard process facilitated changes in individuals' understanding and perceptions of inequities in educational outcomes and, in turn, transformed institutional practices through organizational learning.

Evidence of Change

The two key elements of the Equity Scorecard process—engaging as practitioner-researchers and assisting others' learning and performance—created conditions for cultivating equity-mindedness and learning. In this section we offer three cases as examples that illustrate these elements of the project. The first case exemplifies a practitioner-researcher who initially interpreted student deficits as the source of unequal outcomes and, over time through data examination, became more equity-minded in her interpretations. We then describe a case of a team leader who exhibits various means

FIGURE 11.1
Equity Scorecard framework.

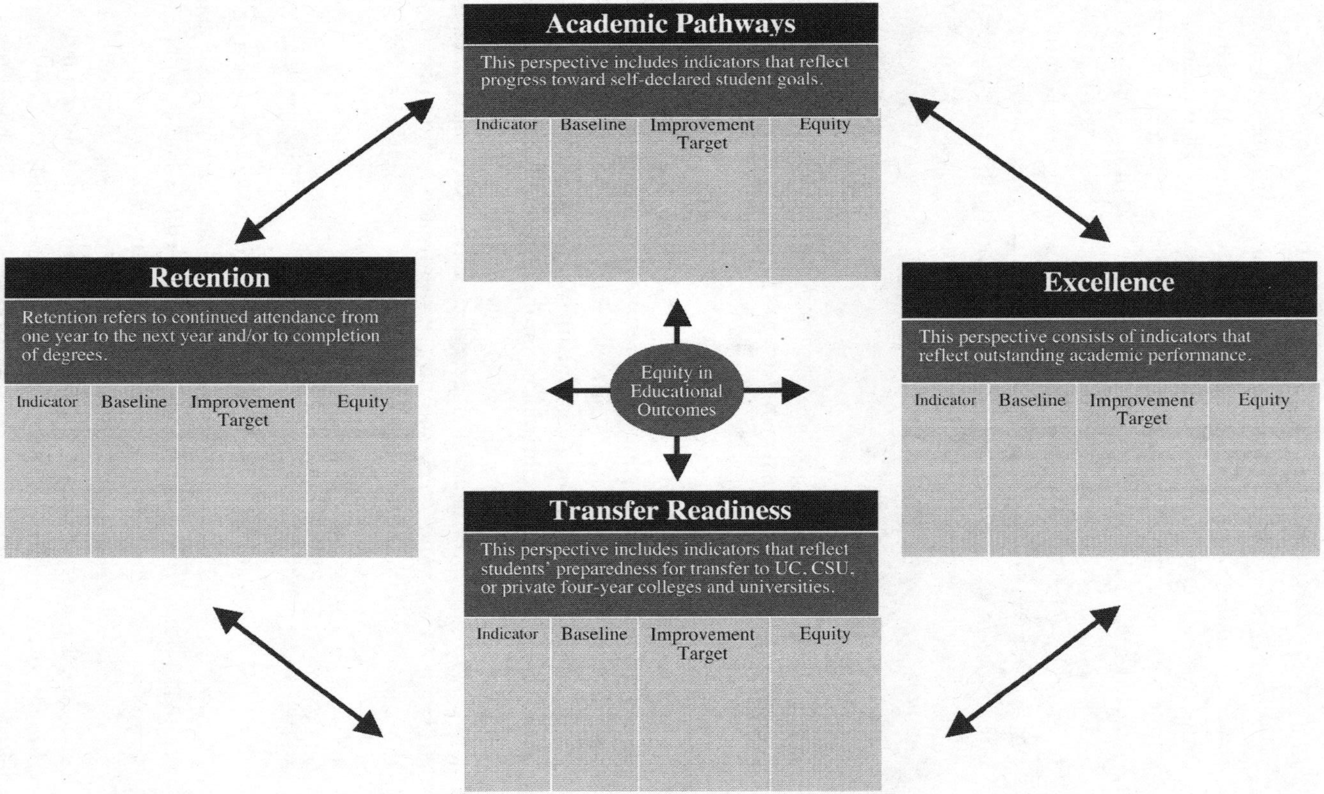

Excellence

This perspective consists of indicators that reflect outstanding academic performance.

Indicator	Baseline	Improvement Target	Equity

Academic Pathways

This perspective includes indicators that reflect progress toward self-declared student goals.

Indicator	Baseline	Improvement Target	Equity

Transfer Readiness

This perspective includes indicators that reflect students' preparedness for transfer to UC, CSU, or private four-year colleges and universities.

Indicator	Baseline	Improvement Target	Equity

Retention

Retention refers to continued attendance from one year to the next year and/or to completion of degrees.

Indicator	Baseline	Improvement Target	Equity

Equity in Educational Outcomes

of assisting team members' performance and learning. The last case depicts an institutional researcher who developed a greater capacity to organize and present data in ways that increased team members' learning and awareness of inequities in student outcomes.

Practitioner-as-Researcher Case: Developing Equity-Mindedness

Vanessa,[1] a vice president of academic affairs at one of the partner community colleges in southern California, remained an active participant from the project's inception. With a stern tone and serious demeanor, Vanessa rarely participated in team dialogue at the beginning of the project. When she did speak, Vanessa asserted her beliefs about the students and the community college unapologetically. During the second team meeting, the team engaged in the process of asking questions of the vital signs data. Vanessa told the team that examining data on students who did not declare the goal of transfer was an unworthy pursuit because "we don't have control of this." Vanessa believed that students who did not initially enter the community college with the intent to transfer could not be persuaded or empowered to achieve this goal. Perceiving the fate of these particular students to be out of her hands and of the institution's hands allowed Vanessa to overlook the institution's responsibility of ensuring that students have equitable access to transfer opportunities. Rather than questioning what the college might do to increase the number of students who wished to transfer—a feat that leads students to more opportunities toward social mobility—Vanessa automatically assumed the issue should be left as it was because, from her perspective, the institution could not influence this important student outcome.

Throughout the course of the project, Vanessa's perceptions about students surfaced during the team's discussion about the data. For example, she advocated examining only those students who entered in the fall semester and were age eighteen to twenty-five because these students in particular were "the more serious students, if you will." Vanessa did not see the value of analyzing data on students who were less likely to achieve the associate degree or transfer. Again, she desired to focus on students who were most likely to achieve successful student outcomes—in her opinion, the students whom the college was truly aiming to serve.

In general, Vanessa focused on students' characteristics at the beginning stages of the Equity Scorecard process. She made sense of students' outcomes by asking questions about their characteristics rather than about institutional responsibility. For example, Vanessa interpreted the data she examined by saying, "The story is that obviously Black students in terms of academic progress are not doing anything much. So my question is, what identifying characteristics might explain some of the low participation?"

When a team member noted that Asians and Pacific Islanders performed low on math courses for the associate's degree, Vanessa attributed this achievement gap to students' deficits. Specifically, she believed "there are preparedness issues there." While Vanessa's attribution to unequal outcomes might have held some truth, she did not stop to consider other reasons for the gap. Rather than considering the ways in which institutional and instructional practices might perpetuate inequitable outcomes, Vanessa jumped to the conclusion that the student group in question did not enter the community college prepared for math. As such, Vanessa once again relieved herself and the institution of responsibility for student outcomes. She then asked the team,

> I have a question about preparedness. It would be interesting to see how many students tested into certain classes. I don't see what we can do about that. They come to us and they are where they are. We have to take the next steps.

In her statement, Vanessa once again reflected her belief that the institution could not assist those students who came in academically underprepared. However, Vanessa closed her comment by adding that the institution would have to "take the next steps" and work with the students regardless of their preparedness. This was a teachable moment. The CUE researcher on this team took the opportunity to reorient the conversation to a perspective of equity. Directing his attention to Vanessa, he said, "The latter part of what you said is really important. First, it's important to know where they are. Second, we have to take the next steps. A lot of other institutions don't know where the gaps are. You do."

We began to notice a shift in Vanessa's sensemaking halfway through the Equity Scorecard process. At this point, she showed signs of becoming equity-minded. The data she examined in team meetings surprised her. She began to think about the ways in which the institution could take a proactive stance to redress unequal outcomes. For example, in collaboration with the team, Vanessa examined data for the academic pathways perspective of the Equity Scorecard that pertained to academic support services used by students who graduated (e.g., attendance in a counseling class, educational opportunity program participation, and academic course assessment status). She said,

> Some of this stuff is beginning to sink in when looking at this data. We can do a number of different things. We can begin to share this information, especially for counselors who do Counseling 101. Think how powerful this would be to share with students. Sharing it with faculty. . . . This would have a positive effect that would translate into the classroom.

Over time, Vanessa became more engaged in the process of making sense of the data's implications than resorting to assumptions or jumping to conclusions about the source of educational gaps. Vanessa moved from interpreting student outcomes as a cause of their characteristics to thinking about outcomes in terms of institutional practices. At one point she said, "It's not just by accident that there's a group not doing well," which was the opposite of how she reacted to disparities in the beginning. She wondered if students who took "the reading classes may do better. There's a lot more going on than specific discrete skills." She later added, "I think we underestimate what happens in the classroom."

By the end of the project, Vanessa became a more active and vocal participant on the Equity Scorecard process team. To improve student success, she advocated for "getting counselors on board," "a curriculum change," and continuing inquiry into student outcomes disaggregated by race and ethnicity with "our newly founded Division of Institutional Planning and Research." She asserted that "the math faculty and the English faculty are a serious part of that discussion." Vanessa believed that the data, when shared with others, had potential to enlighten and empower institutional actors to think and act differently with regard to student outcomes. "I think that this discussion and dialogue," Vanessa told her teammates, "causes people to do all kinds of things . . . they haven't done before."

Team Leader Case: Assisting Team Members' Learning and Sensemaking

Angela, a faculty member and Title V coordinator at a northern California institution, served as the team leader for her Equity Scorecard process evidence team. While Angela gained a deeper understanding of inequities as a result of her participation in the project, she assisted others to learn from data, adopt an equity-minded perspective, and reflect on ways in which to close the achievement gap.

After the first several meetings, Angela made a point to encourage team members to engage in making sense of the data. "Which of the statistics cries out for attention?" she asked the team. Angela desired to make the discussion about the data as interactive as possible. She modeled explanation of the data to the team by offering her interpretation of the data. "The surprising story for me . . . is that Asian males had a low persistence rate and Asian females do not. See that's against the stereotypes and the myths." While Angela shared her new knowledge about students and their outcomes, she also expressed to the team the importance of relying on data rather than "stereotypes" and "myths" to understand educational disparities that students experience. This kind of knowing is based on truth, rather than assumptions.

In addition to encouraging dialogue and offering her own interpretations of the data, Angela aptly made use of opportunities to reorient team conversation when necessary. For example, a faculty member deviated from examining the data to discuss her beliefs about students, which were based on personal anecdotes. Angela stepped in to the conversation to refocus the team's dialogue, drawing from the data's implications and the faculty member's story taken together. Angela asked, "When I think of that—the story itself—[the question] is, what services are we providing for those students? I mean, what is it, you know that they aren't getting that other students are?"

As the project continued, Angela encouraged team members to become "experts" on the data depicting student outcomes. She wanted to ensure that the team understood the data because "the campus community will have the same questions." She viewed the team as holding the considerable responsibility of communicating key findings to various campus constituents in order to foster organizational learning. After interpreting data on student outcomes aloud, Angela told her colleagues, "Yes, I'm being the test case [for interpreting the data]. This will probably be in our report. Someone who hasn't been in our meetings needs to be able to interpret this."

Midway through the project, Angela increasingly shared her own learning with the team as well as assisted their learning by asking team members critical questions about institutional practices. She admitted her own assumptions had been refuted by the data. For instance, after learning that Black students did not progress past basic skills courses, Angela told the team:

> You know why I didn't expect it? Because our college is so diverse, so I just take for granted that everything is diverse. And so the data doesn't necessarily speak to that being true. That was my first impression.

Angela also shared what she learned about the overrepresentation of certain student groups in different classes and programs. "It was my impression that there's some unconscious tracking going on of students by ethnicity at our college possibly." Angela was surprised to learn the institution was engaging in this "unconscious tracking of certain ethnic groups in career paths that do not lead to high-paying jobs." She challenged the team to think about ways in which the institution was responsible: "What are we doing so that we provide students with advisement, career advisement on higher-paying career options?"

Even toward the end of the Equity Scorecard process, team members still felt the need to focus on student characteristics to explain inequities in educational outcomes. In these instances, Angela took the opportunity to shift the topic of conversation to holding the institution accountable. She suggested to the team members that they not jump to conclusions:

> You just can't look at it and say certain populations are not succeeding in majors. But it does help me to say for each of those departments, when this dataset goes out to those faculties, to look at themselves and ask questions about what is going on here—that there will be different reasons for different majors. You can't just take it for granted . . . but we do need to ask questions.

By the end of the project, Angela had exposed her team members to alternative ways of reading the data. She taught them to ask questions about underlying practices of the institution rather than assume students had deficits. Angela shared the Scorecard findings with other committees on campus. She sought to organize a panel to discuss "if there is a racial divide in the college, just to have a discussion about it." The racial divide she spoke of manifested itself in several ways, according to Angela:

> It came about when we looked at program majors. It comes up in the dialogue with staff and faculty. It's an undercurrent. I think it's something that should be brought out in the open. Some colleges say it's not there and that it doesn't exist.

Because of her increased and more accurate awareness of unequal outcomes at her institution, Angela became empowered to confront and engage the campus community with this important topic that had remained largely invisible and unacknowledged.

Institutional Researcher Case: Developing Capacity for Data Interpretation

Although some team leaders, like Angela, consistently assisted others' performance over the duration of the project, most team members needed more time to develop these skills. Jackie, an institutional researcher at a northern California institution, represents one such example. Although she did not begin the project by assisting others' learning on the team, her involvement in the Equity Scorecard process increased her capacity to assist team members in engaging in data analysis and sensemaking. As a result, the team members at Jackie's college were better able to identify and engage in critical dialogue about inequities in student outcomes.

In the beginning of the Equity Scorecard process, Jackie typically presented data on the Academic Pathways perspective using Microsoft Excel tables. Table 11.1 depicts an example of an Excel table Jackie presented at the second team meeting. Data on the completion of degree-applicable English courses, disaggregated by race, ethnicity, and gender, are displayed.

Although Jackie's table was accurate and comprehensive, it was difficult to read because of the overwhelming amount of data. She did not organize it in such a way that allowed team members to understand where the disparities existed. For example, her data displays were not accompanied by graphs, charts, or analytical points to assist the team in identifying and interpreting gaps in the data. In addition, when Jackie presented the table to the team, she did not point out gaps in student outcomes, nor did she invite conversation to collaboratively make sense of the data.

After the second evidence team meeting, the CUE researcher took notice of the lack of discussion on the data. The CUE researcher decided to encourage Jackie to develop her data presentations in several ways. First, she persuaded Jackie to point out the gaps in the data, rather than read the percentages for each group out loud. She proposed that Jackie create charts and graphs to assist team members in making sense of disparities in student outcomes. Second, the CUE researcher asked Jackie to encourage team dialogue when presenting the data. She suggested that Jackie ask team members to take turns interpreting data slides. This shift in data presentation would allow team members to move from passive to active learners.

Jackie shifted her data presentation style and format from simply presenting Excel tables to presenting tables accompanied by charts and graphs using PowerPoint (see Figure 11.2 for an example).

These new presentations graphically displayed data on measures such as the one illustrated in Figure 11.2 on students' completion rates of twelve or

TABLE 11.1

Jackie's Data Presentation at the Beginning of the Equity Scorecard Process

COMBINED NEW STUDENTS 1997–2002

Degree-Applicable English Completion Through Spring 2004: Gender by Ethnicity for All Students in the Cohort Who Completed a Basic Skills English Course

Group	Highest Degree-Applicable Completion Level								Total
	No Enrollment		Drop		Unsuccessful		Successful		
FEMALE									
Asian	33.3%	8	12.5%	3	8.3%	2	45.8%	11	24
African American	35.6%	52	5.5%	8	20.5%	30	38.4%	56	146
Filipino	45.5%	5	0.0%	0	9.1%	1	45.5%	5	11
Hispanic/Latino	43.5%	27	6.5%	4	9.7%	6	40.3%	25	62
Native American	100.0%	1	0.0%	0	0.0%	0	0.0%	0	1
Other Non White	16.7%	1	16.7%	1	16.7%	1	50.0%	3	6
White Non Hispanic	21.4%	3	21.4%	3	14.3%	2	42.9%	6	14
Unknown	25.0%	2	0.0%	0	12.5%	1	62.5%	5	8
Female Total	36.4%	99	7.0%	19	15.8%	43	40.8%	111	272
MALE									
Asian	30.8%	4	7.7%	1	15.4%	2	46.2%	6	13
African American	30.8%	20	9.2%	6	16.9%	11	43.1%	28	65
Filipino	33.3%	1	0.0%	0	0.0%	0	66.7%	2	3
Hispanic/Latino	46.2%	6	0.0%	0	23.1%	3	30.8%	4	13
Other Non White	50.0%	1	0.0%	0	0.0%	0	50.0%	1	2
White Non Hispanic	33.3%	3	0.0%	0	0.0%	0	66.7%	6	9
Unknown	0.0%	0	25.0%	1	0.0%	0	75.0%	3	4
Male Total	32.1%	35	7.3%	8	14.7%	16	45.9%	50	109
GENDER NOT STATED									
African American	50.0%	2	0.0%	0	0.0%	0	50.0%	2	4
Filipino	100.0%	1	0.0%	0	0.0%	0	0.0%	0	1
Unknown Total	60.0%	3	0.0%	0	0.0%	0	40.0%	2	5
Total	35.5%	137	7.0%	27	15.3%	59	42.2%	163	386

FIGURE 11.2

Sample data presentation using PowerPoint.

Transfer Direct: Completion of 12 or More Transfer-Level Units Including English & Math

Of students who successfully completed 12 or more transferable units including transferable math and English within 3 years,

- **Overrepresented:** Asian, "Other," and White students are overrepresented relative to their representation in the new matriculating population.
- **Underrepresented:** African American, Hispanic, and Native American students are underrepresented relative to their representation in the matriculating population.
- **Parity:** Filipino and "Unknown" students are represented at parity relative to their representation in the matriculating population.

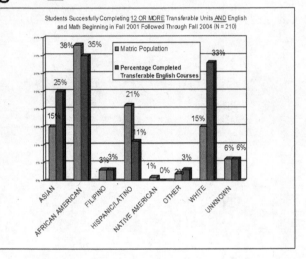

more transfer-level units. In addition, Jackie included interpretive bullet points that made the illustration easier to read.

Although the new graphical representations were clear and well-prepared, when Jackie presented the data to the team, she merely read aloud the percentages for each student group as well as the accompanying bullet points that summarized disparities. Once again, she failed to ask team members to assist her in interpreting the data or ask questions of the data to generate new insights. This form of data presentation discouraged team members from participating. The CUE researcher intervened once more to encourage Jackie to stimulate discussion about data among team members. In this instance, the CUE researcher used her knowledge and skills to assist the performance (Tharp, 1993) of someone new to the process of facilitating the learning of others. Like Jackie, other institutional researchers in the Equity Scorecard process tended to see themselves as data providers and may not have had expertise in helping team members and others to make meaning out of data.

By the end of the Equity Scorecard process, Jackie's data presentation style changed in several observable ways. First, her data presentation slides became more developed, as evidenced by the changes seen between Table 11.1 and Figure 11.2. Summary statements and interpretive bullet points accompanied her new data displays, noting which groups experienced the most significant disparities in outcomes.

Second, Jackie's data presentations during team meetings became more interactive. Her capacity to engage team members in making sense of the data increased. During the last several evidence team meetings, she asked questions like, "So does someone want to take a shot at reading this one?" and "Would you like to read the chart, Harry?" In addition, Jackie began to use other team members' expertise to inform the conversations on data that connected to their line of work. For instance, while discussing data on certificate and transfer requirements, Jackie asked Sam, a counselor at the college, to explain the different kinds of requirements to the team:

> So Sam, perhaps you can explain this whole IGETC.[2] We had a big discussion before—why students would want to get the Breadth certification when IGETC includes CSU and UC. A student can get IGETC and transfer to a UC. Why would they do the Breadth certification? What function does it serve?

Sam became a more active participant during the latter team meetings due, in large part, to Jackie's increased ability to facilitate data sensemaking. Sam's role on the team shifted. He moved from a mostly silent team member to one who expressed enthusiasm to learn and understand the implications behind student outcome gaps.

We found that Jackie's change over time in the Equity Scorecard process project was instrumental to her role as institutional researcher and her role in assisting others' learning. In the beginning of the project, the CUE researcher assisted Jackie's performance to present data more effectively and facilitate a more engaging dialogue among the team members.

Conclusion: Organizational Learning

In this chapter we described three cases—one that illustrated learning and equity-mindedness as a result of becoming a practitioner-researcher, one that

4 CONFRONTING EQUITY ISSUES ON CAMPUS

exemplified a team leader who learned from the data while assisting others
to learn and become more equity-minded, and one that depicted an institutional researcher who increased her capacity to present the data in such a
way that assisted team members' learning. It is important to note that the
learning that resulted from participation in the project varied at each institution. Such differences can be attributed to factors such as institutional context and team composition. Following is a description of various selected
outcomes at the participating institutions:

- All of the Equity Scorecard teams disseminated information about
  key findings to various campus constituents, in addition to their presidents. The teams attempted to create new discourse on campus about
  students of color by engaging the campus community in a dialogue
  about data on inequitable educational outcomes. One team in Southern California created and e-mailed Equity Scorecard process newsletters to inform faculty and administrators on campus about significant
  gaps in achievement. Hard copies of the newsletter were printed in
  color and delivered to committees whose work tied into improving
  student outcomes.
- One English faculty member at a northern California institution discovered startling disparities in transfer rates at her college. In her
  effort to "catch them early," she recruited transfer counselors to systematically speak to students who entered into basic skills English
  courses. The faculty member proactively informed these students
  about steps to transferring in order to empower them to move forward from basic skills to college level English as a way to ultimately
  transfer.
- One institution infused the Equity Scorecard process into its strategic
  plan. A member of the team announced that the "institutional plan
  . . . contains goals directly related to equity and the Equity Scorecard
  process project." Because the Equity Scorecard process became
  "built-in to the institutional plan, [academic departments] will be
  able to discuss data related to student performance in their particular
  area and discuss how to bring about equity."
- A southern California team discovered that a large number of students had reached "transfer-ready" status but never transferred. This
  information inspired action by the Title V committee on campus.
  The committee successfully identified and contacted fifty transfer-
  eligible students, proactively intervening by providing students the

necessary information and tools to transfer. The committee also identified 1,600 students who were close to completing the general education degree requirements. The committee sent postcards and e-mails to this cohort of students to encourage them to petition for the associate's degree and complete degree requirements.

- Another team in northern California became aware from analyzing data on student outcomes that a large number of students do not declare their race on the college application. These particular students were marked as "unknowns," thereby making it difficult for team members to accurately identify the number of students who may have experienced academic inequities. Realizing that students did not have an opportunity to identify as "mixed race," team members believed that many mixed race students opted for the "unknown" category because "they don't fit into any of the [ethnic] categories" listed on the application. The team made necessary steps to ensure that the proper administrator on campus "redo the application online." One team member went as far as to tell the administrator who changed the application that "if he didn't [redo the application], I was going to report him."

- One Equity Scorecard process college is beginning a collegewide focus on improving basic skills education as a result of the data analyses it conducted for the Equity Scorecard process. The team leader for the project has been promoted to a dean position and is charged with leading this effort.

- Several Equity Scorecard process teams discussed the possibility of conducting focus groups and interviews with students of color. They desired to gain a more in-depth understanding of the factors that promote and inhibit students' success in community college. Often, committees do not consider collecting qualitative data to understand how students experience college. These discussions reyflected a shift in thinking for team members. Teams went from automatically placing the majority of the responsibility of unequal outcomes onto students to taking proactive steps to learn from students about their academic lives in order to change the ways colleges served them.

What we have learned from observing the nine participating community colleges is that the Equity Scorecard process empowers individuals to become agents of change because of their new awareness of inequitable educational outcomes. Individuals begin to conceptualize student outcomes from an equity perspective. This shift in awareness and perspective tends to spread to others beyond the Equity Scorecard process teams. Slowly but surely, institutions become drawn in to the alarming and often surprising data, a catalyst for organizational learning. Institutions learn from the information and apply new knowledge to existing practices that are in need of change. We hope they continue to make giant strides in achieving equity.

Notes

1. For confidentiality, pseudonyms have been assigned to all Equity Scorecard process participants discussed in this article.
2. The Intersegmental General Education Transfer Curriculum (IGETC) is a series of courses prospective transfer students attending California community colleges may complete to satisfy the lower-division breadth and general education requirements at both the University of California and the California State University. It was developed to simplify the transfer process for students (University of California–Admissions, 2006).

References

Bauman, G. L. (2005). Promoting organizational learning in higher education to achieve equity in educational outcomes. In A. Kezar (Ed.), *Organizational learning in higher education: New directions for higher education* (No. 131, pp. 23–35). San Francisco, CA: Jossey-Bass.

Bensimon, E. M. (2005). Closing the achievement gap in higher education: An organizational learning perspective. In A. Kezar (Ed.), *Organizational learning in higher education: New directions for higher education* (No. 131, pp. 99–111). San Francisco, CA: Jossey-Bass.

Bensimon, E. M., Hao, L., & Bustillos, L. T. (2006). Measuring the state of equity in higher education. In P. Gandara, G. Orfield, & C. Horn, (Eds.), *Leveraging promise and expanding opportunity in higher education*. Albany, NY: SUNY Press.

Bensimon, E. M., Polkinghorne, D. E., Bauman, G., & Vallejo, E. (2004). Doing research that makes a difference. *The Journal of Higher Education, 75*(1), 104–126.

Dowd, A. C. (2005). *Data don't drive: Building a practitioner-driven culture of inquiry to assess community college performance.* Indianapolis, IN: Lumina Foundation for Education.

Garvin, D. A. (1993). Building a learning organization. *Harvard Business Review, 71*(4), 78–91.

Tharp, R. (1993). Institutional and social context of educational practice and reform. In E. A. Forman, N. Minick, & C. A. Stone (Eds.), *Contexts for learning: Sociocultural dynamics in children's development*. New York, NY: Oxford University Press.

Tharp, R., & Gallimore, R. (1988). *Rousing minds to life: Teaching and Learning in Social Context.* New York, NY: Cambridge University Press.

University of California–Admissions. (2006). *Planning to transfer—IGETC.* Retrieved from http://www.universityofcalifornia.edu/admissions/undergrad_adm/paths_to_adm/transfer/tr_info_ccc/tr_planning_IGETC.html

STAGES OF LEARNING AND PROFESSIONAL DEVELOPMENT

Tharp & Gallimore's stages of learning and development	I. Assistance provided by more capable others	II. Assistance provided by the self	III. Internalization, Automatization, "Fossilization"	IV. De-automatization: Recursiveness through prior stages
Equivalent description adopted for this report	Guided learning	Self-guided learning	Established (& entrenched) knowledge	Un-learning and renewed cycle of learning

Source: First row reproduced from Tharp & Gallimore (1988, p. 35). Second row presents the author's equivalent terms for reference to each stage.

Note: Developed by Dr. Alicia C. Dowd, associate professor of higher education, for the *Equity Scorecard Process: Institutional Responsibility for Student Success* Project.

12

REFLECTIONS FROM
THE FIELD

Georgia L. Lorenz

I n my experience in higher education, I feel confident that everybody
has good intentions. No one wants African American and Latino and
Latina students to achieve at lower, inequitable levels. No one walks
into her classroom on the first day of the semester and thinks to herself,
"This semester I want to hinder the success of my Latino students and make
sure those Asian American students excel." Even the elder statesmen of the
math department who only teach the most sophisticated math courses, who
often get a bad rap, do not desire or *consciously* work toward inequitable
educational outcomes. However, these same faculty members may not be
conscious of the fact that the students staring back at them in differential
equations do not look the same as those in arithmetic, the entry-level remedial course.

The Equity Scorecard brings about that consciousness and, most importantly, the knowledge and will and tools to do something about it—to
ensure that advanced math classes resemble remedial math classes. The Long
Beach City College team, for example, discovered that African American
students did not succeed in the associate of arts degree–level math course at
an equitable rate. However, they also found that African American students
who repeated the course succeeded at higher rates in the second attempt
than any other ethnic group. Thus, they discovered two important points
for potential intervention. First, they should work with the faculty who teach
the course to find ways to increase persistence among African American
students. Second, faculty and staff should reach out to African American

students who received a D or F, or who withdrew from the course, and encourage them to enroll in the course again right away.

I am personally interested in and committed to equity. I went to college in the age of multiculturalism and political correctness. And I learned some difficult and valuable lessons along the way as a White student who had enjoyed a lot of privilege in her life. I spent my days as a student leader and in the early years of my career as a student affairs professional committed to promoting intercultural understanding; creating safe educational spaces for all students; and promoting fields such as Asian American studies, Chicano studies, and African American studies as legitimate academic disciplines.

But I realized rather quickly that the biggest difference in terms of equity in educational outcomes will always be made in the classroom. Every student takes classes. That is the only thing that every student truly holds in common. The classroom is the venue for change in educational outcomes and, therefore, changes in opportunity and life circumstances. The Equity Scorecard brings together teams of people who can make that difference. Becoming a research assistant at the Center for Urban Education (CUE) at the University of Southern California (USC) provided me with an unprecedented occasion to be part of that change.

Not all team members began the Equity Scorecard project "on board," as they say. Many felt that we were calling them and their institutions racist. We encountered a good deal of resistance and there were certainly stumbles along the way. But 100 percent of the team members I encountered engaged in the project fully as professionals dedicated to education. I had the opportunity to witness many turning points and was able to see when it really came together and "gelled" for a team. One example of such a time was the moment in which the California State–Los Angeles team realized what a large proportion of its Latina students were majoring in early childhood education, which proffered the lowest potential financial earnings over a lifetime of any major, because of a gateway math course that the students did not want to take. The Latina students chose the liberal arts, "dead-end" math course rather than the course that could lead to other careers, including those in business and the sciences. Another moment was when the Whittier team began naming the campus "myths" that everyone took for granted but that were proven wrong by the data it studied. These myths, based on anecdotes and personal experiences, had shaped practices across campus for years. No one had checked the data to confirm the myths were true.

There were two major components that made the greatest difference to the success of a team in the Equity Scorecard project: who made up the team and the extent to which the team relied on data. Who the members of the team were made a difference both in the accomplishments of the team and in who listened to their results. It was important for the team members to represent diverse roles on the campus. The teams who had an institutional researcher, faculty members, and administrators on them were more successful than those whose members came predominantly from one of those groups. These diverse roles allowed for a diversity of perspectives on the analysis and interpretation of data, on the questions the team asked of the data, and on the areas of interest pursued. The dean of undergraduate studies may be most interested in retention and graduation rates, whereas a faculty member in engineering may be most interested in discovering the point at which African American students are opting out of science- and math-related majors. These varied interests resulted in fine-grained measures, in-depth discussions, and important discoveries about the educational experience at the institution.

When campus leaders were included on the team, the campus listened. And "leaders" were not necessarily those who had a leadership title. We all know who others listen to on our campus, and it is not necessarily the dean or the senate president. Those people who have informal political influence, whose opinions shape those of others, are critical team members. And when the "naysayers" delivered the team's message, the campus listened. These are the people who have traditionally positioned themselves against things like the Equity Scorecard and maybe even affirmative action. If they are delivering a message about achieving equity in educational outcomes, it is a powerful message.

Those teams who prioritized what the data told them above all else were the most successful. These teams trusted what the data revealed even when it ran counter to their own experiences, the reports of others on campus, and campus myths. This team characteristic is evident in the other chapters of this book.

The practitioner-as-researcher model was critical to the success of the Equity Scorecard. It was of vital importance that the CUE researchers were only facilitators of this process. The facilitator role was valuable for several reasons. As outsiders, we could ask the dangerous and impolite questions that an insider simply could not. We had the benefit of our experiences with many colleges that informed our work with each team. And we had background knowledge on higher education, the achievement gap, and other topics as academic researchers that the team members may not have.

We could have gone into each institution, gathered the data, conducted the analysis, and written a report with our recommendations as to how equity in outcomes could be achieved. Believe me, that would have been easier. But no learning would have taken place at the college under study. Because the team members were the researchers, they owned the process and their results. They reported their *own* findings to their *own* campuses. As the principal investigators, when they wanted to know more about a particular issue, they found out. The CUE researchers lent experiences and resources that helped, but the act of engaging in the research was the true lever of change.

Unlike most special projects or programs, the Equity Scorecard is automatically institutionalized. Because the Equity Scorecard used data that were routinely collected on an annual basis and was conducted by institutional insiders, it is a project that was easily absorbed into regular, recurring institutional processes like program review. Program review requires the use of the same or at least similar types of data and requires a report written by a team of people reflecting on the effectiveness of their program. The Equity Scorecard was, in fact, born out of a type of program review at USC when Estela Bensimon was reporting on the state of the School of Education as associate dean with a team of faculty. The Scorecard process is built on this convention of higher education.

It was exciting to watch the teams make discoveries along the way and figure out how to leverage the resources at their institutions to promote equity. I began wanting to be a team member on the other side of the table rather than a facilitator of the process. And through working with the teams at community colleges, I became committed to the mission of the community college. I feel that community colleges have the greatest potential to make a difference because this sector has the largest number of traditionally underrepresented students enrolled. The tagline for my college is, "Changing lives through excellence in education." And I think we can do exactly that. There is a greater "value added" if we can change a student's terminal education level from a high school diploma to a bachelor's degree. That difference can completely change the life circumstances of that individual student and those of the future generations of his or her family.

In the day-to-day grind, actively attending to equity in educational outcomes is very difficult to do. It is extremely frustrating to realize that you're spending your time as a dean quibbling over who gets to teach what and which data code to use on a course and how many chairs should be in a particular classroom rather than on those things that could more directly affect equity. I hope that in my role as a dean I am able to create clear educational pathways absent of needless hurdles for students to achieve their educational goals. I hope to create safe and open educational environments in which all students can succeed. But upon reflection, I realize that is not enough.

Developing a faculty whose members are dedicated to equity in educational outcomes is the key—the silver bullet in my estimation. This dedication would be evident both inside and outside the classroom. In the classroom, this dedication might mean that one does not treat all students the same. It could mean that the instructor must find the most effective way to reach and educate each student. Obviously, this is not the easiest or most expedient way to run a classroom, but "easy" and "expedient" rarely make a difference. Outside the classroom, faculty members can have a profound influence on the institution and its priorities. In all campus processes, from prerequisite studies to program review, faculty can raise Equity Scorecard–type questions. Faculty members can challenge colleagues engaged in such processes to determine the point at which small changes can make a big difference in the success of our students. Through participatory governance structures, the faculty can pressure the institution to make equity a priority.

None of us will be satisfied until equity in educational outcomes is achieved. When African American students are attaining an equitable proportion of bachelor's degrees and doctoral degrees across disciplines, our priorities can shift. One clear sign we have achieved equity will be when the faculty across the spectrum of higher education look the same as the students they are teaching.

I had the great fortune to be one of the first research assistants for the CUE at USC and was part of the Equity Scorecard experiment from the beginning. My dissertation was one of the first publications associated with the project. Through my experiences with CUE and the project, I learned volumes about inequity itself, how colleges and universities work, and the potential of the community college system. Under the tenacious leadership of Dr. Estela Bensimon, both CUE and the Equity Scorecard have thrived. Dr. Bensimon and the Scorecard have affected hundreds of faculty members and administrators who have changed the educational trajectory for thousands of students, fundamentally changing the way these institutions operate and the life circumstances of those students. In each college where the Equity Scorecard has taken hold, it has become simply "the way we do things," rendering equity in educational outcomes a priority for all stakeholders.

Diana Akiyama was the director of the Office for Religious and Spiritual Life at Occidental College–Los Angeles from 2003 to 2008. She has also held a lecturing post at Stanford University in feminist studies and anthropology and was formerly an associate dean of Stanford Memorial Church.

Estela Mara Bensimon is a professor of higher education and codirector of the Center for Urban Education at the USC Rossier School of Education. Her current research is on issues of racial equity in higher education from the perspective of organizational learning and sociocultural practice theories. She is particularly interested in place-based, practitioner-driven inquiry as a means of organizational change in higher education. Dr. Bensimon has held the highest leadership positions in the Association for the Study of Higher Education (president, 2005–2006) and in the American Education Research Association—Division on Postsecondary Education (vice president, 1992–1994). She has served on the boards of the American Association for Higher Education and the Association of American Colleges and Universities. Dr. Bensimon was associate dean of the USC Rossier School of Education from 1996 to 2000 and was a Fulbright Scholar to Mexico in 2002. She earned her doctorate in higher education from Teachers College, Columbia University.

Laura Palucki Blake is the assistant director of the Cooperative Institutional Research Program at the Higher Education Research Institute at UCLA. She received her bachelor's degree from Smith College and her master's and PhD in social psychology from the Claremont Graduate University. Laura's scholarship focuses on issues access and equity for women and minorities in education as well as assessment strategies that promote improvement in teaching and learning.

Elizabeth Braker is an associate professor in the department of biology at Occidental College. Beth teaches conservation biology, animal behavior, and biodiversity. Her research interests include the ecology and evolution of relationships between plants and insects, host plants and life histories of grasshoppers, and tropical biology and conservation. She earned her doctorate in zoology from the University of California, Berkeley, and her bachelor's in biology from Colorado College.

Leticia Tomas Bustillos currently serves as associate director of the Los Angeles County Education Foundation, which has a mission to provide exceptional educational opportunities to disadvantaged children and youth. In her position, Leticia advocates for policy changes and increased programming in the areas of early childhood and school readiness, science and environmental education, and child welfare services. In addition, she serves as codirector of the Policy Research in Preparation, Access and Remedial Education (PRePARE) project with Tara L. Parker at the University of Massachusetts–Boston. The project conducts research and analysis on policies guiding remedial and developmental education practices in higher education. Presently, PRePARE is involved in a three-year national initiative to improve remedial and developmental studies in higher education in collaboration with the Education Commission of the States and funded by the Lumina Foundation. Leticia received her PhD in education policy from the University of Southern California.

Andrea Clemons is currently an education specialist with UNICEF. She has worked as an assistant professor in the School of Education at Loyola Marymount University and the University of Southern California. She received her master's degree from the University of Toronto and her PhD in international/intercultural education from the University of Southern California. Her work and writing seeks to contribute to improved teaching, learning, and equity in education.

Alicia C. Dowd is an associate professor of education at the University of Southern California's Rossier School of Education and a codirector of the Center for Urban Education. Dr. Dowd's research focuses on political-economic issues of public college finance equity, organizational effectiveness, and accountability and the factors affecting student attainment in higher education. Dr. Dowd was awarded the PhD in 1998 from Cornell University, where her fields of study included social foundations of education, educational administration, labor economics, and curriculum. She was awarded the master of science degree in the field of education in 1997 and the bachelor of arts degree with distinction in all subjects, also from Cornell University, where she majored in English literature as an undergraduate.

Matthew Fissinger currently serves as director of undergraduate admission at Loyola Marymount University in Los Angeles, California. Prior to coming to LMU in 1990, Matt worked for fourteen years in various capacities on the admission staff at his alma mater, Boston College. In addition to his responsibilities in admission, which include managing marketing, recruitment, and selection at LMU, Matt is a senior member of the enrollment management team at LMU, with involvement in the development and implementation of strategic financial aid packaging and in efforts to optimize retention. He has also held responsibility for New Student Orientation. In conjunction with LMU's Equity Scorecard project and as a member of the project's writing team, he has written and presented on LMU's work in the areas of diversity, access, and equity. Matt holds an undergraduate degree in Political Science and a master's in Higher Education, both from Boston College.

Debbie Ann Hanson is a project specialist in the Center for Urban Education in the Rossier School of Education at the University of Southern California. Debbie received a master's degree in Postsecondary Administration and Student Affairs at the USC Rossier School of Education and a master's degree in English from St. Cloud State University, Minnesota. Her research interests include institutional accountability through self-assessment and evaluation, data presentation methods, and equity for underserved student populations.

Frank Harris III is an associate professor of postsecondary education at San Diego State University. His research is broadly focused on student development in higher education and explores questions related to the social construction of gender and race on college campuses, college men and masculinities, and racial and ethnic disparities in college student outcomes. He earned a bachelor's degree in communication studies from Loyola Marymount University, a master's degree in speech communication from California State University–Northridge, and an EdD in higher education from the University of Southern California Rossier School of Education.

David A. Longanecker is the president of the Western Interstate Commission for Higher Education in Boulder, Colorado. Previously he served for six years as the assistant secretary for postsecondary education at the U.S. Department of Education, developing and implementing national policy and programs that provided more than $40 billion annually in student aid and $1 billion to institutions. Prior to that he was the state higher education executive officer (SHEEO) in Colorado and Minnesota. He was also the principal analyst for higher education for the Congressional Budget Office. Dr. Longanecker has served on numerous boards and commissions and has written extensively on a range of higher education issues. His primary interests in higher education are: access and equity; promoting student and institutional performance; finance; the efficient use of educational technologies; and internationalizing American higher education. He holds an Ed.D. from Stanford University, an M.A. in student personnel work from the George Washington University, and a B.A. in sociology from Washington State University.

Georgia L. Lorenz is the dean of instruction at Santa Monica College. She received her bachelor's degree from Stanford University, her master's degree from Northwestern University, and her PhD in education from the University of Southern California. Georgia's work is focused on curriculum, student success, access for students, and the global citizenship initiative at Santa Monica College (SMC), which aims to promote intercultural and international understanding among SMC students.

Donna Kay Maeda is professor and chair of the department of critical theory and Social Justice at Occidental College in Los Angeles. Donna has served as special assistant to the president on issues of diversity and equity at Occidental. She has also served as academic director for Oxy's Multicultural Summer Institute. Donna holds a PhD in social ethics from the University of Southern California; a JD from the University of California, Berkeley, School of Law (Boalt Hall); and a BA in music history and literature from St. Olaf College. Donna teaches and writes about race, gender, culture, and law.

Lindsey Malcom is an assistant professor of higher education administration in the Graduate School of Education and Human Development at the George Washington University. She received her bachelor's degree from the Massachusetts Institute of Technology, her master's degree from the California Institute of Technology, and her PhD in education from the University

of Southern California. Lindsey's scholarship focuses on broadening participation in science, technology, engineering, and mathematics fields.

Michael (Mickey) A. McDonald is currently provost at Kalamazoo College.
He was previously professor of mathematics at Occidental College and also
held a number of administrative roles there. His scholarly work in undergraduate mathematics education focused on how students construct their
understanding of mathematical concepts. He received his bachelor's degree
from Davidson College and his PhD in mathematics from Duke University.

Jonathan Nakamoto is a research associate in the Evaluation Research Program at WestEd. Jonathan received a bachelor's degree in psychology from
Occidental College and a master's degree and PhD in developmental psychology from the University of Southern California. His published research
has focused mainly on English language learners' reading development and
school bullying.

Gretchen North is a professor in the department of biology at Occidental
College. Gretchen teaches plant biology and ecology. Her research interests
include plant physiological ecology, with an emphasis on the water relations
of arid-land species and their responses to projected global climate change,
and the cellular mechanisms of root water transport. She earned her doctorate from the University of California–Los Angeles, her master's degrees from
the College of William and Mary and the University of Connecticut, and
her bachelor's degree from Stanford University.

Edlyn Vallejo Peña is an assistant professor of higher education leadership
in the Graduate School of Education at California Lutheran University
(CLU). She earned her PhD from the University of Southern California,
where she also served as a clinical faculty member and writing advisor before
joining CLU. Edlyn's scholarship focuses on supporting the success of postsecondary students of color and students with disabilities.

Donald E. Polkinghorne is professor emeritus of counseling psychology at
the Rossier School of Education at the University of Southern California
and held the Attallah Chair in Humanistic Psychology from 1997 to 2005.
He served as president of the Saybrook Institute in San Francisco from 1975
to 1987 and was the founding director of the counseling center at the University of California–Irvine. His writing has focused on the relation between

research-developed knowledge and psychotherapy practice. He advocates for the usefulness of qualitative and narrative approaches to knowledge in therapeutic practice.

Abbie Robinson-Armstrong is vice president for intercultural affairs at Loyola Marymount University. She holds a bachelor of science degree from University of Indianapolis, a master of science from Indiana University, and a PhD from University of Toledo. She held faculty positions at institutions of higher education in the United States and Canada including Seneca College, Centennial College, and Durham College. Her research interests include higher education administration, organizational development, and underrepresented students and faculty. Abbie served on the board of the National Association of Diversity Officers in Higher Education for four years. Recognitions for her accomplishments include the Presidential Award for Excellence in Science, Mathematics and Engineering Mentoring from the National Science Foundation, which included a commemorative certificate from President William Jefferson Clinton and a $10,000 grant to continue mentoring activities; and the President's Award for Outstanding Volunteerism from Wright State University.

Robert Rueda is the Stephen H. Crocker professor of education in the area of psychology in education at the Rossier School of Education at the University of Southern California. He completed his doctoral work at the University of California at Los Angeles in educational psychology and completed a postdoctoral fellowship at the Laboratory of Comparative Human Cognition at the University of California–San Diego. His research has centered on the sociocultural basis of motivation, learning, and instruction, with a focus on reading and literacy in English learners and students in at-risk conditions, and he teaches courses in learning and motivation.

Marshall Sauceda is the associate vice president of student affairs at Loyola Marymount University. He received his bachelor's degree in community service and public affairs and master's degree in human resources and industrial relations from the University of Oregon. Marshall's area of expertise involves intercultural affairs with a focus on inclusive excellence and student success.

John Swift is a professor of English and comparative literary studies at Occidental College. Swift's main field of teaching and research is late nineteenth-

and early twentieth-century British and American literature. He also taught for many years an interdisciplinary course on Los Angeles in Occidental's cultural studies program. He has a longstanding interest in undergraduate research in the humanities. He was the founding president of the board of directors of the Southern California Conferences for Undergraduate Research, and he has been a member of the board of governors of the National Conference on Undergraduate Research. He has also served as Occidental's associate dean of faculty and faculty president.

Michael Tamada is the director of institutional research at Reed College. He previously served as the director of institutional research at Occidental College. He received his bachelor's degree in economics from the University of Chicago and did graduate work in economics at the Massachusetts Institute of Technology. He has presented at conferences on topics including measuring the outcomes of diverse student populations, survival analysis of faculty, and multilevel modeling of institutional selectivity and student retention.

Karen Yoshino is the director of strategic consulting at Blackboard, Inc. Her professional roles have included executive director for higher education assessment at The College Board, director of institutional assessment at Occidental College, and executive administrator at Harvey Mudd College. Karen has more than 22 years of experience in outcomes assessment, accreditation review, and diversity management for colleges and universities. She has served on numerous accreditation teams in public and private institutions and contributed to educational policy at the national level. She holds a PhD in education from Claremont Graduate University.

Weick, K. E., 49–50
Wenger, E., 169–170
Wolf, Roger, 117–137
working knowledge, 52
workshops, mathematics, 133

Yoshino, Karen, 96–116

zone of proximal development, 30, 167–168
definition of, 242–243
Zuckerman, Barbra, 156n1

Also available from Stylus

Multiculturalism on Campus
Theory, Models, and Practices for Understanding Diversity and Creating Inclusion
Edited by Michael J. Cuyjet, Mary F. Howard-Hamilton, and Diane L. Cooper

"Not just another book on multiculturalism, this book is a much-needed practical resource on how to prepare a campus to identify the diverse identities of all its students, their commonalities and differences. These seasoned authors have prepared a comprehensive guide for all in higher education, from professionals to students. Examining the student experience with the knowledge provided here could make a positive difference in the retention of all students."—*Gwendolyn Jordan Dungy, Executive Director, NASPA—Student Affairs Administrators in Higher Education*

The book is intended as a text for students, and as a practical guide for faculty, academic administrators, student affairs professionals, and others who want to foster an environment in which all students can succeed. It includes case studies, discussion questions, examples of best practice, and recommends resources to use in the classroom.

Driving Change Through Diversity and Globalization
Transformative Leadership in the Academy
James A. Anderson
Foreword by Ronald A. Crutcher

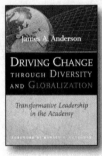

"On rare occasions one finds a book that reframes prior visions. Such books one does not merely read, but one returns to study. Anderson's *Driving Change* is such a book. The first three chapters provide a framework for understanding diversity and globalization, which moves beyond the limits of affirmative action, ethnic studies, and overseas study tours. The theoretical discussion is rooted in the premise that universities' (read also society's) ability to work with diversity and globalization will determine the nature of their futures. Following a discussion of principles, Anderson moves from theory to practice, giving illustrations of campuses that have embraced some facet of this new vision applying it either in terms of teaching strategies and methods, curricular organization, and/or student development. The fact that Anderson is able to draw on working applications gives credence to his theoretical propositions."—*Irene Hecht, Director, Department Leadership Programs, ACE*

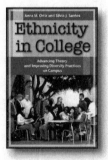

Ethnicity in College
Advancing Theory and Improving Diversity Practices on Campus
Anna M. Ortiz and Silvia J. Santos

"By studying the experiences of 120 Southern California college students, researchers Ortiz and Santos take an in-depth look at the role college plays in ethnic identity development. Their book provides a close look at the divergent developmental paths traversed by students of different ethnicities, and the effect college has on students' understanding of their ethnicity. With smart analysis and helpful suggestions for maximizing the positive effects of campus diversity, the volume is a significant contribution to the literature on identity, diversity, and education."—*Diversity & Democracy (AAC&U)*

While research has begun to document the positive outcomes associated with diverse learning environments, this study emphasizes and more closely delineates just how these outcomes come to be. In addition, the study reveals how the freedom to express and develop ethnic identity, which multicultural environments ideally support, promotes student confidence and achievement in ways which students themselves can articulate.

Sty/us

22883 Quicksilver Drive
Sterling, VA 20166-2102

Subscribe to our e-mail alerts: www.Styluspub.com